Cheryl Claassen, PhD

Whist
A Stud
of Ola͜e͜ɩ ʟ͜ᴇ͜sᴠɩᴀɴs

Whistling Women
A Study of the Lives
of Older Lesbians

THE HAWORTH PRESS
Gerontology and Women
J. Dianne Garner, Editor

Whistling Women: A Study of the Lives of Older Lesbians by Cheryl Claassen

Other titles of related interest:

Lives of Lesbian Elders: Looking Back, Looking Forward by D. Merilee Clunis, Karen I. Fredriksen-Goldsen, Pat A. Freeman, and Nancy M. Nystrom

Faces of Women and Aging edited by Nancy D. Davis, Ellen Cole, and Esther D. Rothblum

Fundamentals of Feminist Gerontology edited by J. Dianne Garner

Old, Female, and Rural by B. Jan McCulloch

Relationships Between Women in Later Life by Karen A. Roberto

Women and Aging: Celebrating Ourselves by Ruth Raymond Thone

Women As They Age, Second Edition by J. Dianne Garner and Susan O. Mercer

Women and Healthy Aging: Living Productively in Spite of It All edited by J. Dianne Garner and Alice A. Young

Women As Elders: The Feminist Politics of Aging edited by Marilyn J. Bell

Whistling Women
A Study of the Lives of Older Lesbians

Cheryl Claassen, PhD

The Haworth Press®
New York • London • Oxford

The Haworth Press, Inc., 10 Alice Street, Binghamton, NY 13904-1580.

Cover design by Marylouise E. Doyle.

Library of Congress Cataloging-in-Publication Data

Claassen, Cheryl, 1953-
 Whistling women : a study of the lives of older lesbians / Cheryl Claassen.
  p. cm.
 Includes bibliographical references and index.
 ISBN 0-7890-2412-8 (hard : alk. paper)—ISBN 0-7890-2413-6 (soft : alk. paper)
  1. Older lesbians—United States. 2. Older lesbians—United States—Interviews. I. Title.
HQ75.6.U5C577 2004
305.26′086′6430973—dc22
                                                                                    2004012953

CONTENTS

ABOUT THE AUTHOR

Cheryl Claassen, PhD, is Professor in the Department of Anthropology at Appalachian State University in North Carolina. She received her PhD in Anthropology (Archeology) from Harvard in 1982 during her radical lesbian separatist years. She has received commendation from the American Association for State and Local History for her study of the U.S. shell button industry. She authored numerous articles in archeology and two books: *Dogan Point*—the results of her seven-year excavation in Westchester County, NY—and *Shells*. She is the editor of *Exploring Gender Through Archeology, Women in Archeology,* and *Women in Prehistory,* and is also the editor of the UPenn Press Series titled *Regendering the Past.*

Chapter 1

Narrators and Friends

In early August 1995 my partner and I were reveling in our freedom. We were both beginning our sabbaticals and planning a trip from our home in Boone, North Carolina, to the Santa Fe Indian Art Market held the third weekend in August every year. Two days before we were to leave, I received a letter from my friend Kay, who lives in Sarasota, Florida. She and my mother had been a couple when I was in kindergarten and first grade in Tulsa in 1959-1960, and I had remade her acquaintance in 1980. I was accustomed to a Christmas letter from her each year, but what could this summer letter be about?

> Dear Cheryl,
>
> I hope all is well with you and Marilyn. I am fine. I am writing to tell you that two friends of mine have bought property in Boone and just moved into the house they had built on it. I gave them your phone number but I hope you will call them. Their address is { } and their phone number is { }. They are both lovely people.
>
> Kay

Boone, North Carolina, and Watauga County are in the Tennessee-Virginia corner of North Carolina—in the Appalachian Mountains, that is—lying between 2,300 and 5,700 feet elevation. Watauga County and Avery County, particularly the town of Blowing Rock, have been popular summering locations for over 100 years for people from Winston-Salem, Charlotte, and Florida. The building of six ski slopes starting in the 1960s in Watauga County and neighboring Avery County, only a minor industrial success, if not a failure, has created an enthusiastic but usually frustrated potential winter tourist. I moved to Boone to teach at Appalachian State University in the anthropology department in July 1983. Gay women on campus were pretty easy to identify using my criteria developed during the previous year in Cincinnati, the prior eight years living in Cambridge, Massachusetts, and the four years before that living in Fayetteville, Arkansas. But those were younger women. I was certain there were older, retired gay women in the mountains and the summer homes all around me and that there might even be a network of older lesbians. Occasionally I'd catch a summertime glimpse of one or two at a town grocery store or an area plant nursery, but I grew increasing frustrated that I knew none of them nor how to crack their barrier of disinterest in me and in things in Boone.

My partner and I are social animals, feminists, academics, and younger than sixty. She helped organize a noncampus group of gay Wataugans. She did what she could to get domestic partner rights for faculty and students. We often hosted potlucks or parties and we adopted (always temporarily it seemed) new gay women faculty. We knew there were other women out there—like a fourth dimension. I resigned myself to mere glimpses of the pixies, and a game of cat and mouse—what did their car look like, which way did they drive off, what was the tag? The excitement that Kay's letter generated in me eclipsed that for our pending trip to Santa Fe. I clutched it like a winning lottery ticket and ran upstairs to read it to Marilyn. Within five minutes I was on the phone to them, but the game of cat and mouse would continue: I got a phone machine. I told the machine that we had gotten a letter from Kay and we'd love to have them over when we returned to Boone. That night, when they called back, the barrier was broken. We discussed where each of us lived in Boone, and then the pixies were named. Did we know Claire who lives on Sugar Mountain or Cindy who lives two houses down, or Ann and Pat in Blowing Rock, or Charlotte and Gail or Betty and Betty or . . . ? I was writing down names as fast as I could.

Two weeks later we four went out to lunch and hatched a plan for a monthly social. They called the women they knew, and I called the Boone nonstudent women we knew. A month later we had the first of many Florida-Boone potlucks on our deck. A calling list was created. The Florida women made plans to go golfing, or out to eat, or to play poker. Someone volunteered for the next potluck. And so we have continued. The few Boone women who come are staff or part-time faculty at the university, lingering undergraduates, or nonuniversity related folks. The Florida contingent and the calling list have grown longer, and computerized.

Half of the women I have met have second homes here and come as early as April every year and stay as late as mid-October, and half of the women are their guests, from New York City, or Michigan, or Florida, or their neighbors in Florida who rent for two weeks or a month in Watauga or Avery County. After several summers of meeting these women, most of whom are retired, most of whom are at least fifty-five, and most of whom live the other half of the year in Florida, I approached several of them with the idea of interviewing them about their lesbian life history, their retirement, and their communities now. Thus, this project was launched in the summer of 1997.

Why a focus on middle- and upper-class women?

Prior to 1994, a number of books appeared in print that chronicled the history and experiences of predominantly noncareer women— *The Lesbian Community* (Wolf 1979), *Odd Girls and Twilight Lovers* (Faderman 1991), *Boots of Leather, Slippers of Gold* (Kennedy and Davis 1993). Exceptions such as *Cherry Grove* (Newton 1993) were something other than life history. Faderman, in *Odd Girls,* believed that middle-class lesbian history was more readily accessible and more comprehensively represented in other outlets, so she developed the working-class information as much as she could in *Odd Girls.* Working-class women are the explicit focus of Kennedy and Davis's inquiry into lesbian experience in Buffalo. It seemed to me that life histories of wealthier women who weren't famous were largely untapped.

Of course, once I got into the literature of academic journals and unpublished theses and dissertations I found that much more information had been gathered about middle- and upper-class women, particularly in university and university town settings, than I had realized, to the point even of overrepresentation of these voices. But therein lay a significant realization—the information on working-class lesbians is in easily accessible books while the information on upper-class and middle-class women is buried in academic journals and libraries—hardly more accessible. A book-length presentation of the lives of middle- and upper-class women—of career women— could bring much-needed visibility to their experiences.

Another research question also directed me toward an investigation of the experiences of career women. In *Boots of Leather,* Kennedy and Davis make the provocative statement that gay liberation grew out of the frustrations and vision of working-class homosexuals (1993, p. 2). I took their comment to implicate women and men without careers, but instead with temporary or menial or unappreciated jobs, or no jobs at all, or individuals raised in such families. They go on to say:

> Lesbians who were independently wealthy and not dependent on society's approval for making a living and a home could risk being open about their lesbianism with few material consequences . . . their ways of living had limited benefit for the majority of working lesbians. Middle-class lesbians who held teaching and other professional jobs had to be secretive about their identity because their jobs and status in life depended on their reputations as morally upstanding. . . . So, they, too, could not initiate the early effort to make lesbianism a visible and viable opportunity for women, nor develop a mass political movement that could change social conditions. (1993, p. 3)

I didn't believe it. Surely these educated, self-confident, older lesbians had helped pave the way for their own liberation and self-actualization, and for mine.

I was fascinated also with the apparent wealth of the women I met in Boone. How had they made their money? I wanted to know the details. I wanted to learn their secrets. How had they made money and held on to it such that they were now prosperous, when several books I read in the 1970s had stated that women were handicapped by their ignorance of finances and investment instruments? It seemed to me in those years that knowing how to read a stock page from the newspaper, keep my checking account balanced, and make and save my own money had meant that I was exceptional among womankind and truly liberated. But I certainly wasn't wealthy after thirty years of liberation and had only dreams of wealth such as I was seeing in the second homes in the Boone area. I had bought and sold land at a profit in 1991 and helped start a women's stock club in Boone in January 1996. I had begun to invest in the stock market in 1995, so I felt somewhat educated about investing vehicles and was very interested in exploring alternative avenues for making money when I began to meet these women and hear their stories.

The final research question which stimulated me to pursue interviewing, and explains largely why I chose to focus on retired women over fifty-nine years of age, was the economic question—How had these manless women managed to attain or retain wealth when supposedly they had been ignorant about finances and investing, as feminist analysis of the 1970s told me? Just how financially savvy were and are women now sixty years old and older? You can find out in Chapters 5 and 6.

As I interviewed the first four or five women, I came to understand the Florida towns of Sarasota, Bradenton, and Tampa as gay communities worthy of histories, and began to move in that direction as well. Gulfport and Carefree, a closed community near Fort Myers, are even more obvious candidates for a history. Pieces of history are scattered throughout the interviews about all of these women-spaces, with most of the information presented in Chapters 6 and 8.

THE STUDY SAMPLE

Although this was not a longitudinal study, it stretched over four years (1997-2001), during which time I encountered many of the women before and after their interviews. It was probably advantageous to me, this extended study period, in giving these women confidence that I was sincere in my interest, my own lesbianism, and my trustworthiness. Several women responded through e-mail as much as three years after their interview to queries I sent, and I stayed in guest houses at two homes of narrators. We encountered one another in Mexico, at the second Silver Threads conference (2001), in Gulfport on morning walks and Women's Energy Bank (WEB) events, at 45+ in Sarasota, at Salon in St. Petersburg, and at potlucks in Boone, North Carolina.

The women interviewed in Florida and Boone were referred to me through three women I knew prior to the project's inception. Ann Davis, of the Clio Foundation, set up sixteen of the interviews, and Kay McFarland of Sarasota, Florida, set up ten of the interviews. Both women also housed me on several occasions and included me in their New Year's Eve festivities. To them I am most grateful. Mary Lou gave me the phone numbers of thirteen women she knew in the North Carolina area. Although the sample resembles a snowball sampling strategy, it wasn't. These three women's (upper-middle class, middle class, Long Island or Chicago, North Carolina second home owners) personal connections highly structure the sampling of stories I present here.

The narrators in this project were interviewed and taped, usually in a single session lasting ninety minutes to three hours. They were interviewed by me, either at the Clio Foundation in Gulfport or in their own homes or rental properties in the Bradenton-Sarasota-Gulfport area, in northwestern North Carolina, in Washington State, or in Arizona. On three occasions both women in a couple were interviewed simultaneously, at their request. I made four interview trips to Florida from my home in North Carolina, beginning in 2000 and ending in March 2001. I interviewed a number of women in North Carolina in the summers of 1997 and again in 2000.

All forty-four narrators were allowed (assumed) to self-identify as homosexual, identify their class status at various points in their lives, their state of coupledom, the extent of their homosexual and heterosexual social networks, and their health and life satisfaction. A narrator could choose any name for her interview and was free to refuse to answer any question or conceal any information. One narrator used her own first name but refused to identify any towns or states. About a third of the narrators used a false name, while approximately half gave their whole names. In several instances, the false name chosen was the same as the real name of someone else—the reader is encouraged not to assume any name is real.

Each tape was transcribed by the Anthropology Department secretary, Teresa Isaacs, at Appalachian State University. The transcript was then given to me and I sent a copy to the narrator. Each narrator had the opportunity to make corrections to the transcript or to reword answers and send it back to me. Three narrators availed themselves of this opportunity. They were sent revised transcripts to do with as they wished. Only two women asked that the transcript not be sent to them. One did not want her partner to read it, and the other was afraid it would be lost in the mail. One woman asked specifically that the tape of her interview be destroyed. Thirty-eight transcripts of women interviewed at the Clio Foundation were mailed in sealed envelopes to the Clio Foundation, where they are to remain for five years unopened.

Each narrator was asked at the beginning of the tape for her consent to be taped and for the name she wished to use for the interview, and was told that our topics for the session were her lesbian life history, her retirement, and her community now. Each woman was also asked for permission to use her words in publications and papers. Only one woman asked to preview anything written using her words. I assured each woman that her testimony would be used in snippets, not as a coherent story, and that much of what she told me would blend, nameless, into tables of statistics or general comments.

Once a year, I sent out a questionnaire on sexuality to everyone I had interviewed since the last questionnaire mailing. The cover letter explained that one could choose to fill out the questionnaire and skip any question. It stated that at least ten questionnaires were being mailed out at that time, which would make it difficult to identify a specific answer sheet. If a woman chose to fill out this questionnaire, she was then to mail it in an enclosed sealed and addressed enveloped to another address in Florida, where the inner sealed envelopes were collected and sent on to me. In this manner I did not know who had filled out the questionnaire nor from where it had been mailed. Twenty sexuality questionnaires made their way to me and are discussed in Chapter 4. Several women inserted their names on this questionnaire.

My criteria for narrators changed over the course of the four years in which the interviews occurred. Initially I sought retired lesbians over age fifty-nine who were upper class or upper-middle class. Gradually the class requirement disappeared and even more gradually the retired status disappeared. The elimination of a class criterion was a reasoned one on my part—interesting stories lie everywhere as does information on women's spaces and finances. The disappearance of retirement was accidental. On one interview trip to Florida several of the women scheduled for interviews were, in fact, not retired or had never worked for pay so couldn't retire. Faced with interviewing or not interviewing them, I let the retirement requirement slide. In the end, this set of papers reflects the stories of forty-four women who are over fifty-nine years old (two women were interviewed who were younger and are not included here) and consider themselves to be, or have been, lesbian. (Only one woman no longer considers herself a lesbian.)

Only one woman offered racial diversity to this sample: Vera, who is African American. There was useful economic diversity in the sample—multiple homeowners to food stamp users. Only one woman was wheelchair bound, three others in poor health, and the rest are quite able bodied.

Many women would not allow themselves to be interviewed in spite of name flexibility. One woman was certain her grandchildren would find out about her through the transcript, two others had suffered in Florida's witch hunts among schoolteachers several decades ago, and countless numbers would give no reason. One woman scheduled an interview and then left when I said one of our topics would be her lesbian life. At the gate to a lesbian RV park in Arizona, I stated that I wished to enter to post a sign seeking interviews with lesbians over the age of sixty. The response I got from a car driving up beside me was that "you won't find anyone here who would admit to that" ["being a lesbian" was my interpretation of "that"].

THE HISTORIC SETTING OF THE NARRATORS

The influences that shaped the lives of all the narrators certainly began with their parents. Dozens of colleges had opened their doors to women students in the last half of the nineteenth century. Their parents were largely young adults when great numbers of U.S. citizens were governed by the temperance movement (1800-1919), the U.S. Arts and Crafts movement (1895-1920), which instructed homemakers to beautify the home using handmade items, and the suffragist movement (1830-1919), which ended when women were given the right to vote in 1919. Margaret Sanger opened the first birth control clinic in 1916 amid a career of public lecturing on women's health, and such clinics multiplied rapidly. Economic opportunities came with education and the expanding marketplace.

Forming a backdrop for all of these advances for women was the person and work of Sigmund Freud, his method of psychoanalysis, and his powerful ideas on sex and one's object of sexual desire. Almost 100 articles and books on lesbians appeared in the twenty years between 1896 and 1916, whereas the century before had produced only one (Faderman 1991). The "romantic friendships" that flourished in the 1800s became contextualized in a language of abnormally repressed and expressed sexuality, as did the "smashes" occurring between women at women's colleges. Women who formed strong attachments to other women became defined as perverts by the legal system and inverts by the medical system. The single, asexual woman became just as suspect as the single homosexual woman. Although the medical literature was relatively obscure to the parents of these narrators, a lesbian love murder in 1892 was not. The story was carried by all the major newspapers and birthed at least three novels by 1895 (Faderman 1991). Instead, the ideal situation for women was the companionate marriage between man and woman, rather than the passionate lovers' relationship.

Franzen (1996), writing about spinsters at the turn of the twentieth century and lesbians of the 1980s, says that the single women in her older age cohort, who reached adulthood at the turn of the twentieth century, sought independence in a society in which reform movements, social work, women living together, and independent women were accepted. There were numerous examples in large cities of women living together, of women working and campaigning, being accepted as women. They saw themselves at the forefront of actions thought valuable by society and beneficial for all women. In fact, it was not radical to stay single; it was radical to leave home for reasons other than marriage (Franzen 1996).

Their parents also experienced World War I (1916-1919), during which time some women worked in nontraditional jobs. The end of World War I brought a new confidence and optimism to U.S. citizens. The Western world was safe again indefinitely. Women now had the right to vote. Clerical jobs, particularly attractive to the middle-class young woman, rapidly expanded in number. The Roaring Twenties ushered in among some groups of sophisticates permission for women to experiment sexually with other women. Bisexuality became a boundary line, with acceptance indicating liberal views. Alcohol consumption and production was controlled by federal and state mandates throughout the decade, finally ending at the federal level in 1933.

Age Cohort I

The fifteen women over age seventy-two, in this case born between 1917 and 1929 (with an average birth year of 1924), constitute an age cohort. They were born into the Progressive Era and the Roaring Twenties. As the reader knows, the 1920s optimism and permissiveness ended in economic disaster in October 1929.

Everyone in the oldest age cohort experienced the Depression (1929-1939). Prohibition ended in 1933, so some of them came of age in a new era of social interactions if they lived in a liberal state such as New York. The Dust Bowl (1930s) made blatantly apparent the dangers of farming and the potential of city life. As the Depression wore on, dozens of government-sponsored make-work programs for men and women were created (e.g., CCC, WPA). The Depression was so wide and deep that only one county in the entire United States did not host a Works Progress Administration (WPA) project. These projects were divided into Men's Projects and Women's and Professionals' Projects and offered stereotypical activities for women— sewing, cooking, mattress making, grounds cleanup, and in some cases archaeological excavation (Claassen 1999) for lower-class women. Individuals with more education could copy county records, record oral histories, paint murals in buildings, or write prose, or they could supervise the manual labor projects. The divisions between manual labor and office labor were probably greatly evident during these years. Commentary on how the Depression and the New Deal affected the narrators can be found in Chapter 2.

The Depression experience generated negative feelings about the stock market, investing, financial planning, banks, and even farming. The family economic standing must have occupied a great deal of attention, and messages about the economy and making a living were undoubtedly being given almost daily to these children and young adults. Employment was as blood in the veins.

To be born in the 1920s, then, was to be burdened with expectations of marriage, college if you were at least upper-middle class, and distrust in investing and the banking system, and to consider drinking, smoking, and bisexuality as the activities of flappers, liberals, and bohemians, and lesbianism as the activity of neurotics. A job was insurance; hard work might not bring prosperity; peace was upon the land.

But when these women turned eighteen, between 1935 and 1947 (averaging 1942), wars were underway in Spain, in Finland, and in Czechoslovakia. The United States was involved in World War II from December 1941 into 1945, and so were the men the narrators were expected to marry. Women could either join the war effort by enlisting in a military branch for women, or work in industries devoted to the war effort or any other task men had vacated. (In this sample, three women joined branches of the military during the war.) The World War II era gave them images of women working in hundreds of "nontraditional" jobs and women living in groups in manless households in cities. The era allowed women to wear pants and made colleges and sports fans eager for their enrollment. The end of the war brought national prosperity, which no doubt contradicted their Depression awareness of limited and fickle opportunity and wealth, while simultaneously they were expected to leave jobs and return home or at most work in the helping/serving professions that men weren't interested in. Overall, their experiences in the 1940s gave many women groups of women friends, urban playgrounds, and some financial independence.

Age Cohort II

The second age cohort is comprised of those women born between 1930 and 1938, twenty-nine in all, now aged sixty-seven to seventy-five. Since the oldest women were nine years old when World War II began, they uniformly came of age in the postwar years, 1948-1956, the years of new prosperity and increasingly strong ideas about the place of middle-class women in a marriage surrounded by children and the walls and roof of a home. The economy was expanding and it was possible for a family to live well with only one working adult. Opportunities for women to mass together were fewer, and the professional as well as pulp literature about women who sought the company of other women was frightening.

Most of these women did what was expected of them out of a positive desire to have a career and family. Simultaneously, most of the narrators had read *The Well of Loneliness*. For both age cohorts, the 1950s were largely devoid of national role models of women leading the charge for political reform, living together or living independently of their families and men. It was even less possible to wear pants. Discussing women's ability to dress like men in the decades before the end of World War II, Franzen says,

Later this ambiguous positioning [women professionals adopting male clothing while at work] was not as possible or as effective because issues of gender and sexual nonconformity were of greater public concern. . . . Because they were forging a new lifestyle for women, it was harder for these women than for men to make clean and complete breaks from their families. (1996, p. 71)

All of the women lived in an America gripped by the threat of nuclear war from the Russians/Communists. Our country was made vulnerable by the activities of some actors, artists, writers, academics, scientists, and all homosexuals. The witch hunts for homosexuals among federal employees and state employees, particularly teachers, strongly tainted the worldviews of women in both cohorts, and some narrators spoke of these events. Some refused to speak to me because of these experiences. They witnessed the rise of black resistance and demands, two even joining in the good fight, and some stepped forward to join the cause of women's liberation. A few of them heard about the Stonewall riots, and some of them were reaping the benefits of the gay rights movement by 1980. Most of them have had little contact with people with AIDS.

Both age groups have had to grapple with the meaning of homosexuality and with coming out. Thirty-four of these women identified their homoeroticism prior to 1969, the date of the Stonewall Riots and the symbolic start of the gay liberation/gay rights movements, when being homosexual still meant having a private sexual attraction. Everyone understood the need to be discreet in public and to develop other, public, aspects of themselves. As should be predictable, not all of these women were convinced by the logic of gay liberation even though they may acknowledge that in the twenty-first century it is easier to be gay. Nine (20 percent) of the women do not consider themselves to be out and three (33 percent) of those are in age cohort I.

Since the early 1970s however, when ten of the women in this sample discovered their erotic proclivity, "homosexual," "lesbian," or "gay person" has been marketed as a public persona that requires "coming out" to maintain a healthy social adjustment. Thirty-five of the women in the sample say they are "out," including twelve of the fifteen oldest women (80 percent) and twenty-three of the twenty-nine (79 percent) younger women. Surprisingly, little difference exists between the two age cohorts in the percentage of Whistling Women who have "come out." This topic is explored in depth in Chapter 7, "Words and Us," and also in Chapter 4, "Lesbian Relationships."

As with attitudes about coming out, when it came time to consider retiring, the two age cohorts again separate. The first group of women reached their sixty-fifth birthdays between 1982 and 1994. In the early 1980s the federal government was downsizing, inflation was outstripping income gains, and computers were beginning to occupy desktops, demanding new training. Companies offered pension funds that provided a predictable and fixed income after twenty-five or thirty years of service. The incentives to retire were strong—avoid the new technology, avoid the constant worry of job security, accept a known amount of annual salary. Why not? They now have had from ten years to work out their new identities, make new friends, learn to budget their money and time, to travel. They are worried increasingly about their health and the cost of health care. Their annual incomes are largely fixed, and, most important, seemingly free of stock market influences.

The second group of narrators retired or passed their sixtieth birthdays in the 1990s. The retirement situation was significantly different. Pension funds had largely been replaced by 401(K) funds, invested in the stock market. Inflation was slowing. The stock market spent nearly the entire decade going up, giving women who had invested or had 401(K) funds a feeling of prosperity and extra cash that could allow them a more comfortable retirement than they had anticipated, even seducing some of them into retiring early. Technology changes in the office were still frequent, but the women were veterans of adapting. One could retire early in the 1990s and reap the benefits of investing and of good health. With fewer than ten years of retirement and the tremendous loss of invested capital that has occurred since 2000, they are worried about having enough money to live at their desired standard, to engage in the activities they retired to pursue. Many of them are still adjusting to retirement—moving, making new friends, scheduling their time, moving between heterosexual and homosexual social circles.

PREVIOUS STUDIES OF GAY WOMEN

Studies of lesbians have taken several forms and had many different purposes. There have been composite personality studies, questionnaires, narratives, and ethnography. Purposes of study have been narrow, such as identity formation, or monogamy, or effects of being out at work, and broad, such as historical reconstruction of communities or decades. The sexology projects of the first half of the twentieth century isolated the topics of sex and sexual practices (e.g., Henry 1948; Kinsey 1948, 1953). For instance, a 1935 study by George Henry examined socially well-adjusted mostly middle-class sex variants among both black and white, many of whom were married. Kinsey (1953) found that 13 percent of all females had experienced orgasm with another woman.

Life satisfaction/whole life studies were underway by the 1960s. The Daughters of Bilitis, through their journal *The Ladder,* collected information on the readership. The Ladder survey (1960) and the Gundlach (1967) survey both found that lesbians tended to have a high level of education, a high professional status, and a stable and responsible mode of living. Both sources reported that most respondents lived with female lovers, while 2 percent were married and lived with husbands, 4.4 percent lived with parents or close relatives, and 13.2 percent lived in other types of situations. Gagnon and Simon (1973) interviewed twenty lesbians about various topics including sex but offered few statistics.

A study of ninety-one women aged eighteen to sixty-plus (25 percent over thirty) primarily resident in the college town of Richmond, Virginia (Albro and Tully 1979), found a median salary similar to the median salary for all women employed full time in 1973: $6,488. One-third earned more than $10,000, and 22 percent had purchased their own homes. Just over half of the women had earned a college degree and 20.4 percent had a graduate degree. Forty-two percent were working in the fields of psychology, social work, nursing, sociology, anthropology, or criminal justice. At the time of the study, 81.7 percent had never married, 11 percent were divorced, 4.9 percent were separated, and 2.4 percent were married. Only seven women had children (8.3 percent), but only two had custody of those children. Eighty-three and a half percent had a woman lover at the time of study. Eleven percent lived alone, 4.4 percent lived with heterosexual female friends, and 52.7 percent were living with a female lover. Forty-five percent of lesbians involved with a lover admitted to having affairs during the relationship. The most common reason cited for why relationships ended was because the lover got involved with another woman. The majority of participants indicated no religious preference.

Ethnographic studies of particular lesbian communities began appearing in 1978 (Ponse 1978; Wolf 1979; Faderman 1981, 1991; Krieger 1983; Kennedy and Davis 1993; Newton 1993). Buffalo, San Francisco, Albuquerque, and Cincinnati have been their focus. Several studies have combined one or two of these foci—sex, life satisfaction, life history, and community—and in this project I cover all four foci (Table 1.1).

Older gay women have been under investigation as a unique group since at least 1978 (Kehoe 1989). The article by Quam and Whitford summarized previous studies of aging among homosexuals as successful in "refuting stereotypes and myths" (1992, p. 368), as well as being too dependent on people active in the gay community, and overrepresentative of white, well-educated, high socioeconomic status urbanites from Los Angeles, New York City, or San Francisco. They collected a questionnaire from thirty-nine women and forty-one men over age forty-nine who were attending a gay aging conference at a local midwestern university. Only ten of the women were older than fifty-nine.

Minnigerode and Adelman (1978) tabulated the problems faced by five lesbians and six gay men aged sixty-six to seventy-seven living in San Francisco in 1978. Seven lesbians older than sixty living on the

TABLE 1.1. Comparisons of Studies of Lesbians Sixty Years and Older

Study	N	Method	Age	Location	Percent married
Kehoe 1988	100	questionnaire	60+	Northern California	27
Almvig 1982	25	interview	60+		
Pollner/Rosenfeld 2000	24	interview	65-89	Los Angeles	24
Whistling Women 2002	44	interview	63-83	Florida, North Carolina	48

West Coast were interviewed by Robinson in 1979 and twenty-five lesbians over sixty by Almvig (1982). Berger bemoaned the difficulty he had in locating older lesbians for his study *Gay and Gray* (1982a), specifying that he interviewed only eight women older than forty and collected questionnaires from only eighteen. Although no women were included in John Lee's 1987 study of forty-seven homosexual men fifty-plus (mean was 60.5 years), he had respondents mirroring the upper age range of my study. A few of these men had retired to Florida and had the same economic range, educational range, and heterosexual life experiences as the women in my study. Seventy percent of Lee's informants had not participated in a gay political activity (Lee 1987). Altogether, the studies cited in this paragraph tabulated the data from a total of twenty-four women.

Lesbians Over 60 Speak for Themselves (Kehoe 1989) is the most extensive investigation of older gay women to date, and was based on questionnaires. One hundred questionnaires were collected from women sixty and older in 1984. Kehoe looked at lifestyle, social life, services, relationships with family and with other women, sexuality, health, and background information. As in this project, she asked about vocabulary, labels, how they spend their free time, connections to the wider gay community, marital history, attitude within family, age of first same-sex experience, if now partnered, present status of religion, finances, politics. After reading this study I modified my own questions and contacted women I had already interviewed for additional information.

Spinsters and Lesbians (Franzen 1996) presents the stories of fifteen women who were well known at the turn of the twentieth century (1900-1920) and who had never married. These women were in the age cohort just prior to the older group in this project. Franzen contrasted them with fifteen women born between 1936 and 1965 who are lesbians living in Albuquerque, New Mexico. These women largely comprise a cohort just beyond the younger one in this project. Six of the women interviewed in Franzen's study were born before 1940 and overlap with the younger cohort in this project. These two cohorts will be used frequently for comparison, as is some of the interpretive material by Franzen. Arlene Stein's book (1997), *Sex and Sensibility: Stories of a Lesbian Generation,* also illuminates the cohort just after the younger one in this study, those women born between 1947 and 1960.

In the late 1990s, Pollner and Rosenfeld (2000) interviewed twenty-five men and twenty-four women aged sixty-five to eighty-nine with wide variations in yearly income. Thirty-three percent had undertaken graduate or professional school, 75 percent were retired, more than 75 percent were single when interviewed, were never in a conventional marriage, and did not have children. Only 14 percent identified as other than Anglo-American. The narrators lived in Los Angeles.

Another precedent for *Whistling Women* is the study by the National Gay and Lesbian Task Force (NGLTF), *Outing Age: Public Policy Issues Affecting Gay, Lesbian, Bisexual, and Transgender Elders,* published in 2000 and authored by Cahill, South, and Spade. This report is a programmatic statement of needs based on estimated numbers of aging GLBT folks. Profiles of individuals are also included. Data from that report are found primarily in Chapter 6 of this study.

WHISTLING WOMEN STATISTICS

Whistling Women appears to be the most recent study of women over fifty-nine and one of the most comprehensive based on interview information. In a nutshell, this project has the following parameters:

Age Cohort I: birth years 1917-1929 (number = 15)

Percent college	60
Percent advanced degrees	40
Percent married	47
Percent bearing children	40
Class distribution at birth	3 upper/upper middle
	6 middle
	6 lower
Relationship status now	40 percent single
Pension received	67 percent
Careers	teaching 33 percent
	nursing 20 percent
	other 47 percent
	none 0 percent

Age Cohort II: birth years 1930-1938 (number = 29)

Percent college	49
Percent advanced degrees	32
Percent married	52
Percent bearing children	41
Class distribution at birth	7 upper/upper middle
	12 middle
	5 lower middle
	5 lower
Relationship status now	21 percent single
Pension received	37 percent
Careers	teaching 33 percent
	nursing 17 percent
	other 40 percent
	none 10 percent

Forty-four women were interviewed, forty-three of whom continue to call themselves lesbians. All but one are Caucasian, and one was born in Canada. The lesbians in this sample in many ways lived lives familiar to heterosexual women and responded to the social expectations of them as women. All but four of the women who married also had children. More women in the older age cohort had careers, and more women went to college in age cohort I, both facts predictable from the historical overview given earlier. More women in age cohort I are living off pensions than are those in the younger cohort. More of the women in the older cohort are now single, also predictable. The women in cohort I are Claire, Kay M, Kay, Carolyn, Joanna, Bing, Amelia, Gloria, Cam, Roberta, Addy, Vera, Sheri, Mary2, and Diane.

WRITING THIS BOOK

Why are books relating the stories of lesbian lives so popular at the turn of the twenty-first century? Why are they appearing in print only now? Certainly part of the answer lies in the fact that many politically identified lesbians have been so for thirty years and they are aging— there is history to be told. It is also because, in spite of a feminist movement and lesbian feminism, feminist literature and scholarship has had more interest in other groups of women than it has had in lesbians. Gay and lesbian studies is largely an academic creation of the

1990s and this is the decade in which gay historiography has prolifer-ated. Although still carrying risks, gay/lesbian/bi/trans scholarship is far safer for the scholar now than ever before. Only since 1996 have I known more than three lesbians sixty-plus years old.

Widening my social circle and in many respects transferring my social life to women sixty and older has been the joy of this project for me. I find their lives fascinating, even though I have been gay and out myself since 1970, first in Fayetteville, Arkansas, and then Boston. I have been lesbian identified longer than several of these narrators and I was/am a lesbian feminist, a perspective shared by only two, perhaps three, of the narrators. Much of what I find fascinating is that our les-bian histories have been so different, which I explore in Chapter 4. I am grateful for the insights into "coming out" that I've experienced through the interviews, as discussed at the end of Chapter 7.

Writing this book was difficult for me. I am an archaeologist by training and have spent twenty years writing and reading that litera-ture, in which the decisions about what to include and what to exclude are far less problematic, and the writing is formulaic at times. Al-though I have done quite a bit of interviewing because I am a fan of oral history, I was not used to the level of reflexivity necessary in this writing, nor the manipulation of lives and memories that was my pre-rogative. In spite of promising many of these women that their narra-tion would never appear in its entirety, I long to break that promise. Many of these stories are so poignant, or so stereotypical, or so un-usual, or so inspirational, or so comical that they beg to be presented in full. Instead, I had to cut and paste information and thus sacrifice the very elements that make oral history so vibrant and so necessary.

It was more difficult than I had imagined it would be to decide on the topics and then how to place them throughout the text. I started out with five chapters and ended up with nine. I changed my mind several times on where to discuss schooling and where to discuss fi-nancial education. Did I talk about careers and gay men in the lesbian lives chapter or elsewhere? I am certain that five other writers would have organized this material in five different ways and that five years from now even I would organize it differently.

I was also bothered by several conventions in oral history and in anthropology. One social science convention that I have rejected is to make myself, the interviewer, invisible. These narrations were col-lected as conversations between me and the woman who volunteered.

My questions often set the tone and the pace, and definitely predetermined the vocabulary and the subjects. The narrators were responding to me and to a particular flow in our conversation. I have preserved my questions, my part in the conversation, and this flow whenever relevant, rather than edit so as to have only the narrator's words available.

Particularly bothersome to me was the argument that fake names must be used for the narrators. Even if the narrator gives permission to use a real name, the researcher should use a fake name, for the narrator knows not what the revelation might bring her.

As a feminist, I must reject this convention. Women are made anonymous in so many ways and lesbians in still more ways and the elderly in yet additional ways. To use a name is a bold move, a defiant move, an honorable move. I asked these women to trust me with their stories—part of that responsibility is the naming of the story. Out of their experienced, lesbian, womanly selves came names, real names, as well as fake names.

Second, these women have lived longer than I, have weighed the world and their place in it longer than I, have wrestled for years with the consequences of their actions, have built numerous barriers and safeguards around themselves. They know exactly what dangers and pleasures their life story and current lifestyle can bring them. I consider the choice to use a real name an intelligent choice, just as is the choice to use a pseudonym. It is not for me to second-guess their perception or their fortitude. When a woman told me to use her real name, I have done so.

> Women have often felt insane when cleaving to the truth of our experience. Our future depends on the sanity of each of us, and we have a profound stake, beyond the personal, in the project of describing our reality as candidly and fully as we can to each other. (Adrienne Rich 1979, p. 190)

Chapter 2

Coming to Be

The reader can surely anticipate the amount of diversity in childhood experiences and families that there would be in a group of any forty-four women born over a twenty-two-year period. Joanna's parents were both professionals while Sappho's parents operated an ice cream parlor, and Sheri's mom cared for foster children while her father went off each day to work. Roberta's mom became pregnant with Roberta while unmarried and living overseas, Cynthia was born in northern Ontario and had ten siblings. Edie and her sister were raised by a single mom in Florida in a tarpaper shack, picking grapefruits and oranges to eat. Mary Lou grew up next to a university campus, while Addy never attended high school. In this chapter, I will develop some of the data for this group of forty-four women that are of interest to social historians. It should be clear to people who would attribute lesbianism to dysfunctional families, child abuse, working mothers, absent fathers, homosexual parents, or unreligious parents that there are plenty of examples of the "better" situation nurturing homosexual children.

This chapter will explore the family makeup, parents, childhood experiences, religious affiliations, and socioeconomic class placement of each of the forty-four narrators. At the end of their high school days, women had the choices to marry, go to work, go to college, stay home, or leave home. These choices are explored here. The treatment of the fifteen women by Franzen (1996) was something of a model for what follows. In many instances the data pertaining to the fifteen women she studied, which constitute a cohort which slightly overlaps the younger one here, are used for comparative comments.

FAMILY SITUATIONS

Birthplaces

Florida, the current location of many of these narrators, has been a
retirement magnet for New Yorkers and the residents of the urban
sprawl surrounding New York City for at least three generations (see
Chapter 6 for confirmation). As a consequence, 10 (23 percent) of the
informants in this study were born in some section of New York
City—Long Island, the Bronx, Queens, Brooklyn. Seven (16 percent)
others were born elsewhere in New York, in New Jersey, and in New
England. Eight more (18 percent) women were born in the upper
Ohio River valley (Pennsylvania, West Virginia, Ohio), and three (7
percent) in the lower Ohio River Valley. Five (11 percent) women
were born in southern states, five in the Detroit or Chicago area
(11 percent), four (9 percent) in Iowa or Kansas, one (2 percent) in the
Northwest, one in eastern Canada, and none in the Southwest or
Northwest.

Family Makeup

The women in this study show interesting differences in natal family experiences that can be summed up in the two age cohorts (Table
2.1). Among the oldest women, 26 percent were raised by grand-
mothers, state-appointed guardians, or in an institutional setting,
while none of the women in the younger cohort had such an experience. The incidence of single moms was slightly higher in the younger group, 7 percent versus 11 percent. Neither that statistic, nor the
proportion of working moms, 20 percent versus 18 percent, however,
varies significantly between the two groups.

Strikingly different is the percentage of women who were raised
by nonworking moms. Among the older women, 33 percent of their
mothers "stayed home" between 1919 and 1939, while almost twice
as many mothers, 61 percent, stayed home from 1930 to 1950, when
the younger women were children.

Seven of the women (47 percent) in the Franzen study (born 1936
or later) had mothers who worked, meaning that 53 percent of their
mothers were homemakers. Only two of those fifteen women (13 percent) grew up in families with a working father, homemaker mother,
and no abuse. Abuse among the women in this study was reported by

TABLE 2.1. Narrators' Primary Caregivers

	1919-1939 (%) *	1930-1949 (%) *	1935-1970 (%) **
Single moms	7	11	
Working moms	20	18	53
Stay-at-home moms	33	61	47
Institution/other family	26	0	40
Only child	33	24	
Four-plus siblings	20	17	
Foreign-born parents	13	10	
Abused	40	33	

*Claassen
**Franzen

eight (40 percent) of twenty respondents to the sexuality questionnaire, although whether that abuse was sexual, physical, or mental was not indicated. (Questionnaires were not coded by age.) Only one woman specifically named sexual abuse, and one named physical abuse.

Perhaps mothers giving up/over the care of babies in significantly greater proportions before 1930 reflects the lack of birth control information and techniques, which were not generally available until 1916 and took time to diffuse through the country.

Pat M's mom died five weeks after she was born from complications with the delivery.

[Grandmother] raised me. She raised me to make me believe that I had killed my mother. I had forced my father into alcoholism at age nineteen. She died five weeks after I was born from an embolism. And at a year and a half, I went out and got polio. All these rotten things this child did before she could even think. So I had no self-esteem. I grew up with no self-esteem. I went to Catholic schools where of course the sisters put you down no matter what.

TALES OF MOMS AND DADS

Seven women (16 percent) commented that they did not like their mothers, while three narrators did not like their fathers or stepfathers. Franzen (1996) found the opposite situation, that between her two age cohorts, one older, the other younger than the narrators in this project, 13 percent did not think they had good relationships with their mothers when they were children, and 33 percent said the same for their fathers. Franzen remarked that the postwar daughters did not as consistently describe their mothers as important role models and sources of support as the turn-of-the-century women did (1996, p. 29).

Several women in this study are first-generation U.S. born. Diane had a father from Ireland, both of Pauline's parents immigrated from Germany, and Sandy's father was born in Portugal. Two of these three women are in the younger age group. Franzen remarked that the "gentle and involved fathers of the earlier women were missing also" among her postwar sample (Franzen 1996, p. 29).

Following are some of the comments heard about mothers and fathers and a grandmother in the present study.

[Mother] worked for the army for many, many years. My mother was the kind of woman who didn't like to stay at home. She was always dressed in hat and gloves and a suit and so forth and she liked to be out and around. . . . She was a woman who was beautiful, bright, active, and involved. She was not terribly involved in family. Somehow I've always felt very much as though she were a person I would like to be. Whereas my sister always felt that she would like a big, fat mama to stay home and cook and clean and what have you. And she resented my mother's beauty and activity. I remember when Mom came to open school week, I was so proud of her. (Barbara)

I don't know how many snapshots of my mother [that I have seen], who was obviously feminine, I mean heterosexual no doubt, in her knickers, in her sailor suits. She was dressing up as a man all the time. (Kay)

[I saw] pictures of my mother and her two sisters-in-law wearing their husbands' World War I uniforms. (Claire)

My mother was a single mom and was a very, very strong woman. She would have been a lesbian herself if she had been able to be free. But she was a person who was stuck in her time, closed in. She didn't investigate, didn't go further into a different route than that proscribed for women. My mother always told me, always, you can do anything you want to do. If somebody else that's human can do this thing, you can do it too. And on the other hand, she wasn't a great mom in knowing how to help me do the things that she said because I couldn't do anything the way she wanted me to. She gave me a double message. If I had had all of that wonderful experience, plus a mom that was really supportive of who I was, that would have been the ultimate of a growing-up experience. (Edie)

My parents were separated and divorced so that I was brought up by a single parent who worked and then decided to go on welfare till my sister, who is seven years younger than I am, was in school for a full day. So my mother worked at all kinds of menial jobs in order to support us but went on welfare because she felt she should be the caregiver to her younger child. Then she worked in banktelling and bookkeeping kinds of jobs. So I grew up in a generation when divorce and separation were, if they existed, they weren't approved of. It was an atmosphere of shame for my mother. (Jackie)

My dad and I were really close. I was daddy's girl and I loved him. He was my best buddy. I could talk to him. My mother and I, so-so. In later years, I mean there was no problem there, but I never felt as close and I think there was a jealousy because my father had a sister that never married, that was a schoolteacher and she'd be home in the summer. I idolized my aunt, so I think my mother had a problem with that, as I look back now. But my mother and I got along just fine. Some of my friends have said my mother could have been gay and probably should have been. She was a lot of fun. (Janet)

And I love my grandmother above everything in the world. She's the one I ran away to because she had lost her husband just before I was born, so I became an integral part of her life. Her whole life was devoted to me. She read to me; she took me for walks. I called her Nana. Nana was more than my mother and father; she was everything. (Mary Lou)

[M]y grandma was at home a lot. It was quite devastating when she passed. (Barbara)

[My father] was a sort of a poet and traveling artist and he couldn't get through a sentence without using an obscenity. He was very Irish, he had a brogue and he was very handsome. And he was never let forget for one moment that my mother had married beneath herself. She was an English lady. I don't know how many years they were together, a long time, maybe sixty years for all I know. She never let him forget for one minute that she'd married beneath her station. And he worked really hard and we weren't as poor later on as we were, but we were always not very well off. (Diane)

By the time I was a teenager, my mother had died just before I was sixteen and I went to live with my brother and his wife. My father said to me one time, "Don't get married." And of course [I asked], "Why not?" Well, he didn't have a good answer. And at the time I just kind of passed it off as most young people do; they don't pay much attention. But later as I look back on it, I think my father was always aware of my being gay. But he never came right out and said anything about it, nor did I. But I think because he knew and because my mother had died and he had to kind of step in and guide. He made arrangements for his sister who was fairly wealthy to invite me to come and stay with her and her husband and go to college. 'Cause I think my dad knew that I shouldn't marry and I would have to earn my own way. (Sheri)

I had an unhappy childhood—father picking at mother, because she was making more money than he was and he was working so hard. They eventually got divorced. I was always bottom rung. Father was mean. He was mean to my mother. My parents weren't doing well. . . . My sister and I were so cowed. I was introverted and it's because of her. One day I liked her, the next day I hated her—we were never good enough for her. I hated them one day then loved them the next. (Amelia)

[Speaking about her guardians] The man was the nicest man that I've ever known. The woman was a true hellion. If there is such a thing as being exorcised, she should have been. She was evil; she was totally illiterate. She was a religious hypocrite. (Vera)

My father had women around him the whole time I ever knew him. My mother died and he married another woman when I was five. He divorced her and married the mother of his two sons when I was in high school. And there were other women in between. When he died, I was standing at his grave, my gay uncle and my present stepmother who was the mother of the boys, my brothers, and across the way were half a dozen women with kids that looked just like my father, all boys. He always said I was his only son. He had other boy children, but I was his only son. (Pat M)

Siblings

The number of only children is surprisingly large, thirteen of forty-four or 30 percent of the narrators (Table 2.2). Family sizes varied from the single child to eleven children. Twenty women grew up with one other sibling (45 percent), giving strong credence to the 1950s to 1970s image of the two-parent, two-child home. Six women had two other siblings (14 percent), and five women grew up in families with four or more children. Two women had gay brothers.

Three narrators reported sisters or brothers who were disruptive forces at home or who were caregivers. Several women noted dramatic age differences between themselves and the next sibling.

TABLE 2.2. Numbers of Children in Narrators' Natal Families

Children	Older Group		Younger Group		Total Study	
1	5	33%	8	28%	13	30%
2	5	33%	16	52%	20	45%
3	2	13%	4	14%	6	14%
4	1	7%	1	3%	2	5%
5	1	7%	0	0%	1	2%
6+	1	7%	1	3%	2	5%

I have a brother who's a homosexual and he created a lot of havoc in the family. So I heard the "wrong, wrong, wrong, wrong, wrong," all my life about my brother because he went into the service. He ended up getting caught; it was against the rules. And my parents paid him to stay away to the extent that he never did earn a living for himself. They paid him off all his life. They went to extremes to get him out of trouble. He was court-martialed and everything else, he was going to get a dishonorable discharge. But because we were politically connected and because my parents knew judges and all this other stuff, they pulled the strings that got him an honorable discharge. (Dawn)

Margaret was born to my mother in Germany during the war and she obviously wasn't married. I think that's why my mother was sent to this country was because she had this baby. So her mother and father, my grandparents, took Margaret and raised her and sent my mother to the United States. And when my parents married, they wanted to bring her over and my grandmother wouldn't allow it. And so finally when my grandmother died in 1935, that's when my sister came over and she was thirteen at the time. (Pauline)

My older sister and I did not get along as youngsters. She had a very difficult time growing up. She always said she felt as though she didn't belong in our family or in any family. And as a result, she was generally very hostile. I kind of stayed out of her way. It's only now that we're older, we're very close. And she got married young, so she married at nineteen. She was out of the house by the time I was sixteen, which was probably better. I felt better about that because I could have whatever relationship I could have with her and it was better when she was not in the house. She stayed out late, she didn't do anything that was terrible, but she just didn't listen and it created a lot of friction. And so when she left everything was quiet and it was easier. (Barbara)

Class at Birth

The narrators were asked to pinpoint the socioeconomic standing of their parents, which was easily done by most women but difficult for some. Some women said they had never given it any thought, and some women clearly disdained the label "lower class," preferring "working class." Table 2.3 summarizes each woman's self-assessment of the class of her parents at the time of her birth. No means of quantifying or verifying these class standings was attempted, and narrators clearly considered actual household income, behavior, and grandparents' standing in their evaluation.

Using this five-class categorization, more of the older women considered their birth families to be in the lower middle class. No one put herself in the upper class. Given that these divisions are highly subjective, combining them into fewer categories eliminates some of the

TABLE 2.3. Socioeconomic Standing of Narrators' Childhood Families (%)

	Lower	Lower Middle	Middle	Upper Middle	Upper
Younger	17	17	41	17	7
Older	13	27	40	20	0
Total	16	20	41	18	5

variation in assessment criteria but does little to change the picture. If I group all lowers together and all uppers together, the difference in the upper class disappears and some difference appears in the lower class (Table 2.4).

There is no significant difference in the percentage of upper-, middle-, and lower-class families of birth for the two groups of narrators.

My mother's side of the family was from West Virginia, different culture. My father's family was from Europe and all schooled. My grandfather was a minister and had a PhD in theology. My father's side of the family was classical, opera. So it was a totally different game than—I want to call them the hillbillies—but they were the upper-class hillbillies because they were monied. (Gigi)

We always lived in rented places and never had anything, just barely lived [eleven children]. We were dirt poor. All I know is my mother used to say to me, when I got older a little bit—I don't remember this—but she said I'd stand with my hand on my hip and I'd say, "When I get old, I'm not going to be poor." That must have been from hating being poor so much, I think. It may be the motivator. I wouldn't say my parents were low class. I think they were very classy people. They had very good values, good morals; they would never steal anything. They would never apply for public assistance—no matter how poor we were and how little we had, sometimes no food, that poor. I wouldn't call that low class. (Cynthia)

We were very poor. That is, we were poor in that we didn't have money. And we were forced to live in poor neighborhoods because we didn't have money, but my mother was originally from upper-middle class here in St. Pete. My grandfather was one of the people who was a city planner and in the newly acquired money rich, not super rich, but in the upper-middle class to upper-class social range. So my mom had a different mind-set. We were poor because we didn't have money. We were poor in what we couldn't buy, but we still had privilege. We were white. We had privilege that we could read, we knew other places, and we traveled. Even if it was the barest minimum, we had visions that were beyond our little poor place where we couldn't economically get out of. I never considered myself poor even though I know that we didn't have money. (Edie)

TABLE 2.4. Combined Socioeconomic Standing of Narrators' Childhood Families (%)

	Lower	Middle	Upper
Younger	34	41	24
Older	40	40	20
Total	36	41	23

The Depression

There were two significant events that colored the economic experiences of the women in this study: the Depression of 1929-1939 and World War II. The federal government's answer to this particular depression was the New Deal, programs that created work for adults. For instance, the WPA, or Works Progress Administration, would employ one person per family if no one else was working. Employment preference was given to men, but when men were absent from the home or incapacitated, women could be employed, usually for no more than eighteen months. One effect of this policy was to cause some men to separate from their families so that they and their wives could get employment. As specified in Chapter 1, typical work programs for men involved construction or digging while for women, sewing, cooking, and cleaning were typical. For more educated workers, programs such as the Writers' Project or Artists' Project, or just copying county records, were instituted. Only two women mentioned a WPA project specifically.

> [Mother] worked for the writer's project of the old WPA and she was one of the 10 percent who got on to that project without having to declare welfare status. Though I think she could have qualified. (Carolyn)

> I studied art at the WPA art center as a child [in North Carolina]. (Joanna)

World War II gave many women an opportunity to work for significant wages. The war is credited with the creation of homosexual urban communities (D'Emilio 1983), and, perhaps most important from our perspective at the turn of the twenty-first century, ushered in a new prosperity that raised almost everyone's standard of living. Because the Depression is recognized by everyone as an economic event, I have included comments about it in this section on social class. However, because most people do not recognize World War II as an economic event, but rather as a social event, I have included narrators' comments on the war under childhood experiences.

The Depression made its impact on the economic situation in several of the narrators' memories. In fact, it likely had an impact on all forty-four women's families, born as they were between 1917 and 1939. Most of the women who commented on the Depression were in the older group, and most of those families recovered. As with the women and families in the two decades before them (Franzen 1996), each with economic slowdowns or depressions and wars, all of these women learned that income was essential yet ephemeral. That experience may have propelled them to make their own income and to save, for each of the women with comments on the Depression is among the wealthiest group of narrators.

Only my mother's relatives [felt the Depression] and she helped them out. But my father was in banking and we never really suffered. We had tramps come to the back door in those days. I remember as a little kid, we lived near a river called the Bushkill Creek and if we'd go down there in our car on the way to church or anything, we'd see all these campfires. And my parents would say that those are the people who are homeless and jobless and are living there on the river, which in those days was very clean. My mother fed the tramps. They called them tramps. I don't mean to denigrate, but that's what they said they were. My mother would always have food and put it out on the back porch for them. They didn't come into the house, but they would eat there. (Mary Lou)

Of course when I was growing up it was Depression times and my widowed mother, who also had to take care of her mother, had a rather rough time of it. (Carolyn)

My father started out with a company and the Depression was tough. But then he moved up in the company and so our fortunes improved. (Claire)

And he worked really hard and we weren't as poor later on as we were, but we were always not very well off. And the Depression of course hit us very hard. It was rough going. (Diane)

I've never worried about money. It's always been there. I was reared in the Depression, but even during the Depression we never lacked for anything. (Gloria)

My parents were very poor during the Depression, but my father worked continuously and did do well. (Jan)

During the Depression my dad was thrown out of work, didn't have a job, but he was a hustler. We lived very comfortable. I would say he gave me my taste for Cadillacs. (Mitch)

Childhood Experiences

Few women commented on their childhoods in any depth. Joyce said she had a wonderful childhood but was eager to leave home. Jan, Gloria, and Gigi all said they had wonderful childhoods as well. Mary Lou commented on the complete lack of displays of affection in her home. Other comments are repeated as follows:

Mother was fifteen years old [when I was born] and she [gave me] over to foster care. At this point I can say I was in foster homes for the majority of my life. And at the age of nine I was placed in a place called Rockland State Hospital in New York. And I was there for four years until I was approximately fourteen years old and then I came out. The reason I was placed there I guess was because my grandfather was . . . belonged to a place called Workman's Circle. And I think being illegitimate I guess my mother at her young age really didn't have too much to say about how my life was run at that point in time. So I was put in this Rockland State Hospital, but my mother never gave me up for adoption in any way, shape, or form. When I got out I went to live with my grandparents because they didn't have much of a choice. It was either take me out of there, which was the Children's Pavilion up to a certain age, or go to a place across the street which as young kids we used to call the Nutsy Pavilion. It's where they kept the. . . I guess they were either insane or on their way. And when I was about fifteen, I suppose, I finally went to live with my mother and stepfather. My mother married him in 1935. (Addy)

High school was the happiest time of my life, still. My childhood was unhappy. My family liked my sister best—I tried not to let that bother me. Father was mean—my parents weren't doing well. (Amelia)

I was born on a farm in New York State, near the Pennsylvania border. When I was small, my people were considered to be quite well to do. And then, through misadventures, that was lost and we went down to what would probably be considered today pretty nearly poverty level. We moved off the farm when I was twelve. I had everything I wanted. I was the youngest of four and seven years younger than my nearest sibling. So I was almost like an only child. I had a pony and all kinds of freedom to come and go and do pretty much as I wanted, a very carefree life. (Sheri)

When we were just in elementary school, she left my dad when I was five and Jane was four. I'm not so sure he was an alcoholic, but what I know is that he spent his paycheck in the bars. And this is still pretty much the dregs of the Depression and she knew she was going to have to go to work to support us and she wasn't going to support him too. So she took us and left. Anyway, she would not leave us with anyone; there was no such thing as child care. So she had to take a job where she was home when we were home. And in elementary school, that means being home for lunch. So she worked at a greasy spoon up on the corner where she could walk home. So that did not bring in very much money. I guess we were poor. Everybody else in our neighborhood was poor too, so I didn't feel poor. Everybody put cardboard in their shoes to go to school in that day. And in Detroit the police department worked hand in hand with the newspapers and Thanksgiving Day all of the proceeds from the newspapers went to what they call the Detroit Goodfellows which were the old newsboys and they would buy clothing and dolls and candy and all that stuff and make up boxes. And the policemen would deliver the boxes. And for years I thought Santa Claus was a policeman. But, you know, I don't feel badly about that because we were close. And Christmas Eve we always went to the movies and on the way home, that's when the gas stations started burning Christmas trees 'cause they hadn't sold them and they'd give them away. So we could carry our Christmas tree home and decorate it Christmas Eve, but that's what everybody did. I don't feel it affected me all that much. I was never hungry, I always had plenty of warm clothes. There were times my mother didn't eat at night. So I personally didn't feel poor. (Dorothy)

I was pretty much the black sheep in my family. In fact, they said that I'd never amount to a damn. So I was always so pleased that my parents lived long enough to come to Shippensburg and see me as an academic, a distinguished person in the community, living in a nice home. I had a lot of problems when I was a child. I was very rebellious and I got a lot of whippings from my mother. She was very strict. Her name was Melissa and I called her Militia. She was very strict. And my poor sister who was just a year and a half older than I was, I would get all the bright ideas about things that got us in trouble. I had four older brothers and they could get away with something and I'd do the same thing and I couldn't and I never could understand that. . . . I saw a picture the other day of me in my teens and I had on nice-looking slacks and shirt and a jacket and Gloria saw it and she said, "My, you were butchy even then." I used to go to church when I lived at home. I had to. My mother saw that I went to church. (Kay M)

I was the tomboy of the neighborhood. I beat up all the boys who wouldn't listen to what I told them. I had a football suit when I was five years old; it was my biggest wish for my Christmas gift. It might have been precipitated by the fact that we lived across from Lafayette College campus and from my bedroom I was able to see football being practiced and my father had started taking me to football games when I was very young. The first sport I ever learned, and I knew all the rules by the time I was five or six years old, was football. And then I used to go over and watch them practice and the football players would toss me a football and teach me how to throw it. The football players from Lafayette College, who were giants when I was that little, tiny, peewee kid, taught me how to throw a football.

We lived so close to the campus and most of my friends' fathers were professors, so I was on the campus continually, using the library facilities, watching the different sports events, soccer, baseball, everything. And the next-door neighbors to us were the purveyors of Coca-Cola and hot dogs and they had me as a seven-year-old working for them after the games . . . . I think I missed camp two summers between the ages of twelve to thirteen or thirteen to fourteen when I had started menstruating. I didn't want to go because when I was in the bunk as a seven- and eight- and nine-year-old, we used to find our counselors' menstrual pads and we didn't know what they were. But we all used the same bathroom in the cabin, you know, and it was a disgusting kind of sight. Once I started I didn't want to be part of that, to have to put my napkin in a can in the bathroom and that was the only place you could put them. I stayed away from camp out of that kind of fear. (Mary Lou)

My mother lived with us and she had a nervous breakdown when I was about four or five years old and then she married an SOB that was my step-father when I was five. And by the time I was eighteen, she had to go to Belle-vue and she was in the state mental hospital for thirty-six years, a living death. She was in and out of private sanitariums from the time I was old enough to remember and she would get better and when she came home, she got worse. But with the environment that existed in the family, there was no way she could have gotten anything but worse. My grandmother, my step-father, my mother, and myself were all living together when I was a child and it was dreadful. It really was dreadful. Then he started chasing me around when I was twelve. He was a child molester and I hope if there is a hell, that he's in it. (Roberta)

I had the polio. So when the senior prom came up, I wasn't going to go. And I was forced into that, I mean the dress was bought. I wasn't even there to say yes or no. And Eddie was dressed up and sent over to take me to the prom. I had, truthfully, at that time, I had two friends—two girls—that was it. One lived downstairs and one lived three or four blocks up the street. That was the whole circle because I spent so much free time at the hospital with the legs, having things done to them. I've had seventeen surgeries on my legs. The last one was when I was fifteen, I think. And so I didn't have a big circle of friends because all I knew was kids from the hospital. (Pat M)

But my grade school life was Girl Scouts, and high school was a private girls' boarding school. All my schooling was women oriented. I realize that I grew up without that knowledge of who boys were. I didn't have any brothers. I had a sister that was my "big" sister—she was nine years older than I was, so she was basically my caregiver too. I realize now what a gift that was—in high school I didn't have to put up with boys; I didn't have to be in that subordinate place to boys. So I was able to see what women and girls could give to each other. (Edie)

World War II

All of the women in this study experienced World War II, the younger ones as children, the older ones as adults. Bing was a Navy Wave and had her first affair with a woman while enlisted. Today the VA hospital provides her with free health care. Narrators for Kennedy and Davis (1993), however, pointed out that they didn't join the military because they didn't want to leave lovers, or a good job (men had job protection if they went into the service), or they couldn't get any friends to sign up with them. The war also created gay communities in port towns and in industrial towns.

Kennedy and Davis (1997) remark that World War II gave unprecedented freedom to women—freedom to socialize, to move away from home, to move about, to dress differently. As those authors put it, the "absence of 16 million men made work and neighborhoods safer" (1997, p. 66). All of these freedoms benefited lesbians greatly while making it more difficult to identify other lesbians.

This historical event, like any other, is made so much more memorable by firsthand accounts. Some of the more unusual information contained herein is that provided by women in the military, the child's perspective, and information about the women volunteers.

[Father] converted to Catholicism when he married my mother. That was a big part of my childhood [in the United States] was World War II and kind of the secrecy, his being Jewish and wondering what happened [to everyone in his family]. I mean they obviously were concerned. My mother's family was there too. But I just remember that period of my life as one great fear about the war. I think I was afraid that the war was going to come to this country. The war was very difficult for people who were German. There was a lot of anti-German feeling and negativity. I can remember being called a Kraut in school. My parents had this really heavy German accent and the name. You can't hide that.

[Then I got polio when I was ten, in 1944]. The house was quarantined; my dad couldn't go to work. They put a big yellow sticker up on the house. So here you have this Jewish father with a big yellow sticker on the outside of the house. (Pauline)

I can remember standing by the window when it was lightning, thinking that bombs were bursting. And I remember my dad, who was in the Air National Guard, putting his gun in the holster—I was so afraid he would shoot his foot. (Nan)

During the war time, my mother used to roll bandages and do all sorts of stuff during World War II. And she got involved in working for the government because of that . . . . And when I met my husband, he had lost his father in World War II in the Battle of the Bulge. And so he was orphaned 'cause his mother had died when he was really young. And we had a lot of sadness in common. (Barbara)

We'd opened a big Air Force base outside of Topeka, and the city was crawling with air force guys, right about the beginning of World War II. So I dated a lot of those guys. (Carolyn)

In 1943 when I was a senior, the boys went off to war and you danced with girls which suited me fine. So I was in a natural setting there for me. I didn't realize it though. I was engaged at the time. I was the first one in the crowd to be engaged. He joined the service after we were engaged [which helped delay the marriage] thank goodness. (Cam)

That was three years that we were together. And then I tried to get a job over there (Paris), which was very difficult. This is right after the war and it was very difficult—couldn't happen—and I came home and decided I was going to graduate school and that was that. (Claire)

My mom was divorced when I was five. We were poor because at first, she didn't have a marketable skill or regular work. She was a single parent through the war years. She got a job in a defense plant in the north during the war. It was after the war—it was 1947 when the boys came home—she was fired and couldn't find another job so she worked independently as a seamstress. Then after the war, our life improved because my dad was sending child support money and she remarried. (Edie)

There were three of us siblings in college at that time. This was 1941. The war had started. I wasn't doing anything in college so my mother came to get me at Christmas and I said, "I won't go back." So I went to a business college briefly and I got a typing job for the Ford Motor Company. Well when I got there, I worked for a few days in the office. But the men in the parts department were being drafted; this was 1942. [So I got the job running the parts department.] I married Paul in 1943 and we went to Utica, New York. He was stationed there for a little while and then we went to New Hampshire for a couple of months. Then he had to go overseas to fly. Pilots on B-17s used to have to fly about 150 missions. This was when we were fighting the Germans.

We lived together for less than a year because we were in one place maybe four or five months and then another place a few months. When he went overseas in 1944, I returned to Shreveport where my home was. I was working in the auto parts business and sharing an apartment with a woman with whom I later became intimate. I remember her very well. Paul was gone about a year and a half. (Kay M)

I met Grace who was a nurse and then she was called to the Navy. [S]he was a Navy nurse during World War II. We were together for a number of years. (Mary2)

That's when I met Sid and we were married the day after I graduated. He volunteered for the Navy because World War II was looming. And he was stationed with the marines in Panama for about eight months. And we were married in September of 1942. Our son was born in July of 1943. (Diane)

First Lutheran Church and then Girl Scout Camps and then YWCA camps—New York City YWCA. They even had a camp for adult women during the war years, end of the war years, and some friends and I that had met in this girls' summer camp worked at that camp for about a week. Of course in twenty-twenty hindsight, the women who attended the camp—a lot of them were wives whose husbands were overseas—but I'm sure there were many lesbians in the adult camp . . . . We went to a junior high school and elementary school and middle school all together, first through tenth grade because of the war. (Marilyn)

Religion of Birth Family

The concentration of narrators who were born in New York City or on the north side of the Ohio River Valley predicts that most of the informants would come from Catholic, Jewish, Presbyterian, or Lutheran backgrounds, and, in fact, that is the case.

Looking at the older age group, a surprising 20 percent of the women claim to have no religious background. Among those who did have a religious upbringing, 27 percent were Presbyterian, 13 percent were Catholic, 13 percent Lutheran, and none (surprisingly) were Jewish. One woman each was born to Methodist, Baptist, and Christian Scientist families. (I lack this information for two women.)

Several significant differences occurred between the two age groups with respect to religious background. Whereas 20 percent of the older group had no religious affiliation as children, only 7 percent of the younger women said the same. Ten of the younger women were Catholic and six were Jewish. Table 2.5 presents the various proportions for religious upbringing. Over one-quarter of the forty-four narrators were Catholic, with Presbyterian and Jewish women also common. One woman in each cohort came from an unknown religious background (9 percent). In sum, these statistics are a bit different from the national figures for religious affiliation in these age groups (Yutema 1997). There are more Catholics and Jews among the Whistling Women, fewer Protestants (44 percent are Protestant versus 73 or 65 percent in the two Yutema groups), and more were raised without a strong religious affiliation.

We were a happy little family. We were brought up as Christian Scientists. I loved it. It was the most beautiful religion as far as I was concerned. When they brought us to Sunday School, my parents would go into church and we sat in Sunday School in a little circle learning about God. And we didn't often go to physicians because we were Christian Scientists. And that's interesting because I had some very bad ear trouble. They wanted to do two mastoid operations which they did in those days. And my father didn't want to have that happen. I was getting ear infections. He brought me to this doctor who was also a Christian Scientist and he used (diathermy) treatment, blast-

TABLE 2.5. Religious Affiliation (%)

	Catholic	Jewish	Presby	Luther	Meth	ChSci	Baptis	Epis	None
Older	13	0	27	13	6	6	6	0	20
Younger	34	21	10	7	7	3	3	3	7
Total	27	14	16	9	7	5	5	2	11
U.S. 70+	20	3	73% Protestant						2
U.S. 60-69	25	2	65% Protestant						5

ing at the ears and it went away. I was lucky, I never had to have any operations. They weren't strict in that regard, but they were believers that a person can heal herself if her faith is strong enough. My dad was very involved in Eastern philosophy. And so at a very early age, I think about eight, he kind of initiated my sister and I into this philosophy of . . . Shiva as the one Lord, definitely monotheistic . . . . We talked about reincarnation when we were really young. It kind of coincided with Christian Science because everything lies within the individual. And so the individual can make changes based on the strength of his faith of the inner self. So that's how we were brought up, my sister and I. (Barbara)

It was rough going. For my first years that I remember, I was brought up in a tenement in Brooklyn that had a mixture of people from all over Europe and from the United Kingdom and it was then that I learned that you could be a Catholic, you could be a Protestant, you could be a Jew, or you could also be an Italian or a German or a Pole or a Russian or French and still be either a Catholic, a Protestant, or a Jew. So I got the whole business about religion and race or ethnicity clear in my head before I was three. (Diane)

Gigi's grandfather was a minister but no other narrator had a close relative employed by a church. Pat M would later become a Unity minister and Gloria would eventually work extensively in the Unity Church. Another narrator worked for a national church office for years.

Three women expressed conflict between religion and their homosexual lives when they were younger, and all of them were Catholics. Two of them resolved the conflict by abandoning the faith, and one found a sympathetic priest.

I was fighting a lot of Catholic issues. I came home one day and I said to my mother, and I was dating, this was in eleventh and twelfth grade. I was dating a boy that was going to the same school. I didn't believe in confession and my mother smacked me across the room. You could never question anything; you just didn't do it. In the confessional the priest would ask me: How far did you go with him? What did you do with him? I'm thinking, *he's getting his jollies from this.* If there is a god, I shouldn't have to tell a man, so to speak, what's going on with me. And I really didn't at that point in my life ever have any sins. So I had to make up sins. Whatever my pattern was, I'd say the same thing every week and I'd have to say a rosary afterwards for all my sins, but I was making them up. It was just hypocritical. (Ellen)

I think I've felt some guilt as far as religion is concerned. But I've managed always to find a priest. In fact one of them said, "Well, how old are you?" at one time. And I told him. And he said, "Well, I'll probably be hearing this from you for the next fifty years or something like that." There was one church where it was known that some of the priests were very sympathetic and understanding. (Mary2)

But I loved {} enough that I didn't care. Now we've gone to church and the Reverend has had a course on homosexuality in the Bible and she's convinced me this is not wrong. So that was a major thing in accepting gay words and "lesbian," knowing that this was not against the Bible. I'm happy with it. (Amelia)

LEAVING HOME

All but three narrators (94 percent) finished the customary primary-secondary school curriculum in the public school system or a Catholic school, and only one of the forty-four narrators did not complete high school in the usual manner. Addy spent her teenage years in a state institution or at home, not going to high school until she was eighteen and then dropping out. She did eventually complete a GED. Edie attended a boarding school as did Liz.

This uniformity in education is usual. All of Kehoe's 100 respondents (data collected in 1984) completed high school, as did all fifteen women in Franzen's study. However, only half of the narrators finished high school in the 1930s and 1940s Buffalo lesbian population (Kennedy and Davis 1997) which had many more lower class informants.

Franzen reports that many of her informants did not like school prior to college. Several women in this project commented on their school experiences and most of those did so favorably. Amelia said high school remains the best part of her life. Addy dropped out of high school because of her embarrassment over her age. Diane reminisced about discovering the library at the school. Sandy went to three high schools because her family was moving. Mary Lou and Sheri attended a one-room school where the ages were mixed. Vera went through high school twice! Ten women referred to high school as the place they discovered sex with women. Several women mentioned their athletic skills that crystallized in high school.

I moved to [the West Coast] when I was sixteen. [Mother] had no friends who had children, she didn't want any of her friends to know that she had a daughter my age. So she put my age back and sent me to junior high school 'cause it was two blocks down the street. I had just finished high school! So I took as many electives as I could take. (Vera)

[W]e went to a junior high school and elementary school and middle school all together, first to tenth grade because of the war. And we were in the elite section that was called College Hill. We had very small groups. Would you believe just last year we had a class reunion for the kids from first grade through tenth? I didn't go. But that group was extremely close. (Mary Lou)

I hated school with a passion. It cut into my free time. I think it's interesting that I went to a one-room school, all eight grades taught by one teacher. And it was a fantastic education. (Sheri)

In ninth grade I was becoming a hellion so they decided to send me to boarding school. It was basically, I'm sure, what saved my life, even though it was a Catholic boarding school with nuns in West Palm Beach and I wasn't Catholic. But that's another place where I realized that although my dad was middle class, he somehow found a way to get me into that school which was for upper class girls. I went to school with girls who were the daughters of presidents, not only of companies, but of countries. There were girls that were from the South American countries that were super rich. The president of the Dominican Republic, Trujillo's niece, Woodward, the daughter of the Jell-O family and Perry Como's daughter—people who were rich. I got a different kind of vision of other parts of society that I never would have been able to see. So basically, in my childhood, I got this look at a very wide range of cultural and economic diversity. (Edie)

My dad always said in later years, "I don't understand how you ever became a teacher. Every night you used to pray the school would burn down." And I did. But I hated school more because it took up my playtime, it took up time away from things I wanted to do. (Sheri)

Franzen (1996) discusses with great insight the desire of the women in her two different age cohorts to leave home. About the women born in the late 1800s, Franzen quotes Smith Rosenberg (1985, in Franzen 1996, p. 77) that for this spinster generation the challenge was to remain single and be independent from their families. "Not marrying did not challenge gender norms but leaving their families for reasons other than marriage did." These women had numerous examples of unmarried women living independent lives working for social causes, feeling solidarity with other women, with their femininity unchallenged.

This social situation was markedly different by the 1940s. By then single women "had been eliminated from the definition of 'real woman'" (Franzen 1996, p. 71) and were thought to be incapable of providing guidance for (as social campaigners), married mothers. Furthermore, psychology had made the single woman a sexual nonconformist, a probable lesbian. Whereas earlier women could wear men's-style clothing to work, or play sexually androgynous roles on stage, "ambiguous positioning was not as possible or as effective because issues of gender and sexual non-comformity were of greater public concern" after World War II (Franzen 1996, p. 71).

Franzen (1996) reports that the women at the turn of the twentieth century left home and sought independence to pursue socially meaningful work and fulfill their potential as women, often with parental and familial support. The fifteen women in this study who were born in 1935 and later left home with no such call to arms—in fact, with no political agenda or sense of solidarity—and often without familial support. They often reported feeling odd, or at odds with their peer group. The only purpose they expressed was to get away from home. That they wanted so keenly to get to away from home is evident in their choice of college or residence after high school—at least 47 percent of Franzen's women, the first of whom reached age eighteen in 1954, left home.

This situation was different among the forty-four women in this study, however. (See Table 2.6.) Leaving home or hometown for school or work was an unusual choice among both cohorts in this study. Among the older cohort, only three, or 20 percent, had left town by age nineteen, and among the younger cohort seven, or 27 percent, were living out of town at age nineteen. Twice as many of the younger women went away to college and less than half the proportion of younger women chose to work in their hometown instead of go to school. Nevertheless, these women stayed home by and large another two to four years. Their lives do not support the picture of women eager for social space and physical freedom or a picture of expanding opportunities for women to live independently.

TABLE 2.6. Narrators' Situation at Age Nineteen (%)

Situation	Younger	Older	Total
Gone away to college	17	7	14
Attending a college in hometown	41	46	45
Married	10	7	9
Working away from home	10	13	11
Working in hometown	10	27	16
In college somewhere	10	0	7

Marriage was the other acceptable way for a young woman to leave home and expresses a different sort of independence. One, or 7 percent, of the older women and three, or 10 percent, of the younger women married at age eighteen or nineteen. None of the women in Franzen's study married.

Perhaps the difference between the Franzen study and the Whistling Women can be explained by social changes over time, since more of the younger women in this study clearly were choosing to go away to college. No one in the Franzen cohort started college before 1954. Confining the comparison to the eight Whistling Women who were 18 in 1954 or later, only two of them had left their hometowns by age twenty (25 percent), and both had done so to go to college, reflecting the pattern seen in this study since 1938.

While the Franzen study participants began college in 1954, they continued to enter college until 1974. In this younger cohort of women now living in Albuquerque, at least 47 percent of the women had left home by age nineteen. Ninety-three percent of the women in that study were pursuing some degree at age nineteen (n = 14). Whereas leaving home to start a new family was acceptable at the turn of the last century, sixty years later it had become acceptable to leave home to go to college and to delay marriage. In the 1940s and 1950s, however, these young women were primarily choosing to go to school or work in their hometowns, and the need to get away from home was less frequently uttered than it would be in the following decades.

Six Whistling Women articulated a burning desire to leave home. Pat N hated her small town, her mother, her father, and her brother, viewing them all as backward and mean. She boarded a bus after her high school graduation ceremony to go to work at the Pentagon in Washington, DC.

> Well, I went off to college but I didn't like it. I ran away from college with my boyfriend. I wanted to get away from home so badly—I went to college and then arranged for my boyfriend to meet me and ran away with him. (Amelia)

> I got [to the West Coast] on December 31, 1939, and realized that as bad as I wanted to get away from the environment I had just left, that this one [moving in with her mother] didn't suit me any better. I hated my mother and she hated me. So I got married when I was eighteen. (Vera)

Planning to go to college or assuming they were going to college was more typical among this set of narrators and their families. It was standard, even by 1940, for girls to go to college in the United States. Newcomer (1959) reports that even by the 1950s daughters of working class families were going to college.

Myself, I'd planned on going to college since I was in about the fourth grade. I wanted to go to school; I wanted my education. (Gigi)

I decided when I was ten that I was going to be a nurse and that was what I thought about all through high school and especially then after my mother died. My mother died of breast cancer. She was diagnosed during my senior year in high school and she died when I was a sophomore [in college]. So that reinforced it. (Pauline)

My sister-in-law was a teacher and she did encourage me to become a teacher. But more than that, she encouraged me to get an education and never tried to really push me in any particular direction. . . . Well, everybody was going to school and I didn't really have much of a choice, so I decided I might as well enjoy it to a certain extent. And some things I did enjoy. I enjoyed writing. I enjoyed reading, always loved to read. (Sheri)

My mother was college educated and that was unusual, but that was back when they had two-year teachers college. My mother was a teacher. My father was in the lumber business. But my mother had a fetish about education. She said, "I don't care where you go or what you do, but you're going to college." All seven of us finished college. (Kay M)

In the older age cohort, 60 percent of the narrators earned an undergraduate degree, 40 percent earned a master's degree, and 13.3 percent a doctorate. In the younger group, the figures were slightly higher (Table 2.7). Altogether, 70 percent of the narrators had at least one college degree. Seven of these women were in college in the 1940s and seventeen in the 1950s. The small percentage of women with two-year or three-year degrees is interesting.

The first women in this project to enter college did so in 1937, and the first graduation occurred in 1941 (Roberta, Mary2). Going from start to finish in a degree program, without interruption, is the typical pattern among this group. There appear to have been few barriers to completing a degree once one entered a two-year, three-year, or four-year degree program in the period 1938 to 1959. The exceptions are few: Kay M and Carolyn both started college, went for one semester, and dropped out. They later continued their educations in different programs at different schools. Two women went to school and quit, never to return. Bobbie flunked out the first year but managed to get back into school the next year. I will explore their reasons for interrupting their degrees shortly. Sappho seems to have had the most difficulty completing a bachelor's degree in this group of women. She began college in 1954 and graduated in 1962, attending classes sometimes during the day, other times during the night.

During the 1940s colleges and universities were eager for women to enter their programs. Even schools such as Harvard opened their doors momentarily to women, but then closed them as men returned to school armed with the GI Bill. Joanna remembers, "While I was [in college in 1947], a corporation came to the college recruiting women to study engineering and then go to work in their companies around the United States. So I did that."

Nevertheless, in 1950, only 24 percent of the bachelor's degrees awarded in the United States went to women, a percentage that had not been that low since 1910 (Franzen 1996). Whereas women had been recruited in the 1940s, throughout the 1950s preference was given to GIs, and women were routinely excluded from programs in the better-paying professions. This exclusion may be apparent in the percentage of women who at the turn of the twentieth century received MD degrees and the decline in those advanced degrees in the very next generation (Table 2.7).

On the other hand, bachelor's and master's degrees for women were much more common after 1941 than they had been earlier.

Delaying College

Some women, a minority, were not able to start school and finish it without interruption. Carolyn dropped out after one semester of college in 1938 to work and support her mother and grandmother. Kay M left school after one semester to spare her parents the expense of

TABLE 2.7. Education of Narrators (%) in Franzen and Claassen Studies

	Franzen 1	Claassen older	Claassen younger	Franzen 2
Two-year or three-year degree	27	7	14	20
Bachelor's	20	60	76	73
Master's	13	40	48	47
PhD/MD	27	13	14	7

her tuition. She had two older siblings in college. Dorothy did not go to college after high school. "There was no way I could do it financially and I felt I was also needed at home; my money was needed at home." While working she married, and then raised her son.

> I stayed home that twenty years, raised my son, went to school. In fact I graduated a semester after he did. He graduated from high school in June and went off to college and I graduated the semester after in January. (Dorothy)

Jan didn't go to college, opting instead to work in her community theater and eventually to get a job at the local medical college. With the tuition benefits of her employer, she did begin a bachelor's degree in 1970.

> I graduated in 1980. I started in 1970 and became very frightened and dropped out. And then went back and dropped out. And then completed it. Well first of all I didn't go because I'm involved with women and that took up all my interest, which I blame myself badly for. But I wasn't ready; I was frightened. I went to the University of Pittsburgh and I walked into the big cathedral room and I was so overwhelmed by the building for one thing and figured that everybody there knew far more than I did and I was just totally overwhelmed by that and I had to keep dropping out. Until I took a class, I wanted to have a degree in art, I took an art class and a behavior modification class together and that helped me control myself and stay there. I was working at that point in Pittsburgh at the university, so I was getting tuition assistance.... I was very angry with myself for always dropping out. I did that a couple of times. Then I got into a Women Over 30 program and they were very helpful with keeping me focused on my goal which was to get a degree in art. And I got two degrees in art, but that was difficult because the chairman did not want women in the classes and did not want older women in the classes. And I thought, *I'm coming through anyhow, no matter what you say buddy.* And the Women Over 30 helped me with that. (Jan)

SUMMARY

With a sample of forty-four women's life stories, it is possible to explore U.S. social history. There are reflections here of the changes in social possibilities for both the narrators and their moms. The oldest moms abdicated the care of their daughters more frequently and worked while mothering more often. We will see how circumstances treated their daughters in the next chapter. The Depression was a formative event in several of the narrator's lives, and World War II affected all of them—some as girls, some as spouses, some as workers, some as students.

All of these women finished high school or earned a GED, and most of them chose to stay in their homes or hometowns in the two to four years following high school. A minority of them married, or left town, and expressed a strong desire to "get away." Sixty percent of the narrators earned a bachelor's degree and the vast majority of them went to school for four uninterrupted years to earn that degree. Most of the women who did not go to college were from working-class families.

As for how a lesbian is formed, there is no answer in the tales of forty-four women coming of age. It isn't due to working mothers, clearly, since 61 percent of the women in cohort II had stay-at-home moms. It isn't due to feminism, because feminism was in a lull from 1930 to 1950 when these women were girls and young adults. It isn't due to bad relations with mothers, since the women in the Franzen study liked their mothers, and it isn't due to bad relations with fathers, since only 7 percent of the Whistling Women disliked their fathers. It isn't due to lack of religious instruction as youths, because only 7 percent of the women in the younger age cohort said there was no religious teaching in their homes and because 5 percent of the general U.S. population aged sixty to sixty-nine said the same thing.

Whether after high school or after college, twenty-two of the Whistling Women chose to get married and eighteen had children. All of them eventually divorced. Their married lives are the subject of the next chapter.

Chapter 3

Marriage and Families

Numerous studies in the latter half of the twentieth century have shown that women who identify as gay or lesbian have similar life trajectories to straight women (e.g., Gagnon and Simon 1973). At the end of the nineteenth century and the first half of the twentieth century, scientific and academic wisdom made the opposite claim, that lesbians were more like men than like women. In this chapter it is perfectly clear that nearly half of these lesbians did have lives very familiar to straight women and men, because they were married.

The stereotype that ruled the 1960s and 1970s was that women were only in college to find a husband, or that women would marry soon after graduating or starting a job and then drop out of the workforce. In fact, three women married someone while in college and five narrators married within two years of graduating from a degree program (Table 3.1). Of the forty-four women in this project, twenty-two (50 percent) married at least once. Of this number, three married twice, and one married four times. Seven of the twelve married women with degrees dropped out of the workforce during marriage but all but two of them reentered the workforce upon divorce.

Forty-seven percent of the older women married and 52 percent of the younger women married, possibly reflecting a greater emphasis on marriage after 1950. In both cohorts, if a woman hadn't married by age twenty-nine she never married. Gigi divorced as soon as the honeymoon was over, after about six weeks. Three women inadvertently married gay men and two intentionally married gay men.

Twenty-two (50 percent) women never married, but many of those women did date. None of the women in the Franzen study (cited extensively in Chapter 2) chose to marry, and only 27 percent of the women in the Kehoe study (women who were sixty or older in 1984) married. That 50 percent to 100 percent of adult women in these samples did not marry is in sharp contrast to earlier age cohorts. Only 4.8

TABLE 3.1. Age at Marriage for Narrators (%)

Age	Older Cohort		Younger Cohort	
17-19	2	13%	2	7%
20-21	0	0%	7	24%
22-23	2	13%	2	7%
24-25	1	7%	0	0%
26-27	1	7%	1	3%
28-29	1	7%	3	10%
30-35	0	0%	0	0%
36-40	1 second marriage		1 second, 1 third marriage 1 fourth marriage	
41-50	0	0%	0	0%
51-60	0	0%	1 second marriage	

percent of the Franzen women born between 1915 and 1918 stayed single but that this figure represented a decline from the previous fifty-five years (Franzen 1996).

Other projects that have examined lesbian lives have either failed to sample women who married or downplayed this aspect of their lives (e.g., Gagnon and Simon 1973; Franzen 1996; Kehoe 1989). In this chapter I explore their heterosexual lives and marriages, their choice to have children, and their divorces.

DATING MEN

Ninety-one percent of the women in this study dated men sometime during their lives, and most of them talked about it during the interviews. One younger woman said she never dated men. One younger woman and two older women made no mention of dating men and did not marry, so perhaps they did not date.

Most of the daters saw dating as the natural thing to do, and many of them commented that it was the appropriate thing to do. Several women self-prescribed dating as a cure for loneliness or perceived difference or heartbreak. Sources of dates were often dances in their hometowns or through the business they worked at, and on several occasions the dates were military boys. Kay M, Pat N, Carolyn, and

Sandy specifically mentioned attending dances that were populated by male enlistees and/or meeting their future husbands at base or community dances.

> Then she left college and I started dating. I tried to date. It was just easier to be normal. (Bobbie)

> When she graduated, [my lover] went on to college and when I graduated, I started dating because I figured this is what you have to do. This is what women were supposed to do. And I dated and met a very nice young man. (Dorothy)

> Oh yes. I dated. I went along. I did it because basically it was the thing to do. But I had crushes on girls, you know, mad crushes on girls and, of course, could do nothing. (Claire)

> And I thought that if I got away from her, I wouldn't be that way [homosexual]. I dated; I dated guys. We went out on double dates, this sort of thing. (Cynthia)

> Well, in terms of what I knew what I was supposed to be doing was going out with guys and socializing and things like that. I never really enjoyed that. I just wanted to be with her, spend time with her. (Kate)

> When I was in high school I went out with guys. There was a rule. When you went out with someone, on the third date you kissed—not on the first, not on the second. So I went out with guys twice and I didn't have to kiss them. (Mitch)

> I was engaged to him and I was going to marry him, but I think I was just in love with love and I wanted to order him around, which I did. I was engaged three times, but I really knew in my heart I would never marry any of these men. I just wanted to be able to say, yes, I'm engaged to him. (Amelia)

> I just don't want to sleep with them, that's all. But I like men, I'd rather be in their company, straight men. I'd rather be in their company than to be with women. 'Cause I think women for the most part are pretty shallow, a lot of them. You don't find too many in my generation . . . (Roberta)

> I was the typical coed—I even kept track of . . . I dated seventeen men my freshman year in college and went steady with five of them. (Mary Lou)

Deciding Not to Marry

Some women did not date men, and some women decided to stop dating men. Several women expressed confusion in their young adult years created by dating boys and loving girls. But most narrators who stopped dating expressed dissatisfaction with the men they met and with those men's images of the wives they wanted to have at home.

Well, I had a feeling I was always . . . I went out with men later on when I got to be eighteen up till I was about twenty or so. And then just one night it got to be . . . I just thought I wasn't happy. This one night that changed everything, I sat in the car and I started to cry because I didn't want to be with him. I wanted to be with so and so. And then I thought, look, this back and forth business. I mean, one way or the other. So, that was it. (Chris)

I think the men that I was involved with by and large, I thought of as weaker than I was, let me put it that way. I knew I wanted a career. And the men that I was attracted to, the first man that I was dating in high school was very career oriented. But I really didn't have strong sexual feelings for him. Then I was involved with two other men particularly while I was in college. They were not going down this same road that I was interested in going down. And one of the men I was very sexually attracted to on the undergraduate level—I really was. But I just knew it wasn't going to work. (Ruth)

Oh, I dated and was very much involved with an English fellow. The main reason that we did not get married was in the process of talking about our lives together, it became clear to me that his intention was that his wife would never work. She would stay home and have babies. And I didn't think I would be happy just staying home and having babies. I didn't either accept or reject having babies but, you know, it was sort of the way things were. What didn't fit was not having a career, not working, not having the kind of intellectual stimulation I wanted. By the time I knew him, I was teaching and I was enjoying it enormously. (Judy)

And I got engaged a couple of times, but I just couldn't do it. The thing that saved me was, two things. One, the *Leave It to Beaver* program that I used to watch. It all centered on the two boys and the man. I kept looking for the woman who was always in the kitchen in her apron taking care of the boys' needs, you know. I thought, *Not for me.* And the other thing that saved me was every summer I would go to camp, which was lovely. And I would have these great emotional attachments to these women. And I'd come home from camp and give back the ring to the guy I was engaged to because it just wasn't the same, you know. (Bobbie)

I was engaged and went off to run a camp and fell in love with this woman. She talked me into not marrying and then he did several things I didn't like so I called it off. For one thing he sold my car without asking my permission and said I should put the money toward the car he bought "us." Then we went to a party and he got drunk and I walked home. It was a scary walk and I said that was it. (Mary Lou)

At this point it is appropriate to ask if the women who had women lovers in high school or college married. Eighteen of the younger women had female lovers by age twenty-three. Seven of those women married men. If we discount Joyce who married a gay man for convenience and Gigi who married for only six weeks, then only five of the eighteen women (28 percent) entered into matrimony with men. Among the older women, eleven women had sexual relations with women before age twenty-three and six of them (40 percent) married. It does seem that same-sex sexual experience at an early age is a good predictor that a woman will not marry a man. The average age for first same-sex sexual experience for women who never married is twenty-one and for women who did marry is thirty in this particular study. None of the narrators who did not marry expressed any regrets with that eventuality.

MARRIAGE

One half of the women in each age cohort married, reflecting the persistent expectation that women marry. For the twenty-two women in this study who did marry, several points must be considered in their satisfaction and experiences. Several women expressed glee, a sense of accomplishment, with being engaged and going through with the marriage. A few women felt pressured by their fathers to marry, and a few others used marriage as a way to get away from home.

Living as a married woman, particularly as a housewife, was pleasurable to a few of the narrators, as were going to parties and on business trips and having nice incomes. Having children was almost unanimously fulfilling for women who became mothers. But emotional fulfillment was rare from husbands and was far more often provided by a woman lover during the marriage. Divorces were generally painful, sometimes nasty, and usually instituted by the narrator.

The Decision to Marry

I went to work for the airlines. Everybody was partying and that was what it was all about, and then I got bored with that. I went home to visit and ran into this guy at the country club and everybody had us married off right away. I just fell into it.

I never did [like him] from the beginning. I didn't love him when I married him. The reason I married him, I hate to admit this, but my father sat me down and said I shouldn't string this fellow along, that he was a good provider, he was a good guy, he liked him, he'd make a good husband for me. It was the first time my father ever sat down with me. Well, gee whiz, so I married him. (Dawn)

And they just kept pushing both of us. Ruthie and Joe, my uncle and aunt, sister-in-law and brother-in-law, however you want to call them, kept pushing [him] and my grandmother kept pushing me and my other uncle kept saying, don't do anything you don't want to do. But I got to the point where my grandmother and I couldn't live in the same house. We're both hot tempered, we're both Aries and it had got to the point where I didn't back down anymore. I fought. So the easiest way to get out of that situation was marry this clown and I did. (Pat M)

Before this even happened, we thought we were happy. But I was being pressured terribly by my family to get married. This was seven years I think after we had met. Of course I didn't. Then one day at a party, I met a fellow, a gay man. He started telling me that he has to get married because his family is pressuring him to. This was the first time we met and he's proposing marriage 'cause he was with a very nice, good-looking Swedish boy. I don't know if he truly loved him, but he was looking for a situation where two gay men and two gay women could do something like this because he was a vice president of a very large company. And I liked him very much because he really seemed sincere and the way he figured it, it could work. At least it would work for a few years. 'Cause we're talking about 1963 or so, things were pretty tough for [gay] guys, especially in business. But anyway, we started seeing them as a foursome and we liked each other very much and we decided, okay, the two of us are going to get married. But his boyfriend was from Sweden; said he didn't need it and, he didn't want it. So we got married, which was a terrible guilt trip, so bad that before the wedding, I went to the hospital with a fever of unknown origin, which was stress. I finally got better and we got married in Chicago. And my family just went insane for him, buying him all kinds of presents. He was a very good-looking, very nice, very sweet man. (Joyce)

It's really surprising I ever married him. He was a fireman at the time and had a business that he was doing on the side. And he was the one fellow that never showed up on time. [O]ne night he was supposed to come at seven o'clock or so, and I told my father that when he finally showed up to tell him I was gone. And my father gave me a long lecture on what an enterprising guy he was and the fact that he was a full-time fireman and working at his new business, that I was making a big mistake. Anyway, after my father lectured me, I waited around and apologized up and down. But [being late] was a pattern he always had when I was dating and carried over into our marriage.

We had a Polish wedding. To this day, several of the events that took place, I don't know what they meant. I never wanted a big wedding. I always wanted to run away and get married. We tried to talk his mother into allowing us just to elope. But no way, too many people owed her weddings and she felt she was owed back and this was the way it was going to be. So there were 600 people for breakfast and a big band playing. All our pictures were taken on fire trucks. It was a hoot for somebody that likes to sink into the bushes. It was quite an event in my life. (Ellen)

I finally ended up at nursing school and I met this man there. And I guess then is when I fell in love with love. He looked like Alan Ladd; he was very handsome. He had very suave manners. Well, needless to say, I ended up marrying him. (Amelia)

Because in those days that's what you did, got married. It was assumed that you would get married. And so you did. But truly speaking, I wouldn't have gotten married had I not wanted to. I was in love with this man. I cared a lot for him. He filled a lot of needs for me emotionally at the time, till I grew up. Once you grow up, you know. (Barbara)

So I got married [the first time] when I was eighteen. Got me out of the house. And I continued to go to school and they skipped me of course [because I had already finished high school]. So I got out of high school in June of 1942, but I was married. But nobody knew it. They wouldn't let you go to school then if you were married. (Vera)

Having worked for county government at that time, I went down to the divorce records and I pulled every divorce paper and I read them [about my second husband]. And in every one of them there was a common thread that said, sexual incompatibility. His first marriage lasted a year and a half, his second marriage lasted six months, and the third marriage lasted just barely two years. So I knew all I needed to know. So the next time I saw him I said, "You said we were going to get married on April 10. Are you sure that's what you want to do? Because it sounds like a pretty good plan to me." And he said, "Well, maybe not April 10, but sometime close by." And so we gathered up all these people, the couple that was there when he made the statement and two other couples. And we all had a brand new Thunderbird and we all took off and went to Las Vegas. And we got married [second husband] in a chapel in Las Vegas.

I married [the second time] because I was living in an apartment. I had never lived in an apartment before. We had always had a home. And this was a way to get out of that apartment and get into a home. We had a two-bedroom, two-bath place. It was a good way to get my son out of the city and into the suburbs. (Vera)

January of 1950 I got married [at age seventeen-and-a-half]. My parents were terribly against it 'cause they had high hopes that I would do something great, intellectually in school or what have you. And they were very much opposed to my getting married, but somehow I did. (Barbara)

Well, in college I met women 'cause I went to a women's college. Well, I guess one reason I decided to get married was that I didn't know how to meet women in Washington, DC. (Joanna)

Married Life

I was married for a year and I was pregnant and at the end of the pregnancy I just knew that I could not be straight, that I was gay. During this time I had met another very wonderful person. We talked this over, chewed this over, digested it, spit it out, and decided that I should stay married for the sake of my son 'cause he needed a father. We were indoctrinated into that theory and we believed it, which is not true at all. So we were married until Paul graduated from high school and he went off to college. And at that time my husband and I were divorced and I went and lived with this friend of mine. Now I also had a gay relationship with her all through the twenty years that I was married. And this was whenever we could get together. (Dorothy)

I'd like to start off with is what I consider a preference since I was married and enjoyed married life quite a bit. I was very heterosexual. I was married to a very nice man. We had an extremely close and friendly relationship, a wonderful friendship and [I] was treated always as an equal, no power plays, no controlling. We each contributed to our relationship and we had tremendous bonding even if we would not have had two children, which of course strengthened our bonding. I've been divorced now for twenty-nine years and I still feel very close to my former husband. (Nan)

We were busy. It wasn't as rewarding to me [as my gay social life] and it was something I felt we had to do. My husband and I gave parties once in a while. We gave New Year's Eve parties and there was always a crowd over Christmas Eve and Christmas Day. We went out to dinner a couple of times a month with people that he worked with. When he would fly out of town for the weekend, sometimes I'd go with him. He'd win contests and trips and stuff and we'd go to New York and Chicago. So it was certainly there. It wasn't very rewarding for me, but it was something I had to do. (Dorothy)

Anyway, I married him and we thought this was going to be the end of our troubles. It was only the beginning. We took two apartments in an apartment building in Queens, New York. One above the other. And it was very difficult, not with my family so much 'cause they were in Chicago. But his family lived in New York and we read the riot act to them that we're private people and they must never come over without calling, never. And we decided his apartment would be the marriage apartment. And we both furnished our apartments nicely. His was quite masculine and mine was quite feminine. We put a common telephone between and you can't imagine what an interview that was with the telephone company, trying to explain to them why we needed a phone in both apartments that would ring in both apartments on the same line. We told them it had something to do with business, we were in business together and we needed this communication thing. We had three telephones, each apartment, my private telephone, [his] private telephone, the marriage phone. And we placed them in the kitchen of the apartment so that if it would ring in either apartment, if I were home, I would stomp on the floor three times so he'd know I'm answering it. If he didn't hear this, he would answer. And every time I would get out of the elevator—we were on the seventh floor and he was on the sixth—I would have to look around the hall to make sure nobody saw me going into my apartment. That can make somebody very neurotic. Anyway, this marriage lasted ten years and I knew of two other gay couples doing this. (Joyce)

And truthfully, when we first got married, it was okay. We were okay. It was just that after Paul was born, he started acting strangely. Not coming home and then he'd come home like at 2 or 3 o'clock in the morning. And the kicker was I always knew where he was. He was at work. He was a workaholic and he just wanted to stay at work and not come home. And on and on and he kept going through all of this stuff and he always wanted me to go to church. Every night, go to church. There's something going on over at the church; go to church. And I have never been one to run through the door every time it's unlocked. And then I sort of dug in my heels and I wouldn't go at all, not even on Sunday. Whoever heard of a Catholic not going to church on Sunday? I found out that the spirituality I needed was within me. It wasn't down the street in an edifice. And that caused problems of course and then there were other problems. He then decided that we should get into some kinky sex and I said no, absolutely not. (Pat M)

That baby was born February 12 and [first husband] went into the service six weeks later. He and my mother got together and got this notion that I should move in with her. I wasn't as strong willed then, I guess. So they kind of overrode me and I did that and that was another major mistake in my life. Then his grandmother died and so I moved in with his grandfather. And I stayed there. I didn't get along with him. There were two other girls whose husbands were in the military and I found a place with one of them. I stayed there until I knew he was coming back from the service. . . . And then I started encountering all of these difficulties. I loved the house; I loved cleaning and making the home; I loved nesting. But I couldn't stand the intimacy. Every time we got into an intimate situation, I'd end up running into the bathroom and throwing up after the fact. I just couldn't stand it. So I thought, there's something wrong with this picture but I don't know what it is and I don't know what to do about this. (Vera)

[The second husband] was really good-looking. Everybody thought we made the perfect couple. I was involved in all of these civic and political organizations and he was a perfect escort. And we did a lot of entertaining. Well, occasionally we'd go to some social function and you know how in the heterosexual community, the guys are hanging out over here and they're telling dirty jokes and the women are hanging out over here and they're talking about their last delivery and their last surgery and all of that other crap that heterosexual women talk about. And I was bored to death, so I would leave and go back where the guys were to hear the jokes. And I walked into one of those sessions and at the time I walked in, he was saying, "I'm going to get rid of this one forty and replace it with two twenties." So my ego just went completely nuts and I said, "And what in the hell are you going to do that for? You're not doing anything with the one forty." You could hear a pin fall in that room. I don't know why I was so angry. (Vera)

So even in the previous city we lived in, where I knew [he] was meeting men on the side. I felt like the jerk whose husband is going around. I just felt like those guys all knew and there I am the stupid wife going along with all this. (Marilyn)

But a sad, sad mistake [marriage] was. What I didn't realize, he was so nice to everybody else and our home life was miserable. (Amelia)

I didn't hear much about gays but I knew that I loved girls and women. That's the thing, I think that I chose the closet of marriage. I was really closeted in my marriage. My marriage was one of those, as Sonia Johnson says, one slave/one master, one prisoner/one guard. I really felt like I was a prisoner in my married life. (Edie)

I asked him one day, I said, "if the business and the house were burning down, where would you go first?" He said the business. The business will make the money. Honest to God, that was a point where I thought, I don't need this. . . . She was the one I think that really drove me to suicide. I'd gone off to a motel with a bottle of vodka and a bottle of pills. My husband missed me and came out looking for me. And he and his friend were driving around looking for me and they found me and came in and broke the door down and took me to the hospital. And when I woke up, she was yelling at me, "What the fuck's the matter with you? Why did you try to do something so stupid?" Oh, I told her I was crazy about her. I thought maybe that would turn her, but it didn't. (Ellen)

I wanted to spend time with my kids and do things with them. I hated going on vacation with my ex-husband. He was boring. He just was very unemotional and he didn't spend too much time with the kids. And basically he left that up to me. I emotionally got all my satisfaction having these relationships [with women] that I had. (Kate)

The third husband, he was working, I was working and we had about the same income. No, he made a lot more than I did, but we had the same way of thinking about money. One thing we did, he did not want me to work when we were married. However, we were married just short of a year and I got a hold of this job I could do. I had gotten a license in the meantime. And he said, all right, as long as I don't notice it around the house, you can work. So I did. This was the country too and he wanted to get a Troy-Bilt tiller and they were $500 and this was in the 1970s. He said, "But I don't have the $500" and I said, "But I do." All this time he didn't care what I did with the money. He didn't know I was saving it. So, anyway, he got that and now he's interested in my work. So then we began to work together. See, his first wife had spent everything and he thought all women were like that. She just ran up credit cards and stuff like that. So we accumulated quite a lot. (Sandy)

I'm finding out who I am. I had to sublimate my life all the time I was married 'cause I was busy raising children, moving around from place to place and, of course, my husband was not a handyman or anything. He was a workaholic and an alcoholic so he was gone most of the time. So I was the one who ended up redoing the whole irrigation system on the yard or fixing the roof or doing the plumbing or the electrical or the painting or whatever had to be done. I did that because I was just mechanically inclined anyway. (Dawn)

Bing enjoyed being a housewife, particularly remodeling and sewing clothing. She had three sons, the first in her second year of marriage. She continued to run around with a group of friends from Ohio State. Pat N's husband hid from her two previous marriages, didn't want her working after he got a job, spent school loan money on a car rather than tuition, and was busted for writing bad checks. He was also physically abusive.

CHILDREN

No, to me it was that sense of, that's what I wanted to do [to marry] and I wanted to have children. I wouldn't have given that up. I didn't get a chance to have a girl. I had three boys—all men. (Edie)

My first son was born when I was twenty. I was burning to have children, I wanted children in the worst way. I waited for a little bit until I was nineteen. We used contraception. And by the time I was twenty and half, my older son was born with much difficulty. . . . I wanted to be the first one [in my crowd] to take my baby strolling in a carriage as a young mother and I couldn't, I was lying in bed for six months . . . . I was really told not to have any more children because of that. But when he was about five, I decided that I wanted another child. And so, I had my second son. . . . I've always felt that the little guy, that for some reason I knew him. I looked in his eyes when he was just about a week old, and he had these big black eyes with long lashes, and there was such recognition, the most amazing recognition with this baby. There's a different kind of feeling. The older one, like he's my child, my baby. With the younger guy, there's a different relationship. (Barbara)

Of the twenty-two women who married, eighteen had children to raise. As Edie and Barbara stated, many of the women expressed interest in their children and satisfaction from mothering. The older women birthed nine sons and three daughters. The younger women birthed at least twenty sons and ten daughters (gender of two children unknown). Table 3.2 offers a look at the number of children birthed by the narrators, compared to their own family size as children. The smallest household had one child and the largest household had five children. Including the children raised by Mary1, who never married, the largest household had six children.

A smaller percentage of younger narrators had no child. In fact, the younger women had larger families than did the older women and larger families than they grew up in generally. Among the mothers of the narrators, forty-four women birthed 102 children, an average of

TABLE 3.2. Numbers of Children Birthed by Narrators Compared to Their Own Childhood Families

Children	Own Birth families		Older Group		Younger Group	
0	NA		2	29%	2	13%
1	13	30%	1	14%	3	20%
2	20	45%	2	29%	4	27%
3	6	14%	2	29%	4	27%
4	2	5%	0		1	7%
5	1	2%	0		1	7%
6+	2	5%	0		0	

Note: Twenty-two women married, eighteen birthed children

2.32 children per mother. Excluding the women who married for less than a year or knowingly married a gay man (n = 4), the older group of narrators averaged 2.20 children, and the younger narrators averaged 2.46 children. As the 1950s to 1970s stereotypes predict, women married in those years in greater proportions, stayed married longer, and birthed more children than had mothers since the 1920s.

In a survey of people fifty-five and older published in 1997, Yutema found that 45 percent of women sixty-five and older have at least three children. Among the Whistling Women this figure is 41 percent. Sixteen percent were childless in Yutema's sample; 53 percent are childless in this sample.

Three women who did not enter into heterosexual marriages raised or helped raise children they did not birth. Mary1 took her brother's four children when he and his wife decided to give them up for adoption at their divorce, and she also simultaneously raised two children belonging to her lover. Gigi took up with a woman who had five children and co-parented them for eleven years. Sheri, of the older age cohort, adopted her lover's grandnephew and may have been one of the first single women to adopt in the state of New York.

Bing had a son who was gay and died of AIDS in the 1990s. She has gotten involved in the AIDS Quilt project. One of the children Gigi raised is gay also.

And when I was living in Phoenix, my youngest niece came to live with us. She was fifteen. When I had lived in Boston with the woman with the two kids, I had my brother's four as well because he and his wife split up and they were going to put all the kids up for foster homes 'cause neither one of them wanted them. So I took them.

Sooner or later they went with the mother. She remarried and they went with her. The youngest one I guess was still giving her a lot of trouble, so she wrote me a letter and asked if I would take her back. And so she came to live with us in Phoenix. (Mary1)

He was her grandnephew. Her niece, when she was a teenager, had gotten involved with a guy and begged him to marry her, which he did, but it was a fraudulent kind of thing. So Jane and I helped her get an annulment and bought her a car and started taking care of Scott on weekends and things like that. His grandmother really didn't want to get involved. His grandmother was Jane's sister. So anyway, we took him more and more. Of course, vacation time, I had him. And I said to his mother, look, he's a bright little boy. He wasn't a year old, but you can tell. I said, you can't bounce him around, it'll destroy him, he's got to have stability. And I said, either you put him up for adoption or you find a way to make a stable life for him or let Jane and me adopt him. And she thought about it for a week or so and then she said to me, I would like you and Jane to have him. . . . I did because Jane was too old by state law. In fact the laws were just changing and I was probably one of the first single women to be allowed to adopt a child.

The adoption proceedings were started when he was about four years old. So that would have been 1966. He was born in 1962. But the actual adoption was dragged out forever. We had two different lawyers. One old guy quit and he said, "The laws are changing and I'm really not interested." And so we got a younger person and then he got sick. I wanted the adoption done by the time he started school because I know that name changes follow forever. . . .

But I think raising a boy too gave me the excuses that I needed to go ahead and do some of these things. I bought him a trailbike when he was eight years old. And then when he was ten I traded that and got him a street legal. Only he wasn't old enough to drive it, but I got my license for it. . . .

I knew Jane was picking up with other people at that time, but by then we had the boy to raise and I didn't make a fuss. I'm very nonconfrontational and I didn't want to upset anything because I was busy working as hard as I could and enjoying raising the boy. But I also knew enough to know that if I had to do it all by myself, I couldn't manage. It would be difficult to manage all by myself. So I just shut up. (Sheri)

Usually it was just one [boarder]. There was a time we had two, but usually it was just one man and he had his own room and I did all of his laundry and his meals and everything. And I was breeding dogs at the time also, little Boston terriers. And I had little puppies and I had to get up in the night and sometimes they couldn't nurse, you know, and so I would lay down on the floor with them 'cause I would be afraid I wouldn't hear them. And we had bitches' milk—even in those days you had to mix it with water. And they would peep about every two hours and I would just lay there with them and give it to them. . . . I did this until my fourth child was born.

Yeah, up until the fourth child was born and I couldn't do it anymore. Because these kids were born like shotguns, boom, boom, boom. And I had the fourth child and the oldest one was still not in school. And yet it is biologically easier to have—I could have had another two or more in that time. And then along about two and a half years after the last one, I had the fifth one. And after that, my husband didn't want any more either. I didn't do any more with boarders or dogs or anything after she was born. I just couldn't do it. (Sandy)

I just felt like, this was what I chose. I came from a divorced family when I was a kid and I made kind of a pact with myself that if I ever got married, I was never getting divorced. I was not going to do that to my kids, what was done to me. So when it came time, and I realized that this marriage was no good for me, I stayed in that abusive marriage anyway. One of the reasons, I think, that I just didn't strike out on my own before that was because I just couldn't see how I could be a single mom and how I could do all that by myself. (Edie)

Birth control is a topic that came up several times, and its use allowed the narrator to take some control of her reproduction.

I got married in March and six weeks later I guess it was, I got pregnant. I had never heard of birth control. I stayed married thirteen years. (Vera)

I have three children, two boys and a girl. They were all under four years of age. It took me a while to figure out what was happening here. But he was Catholic and I was not, so one didn't use birth control. And finally I decided, yes, one must use birth control. This is getting ridiculous. (Amelia)

I had my tubes tied after the fourth child. . . . I had him tie his tubes at one point after we had our children. But we started swinging; we went to swinging clubs and I didn't want him to start procreating anymore. And I thought it would be safer for the future of our children. I look back on it now and I don't know how I ever talked him into it because I had already had my tubes tied. But he didn't seem to question it and he went ahead and did it. (Ellen)

So when that time came, there wasn't any more talk of religion—of the church or anything. And the whole thing was about birth control. There's such a thing as being a little too religious, if you know what I'm saying. I know there are a good many Catholics now that run right over this birth control stuff and they take the pill and stuff like that. Well, I was pregnant with the last child when I heard of the pill and that was in December 1962. He was born in

January 1963. And I knew I was never going to have another baby when I heard that. You know you hear about these abortions that people have and I can understand that. Not that I would say I would do it myself, but I can see why people. . . . I was desperate. (Sandy)

What kind of moms were these narrators? Reviewing the categories in Table 2.1 in which the moms of the narrators were the subject of inquiry, it is interesting to note now what kind of moms the narrators themselves turned out to be (Table 3.3). Not surprisingly, none of the mothers referred to themselves as abusive.

More of the Whistling Women were single moms and more were working moms. Two of the narrators with children abdicated their mothering responsibilities either permanently or until the children were adults, and one mother did so temporarily. Pat N became a single parent with a two-year-old at her divorce and, while going to community college, placed the child in foster care. She became gay when her daughter was six and enjoyed gay life, but thought that it was no life for a child. She moved away from her lover to a teaching position on the West Coast where the child spent many evenings with baby-sitters while she went out to gay bars. When Pat N was admitted to a master's degree program in another state, she gave up the girl for adoption before she moved. She did not want to parent.

TABLE 3.3. Narrators As Moms Compared to Their Own Moms' Situations (%)

	1919-1939	1930-1949	Narrators*
Single moms	7	11	14
Working moms	20	18	43
Stay-at-home moms	33	61	52
Institution/other family parented	26	0	10
Had only one child	33	24	24
Four-plus children	20	17	14
Foreign born	13	10	4
Abusive	40	33	0

*Percentage of twenty-one narrators who raised or birthed children. Determining a figure for single moms is difficult. I have restricted the count to women who lived alone for at least two years. Cynthia was (foreign) born in Canada.

DIVORCE

The reader might suspect that marriages with gay women would be short-lived and that marriage between gay women and gay men would end quite quickly. However, this was not this case among this sample of gay women (Table 3.4).

A significant number of the younger women stayed married much longer than the older women. Sixty-seven percent of the married younger women were married for at least seventeen years versus 17 percent of the older women. All but one older narrator ended her marriage after thirteen years. They even persevered longer in their marriages than do "heterosexual women" in general. The average length of first marriage for a heterosexual couple in the United States in 1998 was eleven years but was 13.41 years for these twenty-two lesbians, while the average of all marriages in the United States is 7.2 years (www.unmarried.org/statistics.html) and 12.64 years for the Whistling Women. Dawn was married for thirty-five years. After twenty-two years of loyalty to a husband who turned out to be gay, Marilyn was served with papers for divorce alleging unfaithfulness due to her recent feelings for women.

TABLE 3.4. Length of Marriages Involving Narrators

Years Married	Older	Younger
< 1		Gigi
2-4	Addy	Sandy 2nd, 3rd, Pat N 1st
5-6		Pat N 2nd
7-8	Pat M, Kay M	
9-10	Vera 1st, Diane	Joyce, Nan
11-12	Bing, Amelia	
13-14	Vera 2nd	Sandy 4th
15-16		
17-19		Pauline, Liz, Ellen, Kate, Sandy 1st
20-21		Kathleen, Edie
22-25	Joanna	Marilyn, Barbara
> 25		Dawn

As a matter of fact, it was a big surprise that I felt anything for my ex-husband. And I did love that man and I still do as a brother or a friend. He's a good man. We had a deep and a very sweet relationship, even when we divorced. (Barbara)

I think I could have had seven [children] and he wouldn't have said anything. He wasn't doing anything and we could afford them. It wasn't a matter of money; it was a matter of how long my nerves would hold up. I was doing it all.

We had a little gun and I took the gun one day and pointed it at him. Well, he called the police and the police came and took my little gun away. I picked up a butcher knife one night; I was going to kill him. I was drinking and I said to myself, "The only way I'm ever going to get rid of him is kill him." I picked up the butcher knife, walked down the hallway, looked at him sleeping and I thought, *I am an absolute loony.* I shocked myself. (Ellen)

I graduated in 1970. It took me four years to do this two-year course. I started in 1966 and I graduated in 1970 and this is the only thing that saved my sanity. I was about psychotic by the time I left him. I mean that's the other side of the story. I can remember some of the things I said, some of the things I did, and I really did not have a sound mind. Just over a period of time, this constant verbal stuff gets to you. It's very abusive.

He wanted to get the divorce because I left him, that's why. I did my share of stuff too, see. And the reason that I did that was because he wasn't with me; he's emotionally distant anyway. I mean, it was like living in a desert emotionally. But still you shouldn't do those things.

[He would say] These were somebody else's children that I was pregnant with, things like that. He did a lot of that. I went up to visit with my mother in 1962 when I was pregnant with the last child. And he says, "Well, I guess it's all right for you to go up there while you're pregnant because you can't get pregnant while you're pregnant."

Then he still asked me to go back. Now I didn't want this other guy anymore. But I didn't want to go back either. Now I had a way of supporting myself and it looked as if I had gone to school to leave him. It looks that way but that's not why I did it. I did it because I had to do something. I was going crazy, literally, in that house. And getting out there and going to school was a salvation to me. Because if you're going to graduate, get these classes down and get the grades, you've got to apply yourself. And even though it took me a long time to do it, it was still a lot of focus. And at the same time, although I didn't realize I was doing this, I was making an example for my children. (Sandy)

When the children all grew up and went away, I had no more reason to stay with this person whom I had no interests with. (Dawn)

[Second husband] was a terrible person, not only verbally abusive but every other way. He was worse than what I left. He was an alcoholic. I was supporting him; he wouldn't work.

I was working at the hospital in Bradenton. He was very abusive sexually and financially, emotionally, physically. I was getting socked every once in a while, you know, very poor self-image at the time. But this is all because of what I had when I was married. I was just primed for somebody like this. But he paid attention to me; this was the big thing. Even though it was negative attention. We moved to California twice, gold mining and things like that. There was things that he did like paying attention. Even though it wasn't good, it was something. I didn't have it; I was ignored. It was like I wasn't even there sometimes [with the first husband]. So anyway, I did heal myself on that and I didn't have anything to do with him after a while.

So a few weeks later, the kids are away, the dog is with me and I'm getting the clothes off the line, late at night, about 11 o'clock. . . . I happened to turn toward the street and I saw his car come by. I ran for the back door. I didn't make it. I just dropped everything and I got in the house and I couldn't close the door. He got in the door before I could close it. And the dog is right there. . . . And so after a few minutes of that, he just let go of the door and I shut the door and that was it. And I never heard from him again. He never came back. (Sandy)

He started going out with other women and I know three in particular. One used to phone me at home all the time and say, "What can I do?" I said, "You got yourself into this; you get yourself out." I started to divorce him once but my mother came down. Mother was ruler of the roost, very matriarchal. . . . She came down and said, you cannot divorce him because we've never had a divorce in the family, blah, blah. So she talked to him and he decided he would behave himself, which lasted maybe all of two weeks. Anyway, then we moved to Orlando and I did divorce him at that time, 1964. (Amelia)

When I left him it was because I found I was attracted to women and I had asked him to go into therapy with me because I was very interested in resolving with him to further our marriage. He just couldn't bring himself to do something like that; he didn't understand going into therapy and talking. I decided I needed to give him his freedom and I divorced him even though I still loved him very much so that he could have a complete life. I never felt that I was giving him a complete life after I became sexually involved with a woman.

I believe the reason that I sought the affection from a woman is maybe I didn't feel I was being as unfaithful to my husband. I'm not sure about that. Being young I sought more affection in more physical closeness than I was receiving. Otherwise I received everything else that should be involved in a relationship, the friendship and the caring and understanding, just being there for one another and the communication. It was mainly because of the physical that I left my marriage. (Nan)

I mean she was still dating her fellow. I did something really stupid. I didn't want to go through with it and my father made me. 'Cause I knew I did not belong with this man. When my dad came to pick me up [for the wedding], I said, "Dad I'm not going. Please don't make me go." He says, "Oh yes, you're going." So I was late for the wedding. I was only married about six weeks. 'Cause when I came home from the honeymoon I filed for divorce and moved back in with Mary. So we got a divorce and it was the same judge that had given him his other divorce and told him if he ever saw him in divorce court again, particularly with a young woman, he was dead meat.

Oh God, yes, [he resisted the divorce]. He was terrible; he was awful. He changed the locks on the apartment and everything. I had to get my mother and the police to break in to get my clothes out and stuff. He tried to sell my boat while I was gone. I was in the hospital, ill for a couple of weeks. I came out and he was trying to sell my boat. He had wiped out the bank account, everything. He wanted the ring back. I said, "Guess what, you'll have to chop my hand off," and I walked away. (Gigi)

Mine [divorce] was not a problem, because my ex and I had grown apart over the years. Actually, he asked me for a divorce and I was thrilled that he did because at that time I was going with Joan and I just couldn't bring myself to say I wanted a divorce. But he did. He asked me if I was happy and I said no. He said, "Well, I'm not either. Maybe we should separate." And I said, "Maybe that's a good idea." And that was it. It was just as simple as that. (Barbara)

When we separated—it was a separation—we'd see how we did because here I was ready now to go out to teach. He wasn't so sure he wanted me to do that because who's going to put his dinner on the table at five o'clock at night? Well, I don't know, we'll have to work something out. So we were battling these kinds of things. So we separated for a year and at the end of that year then he wanted to reconcile and I said, "No, no way." So I really don't know what he thought. Once he did ask me if I was bisexual. And I said no. If anything I was probably asexual, which I probably wouldn't do now. (Dorothy)

About three months into my lesbian relationship—we were each living in our own separate houses with our kids and our husbands—I finally told my husband I wanted a divorce. And he said, "Well, I know what's going on. I know that you're in love with Doreen." So he said, "I'll tell you what, I'll leave for a month and I'll be back in a month and you'll see how much you miss me." But he never came back, and I never missed him. Then it took a long time— in those days you had to have a legal separation in order to get a non-contested divorce in New York State. (Edie)

It is clear by now that these twenty-eight marriages by twenty-two women ended for various reasons. Some marriages lacked any intimacy, or even fondness. Other marriages were viewed as restrictive. Kate's husband didn't want her owning a restaurant because he made enough money. Pat N's husband didn't want her to work, nor did Sandy's third husband.

It could be that these marriages lasted so much longer than those of "heterosexual" women because these women found emotional outlets with other women, allowing them to tolerate the marriage. Not only did a number of these married women have affairs with women during their own marriages, but the narrations indicated another fourteen women in marriages to be their lovers. Henry's study of homosexuals, begun in 1935, also found that many of the women were married while having affairs with women (Faderman 1991).

For several women, attraction to women or an attraction to a specific woman led to the divorce. Ten women had affairs with women during their marriages, and one had sex with several different women in swinging clubs but not in relationships. For Dorothy, an affair lasted twenty years, and for Liz, seventeen years, the duration of both marriages. Kate, Diane, and Bing also had several affairs during marriage. For the other five women, the affairs happened quite late in their marriages. Liz divorced her husband for reasons that included a waiting lover. When she called to tell the lover she had just left her husband, the lover ended their relationship.

Marriages were also abusive in some cases. Pat N (first husband), Sandy (second husband), and Liz each found themselves in physically abusive situations. Amelia experienced verbal abuse as did Sandy. Sandy also identified financial abuse in her second marriage.

The Economic Impact of Marriage and Divorce

The women who were married for longer than a year were asked to identify their socioeconomic class while married, as were the never-married women (Table 3.5).

As expected, married women seem to have fared better economically than unmarried women, but only slightly so and not to the extent that was the situation in the nineteenth century, or even in the first quarter of the twentieth century. It seems that by 1950, a woman didn't need to marry to live a middle-class or even an upper-class lifestyle.

TABLE 3.5. Socioeconomic Class in Midlife

Class	Married Women		Never-Married Women	
Upper	3	16%	2	8%
Upper middle	4	21%	6	24%
Middle	11	58%	15	60%
Lower middle	0	0	2	8%
Lower	1	5%	0	0

Even the three women who were not married but raised other women's children were in either the upper class or middle class. A job, or a husband, can explain a woman's class during her working years among this group. More subtle impacts of marriage on a woman's later years are presented in Chapter 8.

Economic Impact of Divorce

Divorce has many economic ramifications. Immediate economic freedom occurred for some women, immediate economic hardship for more. Although many of them didn't think about it at the time, the marriages and divorces, in many cases, have affected their retirement monies. A number of women likely had no credit record once they were divorced (Ellen) making starting over difficult in some cases. Ellen got money from the sale of the house but was uncertain what to do with that money to guard it, seeking advice from six investment advisors. Several women opted to divorce without alimony, and a few others lost child support monies when the children turned eighteen, as well as the house they had been living in.

Divorce failed to change appreciably the economic status of women who were already in the lower classes or who were working or recently educated at the time of divorce. It did significantly impact those women who had three or more children and were marginally employed.

[The divorce didn't change my economic status substantially] because we were a striving young couple with children. When I was married I wasn't working. After I was divorced, then I started to work, gained a lot more self-esteem. And it was very interesting years because they were very lean years, didn't have much. I did part-time jobs. I got involved in a couple of businesses before I got involved in real estate. The businesses weren't big businesses. They were more of a physical nature, like vending machine business. (Nan)

The first divorce—actually I was better off because I know how to handle money and he didn't. Now I had an income and I could manage it. I wasn't really saving that much but I did all right. I always said that all I wanted was enough money to be able to get a pizza once a week. But we [when married] couldn't; we didn't have any money. We had trouble even buying bread. I had to take bottles to the store to buy bread, I remember a few times. So I now could support myself and that was a big thing to me. (Sandy)

Yes [divorce dramatically changed my financial situation]. It should have been $300 a month from him but he would only give me what I needed to buy groceries and clothes. And then Mother said, "If you come up here I will give you $300 a month." Plus I went to work. So mother gave me an allowance of $300 a month. (Amelia)

I didn't get any kind of a settlement when I left my first husband. He was supposed to give me $3,000 and he didn't—a one-time thing. And he got the house which was paid for, which I felt was fair because he had the kids there. I felt that was fair. I had to take him to court two years later to get that money. I was bound I was going to get it.

The second husband, there was no money there. . . . I left him very well provided for. He had twenty acres with sixty pecan trees—producing trees. They were big. And a big house that he had built himself; it was a big house. And he had three bathrooms and two kitchens and I don't know how many bedrooms—enormous fireplace, big stuff. And it was probably worth about $150,000 plus the land. So I got from that marriage $50,000 worth of stock certificates. He gets the house and the business. It seemed like a lot, $50,000, however, the stock went down right after I got it, so it wasn't worth that much. But I was glad to get out of there.

I realized I really shouldn't have gotten a divorce because I didn't really want it. I just wanted to clear up loose ends. If I had waited until he wanted it, to get married again, I would have gotten more out of [the divorce]. In the meantime, he gets all this stuff and he had a good job too. So I cashed in most of what I had and reinvested it. It wasn't but $50,000. And you know he had a lawyer try to get $20,000 out of that from me from utilities [companies] that was in there because I had told him I would give it to him. I talked to my lawyer, who was a gay lawyer, a woman. I told her, "I said I told him I would do that." She said, "I don't see it here in the papers. There's nothing in writing." She said, "You don't have to give it to him." So I didn't. (Sandy)

I had a lot of insecurity about leaving. Not him per se, but worrying about money and worrying about how the children were really doing. When I was going through my divorce, all the children saw a psychiatrist and he deemed them all to be doing fine. I can honestly say in all the years of raising children and after them growing up, they all seem to be doing all right. I guess it was leaving a stable environment that did the most damage to me. (Ellen)

I gave up an expensive house that my parents had helped finance. But I'm an only child and my parents had some means. They were upper-middle class, and I had the security to walk out of there knowing that it was not a financial hardship. In fact, I think I enjoyed simplifying my life and moving with the old furniture from the house into this one-bedroom apartment.

[In realizing a portion of the house sale] I gave up a portion of his retirement. He filed for the divorce and I got this paper that said "gross neglect of duty," which just really ticked me because I had been so dutiful for so long [twenty-two years]. The divorce didn't happen until 1979 and it was right after that that real estate really rose in value, so he made off very, very well. I fought it some in the courts too. I should not have had to split up all of the things that my parents had given me. He came out very well. (Marilyn)

When I left him, I hadn't been working at all. I probably said something like, go to hell son of a bitch or something, just left . . . I went to work as a bartender after I left him. [I had nothing that I would consider my own money while I was married.] My dad gave me $500 shortly after I left {}. And he said, "I wish I could give you more, but that's what I've got."

The divorce papers said "location unknown." Of course {} knew where I was because my brother was between us and occasionally would hear from him. He divorced me. This is very funny. He divorced me, but he waited seven years so he could get me for desertion. In doing so, he made the marriage last fifteen years and I'm now collecting widow's benefits, so there. It took a while, believe me, to get the divorce records. I knew where but I had no idea when he got the divorce.

No, I'd never used [the $500]. I found a bookkeeping job in a place in the southern part of Manhattan around Canal Street for a man that sold and bought rags and he had this funny little building, I can still see it. And I went to work as his bookkeeper. When he offered me a salary I almost fell over, it was three times what I expected. (Pat M)

[The divorce didn't do a whole lot to me financially.] I was working and going to school. I got an alimony arrangement from my husband. Not only that, I had wealthy parents who would always help me out if I needed it. And my school was a private school and my parents paid for that whole thing, until I really got a scholarship. I got a stipend for my master's and so that didn't cost anything. And anything I wanted to do extra, my parents were always there to help me and they did. They were very generous. If I needed anything, they were there. I didn't live high on the hog, but I certainly wasn't in trouble. (Barbara)

Well, actually, [the divorce] had little impact in the beginning. . . . My husband settled with me for a property settlement. And he was very good up until I turned sixty-five this last June. And all of a sudden all of the payments started going in arrears. So I've had a hard time with him for the last six months. He's two months in arrears right now. (Dawn)

I was doing good for about four years [after the divorce] because I got child support, even though he had the boys at some point. I got child support and I got alimony. As long as I had child support, I was doing quite well. I managed to buy some real estate. I bought a condo and kept it about one year and made like $9,000 in one year, which back then was good. I bought it to live in and I thought I'd stay there, but I started getting in trouble again, emotionally. I had never been on my own, making my own decisions and worried about the future. So once I was on my own, it was scary. (Ellen)

Well at that particular time when I had sold [the restaurant], I was going through a divorce. And a lot of funds were cut off and I had to use [the sales proceeds] to live. [The custody trial], it was a punishment, that's exactly it. Because after he lost the case, he did not pursue it on appeal. So the whole thing was really for naught. But it did not get me a good impression with the jury. It was a mess. He did not win custody of the children, but he got the divorce which meant that I was cut off totally, which was a hard blow. It's a good thing that I had my own things going and I was able to sustain myself, besides the fact that the judge awarded that he pay for all the various things in the house until the children were old enough to, of age, which I think was eighteen. But that was it. (Kate)

The freedom I gave myself really wasn't freedom because I was carrying all these strings with me. The children were older; they were teenagers and things like that. I wasn't there at home. I was connected with them, I mean they knew where I was and everything, but I couldn't live there. The kids stayed with him because I didn't get a lawyer. I kept after him, saying to him, "Why don't you go get an apartment?" and he wouldn't do it. He says, "We can't afford that." So I did it after a while.

One of these two women, the mother-daughter women, she made an announcement one day at the bowling alley. She said, "I've got an apartment to rent." And I rented it for $200 which even at that time was cheap. I rolled the first ball and I said, I'd love to do that. It's too bad I can't do it. Then I rolled the second ball and I turned around and said to her, "I will." I guess I am kind of impulsive, but it was in my mind anyway. So now I look at the house. We went to church the following Sunday at eight o'clock; I was going to Sunday church at eight with my husband. We would go out to eat and then I would go to church at eleven with Nan. I did that for a long time. But this time after we came back from church, instead I said to him, "I'm going out for a while alone" and I just can't seem to lie to people. He said, "Why are you going?" I said, "I'm going to look at a house to see if I can rent it." He said, "What? Are you going to leave me?" And I said, "I will if I like the house." But you know we had such a lack of communication, when I came back from that and I gave her a $50 deposit . . . he never asked me. So anyway, I moved in on the first of December 1985. (Sandy)

Divorce did little to Joanna's economics but significantly lessened the income of Diane.

Who initiated these divorces? In three cases at least, it was the husband. But seventeen narrators initiated their own divorces. That they would do so is a testament primarily to their dissatisfaction with their marriages, their sense of their earning potential, and the fact that in most cases children were college age or older.

Custody Hearings

Three women had custody of their children threatened by their divorces. Kate managed to win the court hearing about custody but not before her lesbian relationship was made the issue. Ellen lost custody of two of her three children due to her lesbianism and a suicide attempt. Pat M chose not to fight her husband and let him retain custody of their children. He was a wealthy man and had been a good father. Once divorced, she had no resources to fight for custody or to support the children. After a separation of thirty-six years, she was recently reunited with her children.

Actually they were accusing me of being gay and they wanted to take my children away from me. I guess sexuality was on trial indirectly because they were trying to prove that because of my relationship with Barbara that I was an unfit mother. What happened is that Barbara and I went to California and we were followed. And I noticed that someone was following us in California. Because, as I said, I'm a very suspicious person. And I saw somebody following us and we called the police and the police got them. And they said that they were hired by my ex-husband to follow us. And we happened to be visiting some friends of ours that lived in. . . you know 42nd Street is very, very nice and there's a lot of restaurants around. They were trying to prove that we were in a very seedy area, which didn't work . . . I was looking over my shoulder all the time, you know, and things like that.

We had a trial that lasted six weeks with a jury. It was very painful. [At the trial] I just was myself. I wore dresses that I wear anyway. I wore jewelry that I wore anyway. I was just myself. I had to bring in my children's teachers and all kinds of different people at that particular time to show that I was a good mother. And they were trying to prove differently. It didn't work. I didn't lose my children, but it was hard. (Kate)

The letters the women wrote me, my husband found them. That was the reason that I lost custody of the three boys. The lawyers made the divorce dirty as usual. My lawyer told his lawyer that I was going to go after his business and his business was his first love. If he had to choose between his family and his business, his business would come first.

Well, I was so screwed up at that time, you know, with the suicide [attempt] and I wasn't stable. I had mixed feelings about leaving the marriage. The youngest child was thirteen. I got myself together with this woman that I was with. I was awarded Collette, but she was still in school and didn't want to leave. So the oldest boy child came up to Michigan. So what we did was we just switched kids. Collette stayed down with her father and I took my son up with me. And the kids seemed to be pretty well balanced. We lived on a lake up there. She loved children. (Ellen)

Recovery

All of these women survived their marriages and their divorces. Only one woman mentioned attempting suicide, once before the divorce and once after. No one admitted to being addicted to drugs, but a few said they had been alcoholics. Most of them would say they are far happier now with their lives than they were with their married lives.

Their new lives would include intimate long-term relationships with other women. Some of those relationships had started before the divorce, some supported the newly divorced woman, some had yet to be discovered. Some women entered the workforce for the first time armed with skills they had learned before marriage, and others were armed with skills they learned during marriage or shortly after divorce.

Most of the divorces took place during the 1970s (Table 3.6). The 1970s was the era of the women's movement and gay liberation. The atmosphere in the 1970s was ripe for women breaking out of marriage and housewifery, for women meeting one another, supporting one another and hearing about the activities of other women. In the next chapter we will go in depth into their lesbian lives.

TABLE 3.6. Calendar Years for Divorces

Year	Older Women	Younger Women
1950-1951	Kay M	
1952-1953	Diane, Addy	
1954-1955		Pat N 1st
1956-1957	Vera 1st	Gigi
1960-1961		Pat M
1962-1963	Bing	
1964-1965	Amelia	
1966-1967		
1968-1969		Nan
1970-1971		Kathleen, Sandy 1st
1972-1973		Joyce, Sandy 2nd, Barbara, Pauline
1974-1975	Joanna	Sandy 3rd
1976-1977		Marilyn, Ellen, Edie, Kate
1978-1979		Liz
1980-1981		
1986-1987		Sandy 4th
1994-1995		Dawn

The second marriages of Vera and Pat N ended in the death of their husbands. Pat N no longer considers herself to be a lesbian. The rest of the women became involved with other women.

After the divorce, Pat M left New York and got a job as a cook. Liz got a job in publishing and moved to a new state as her son went to college. Dawn, Nan, Liz, and Ellen lived on alimony, or investments, and Ellen moved to another state with a woman lover. Barbara continued working and received alimony. Vera and Marilyn continued the jobs they had had while married. Pat N became a single parent, moved back home, and went to junior college, then college. Diane continued working and getting advanced degrees and worked in the Virgin Islands on two occasions.

> So my mother finally said, "Yeah, you must divorce him." So she said, "You must go to school." Well, I didn't want to go to school. But, anyway, Mama said, so you do what Mama said. Well, I went back for business, shorthand, and all this stuff.
> It was junior college and I took algebra and all this good stuff and I made the Dean's List. Well, look at this; I'm not so dumb after all. What a relief that was. You know, I'm just not as stupid and all the things that he would tell me. (Amelia)

SUMMARY

Half of the women in this project married, three more than once, and eighteen birthed children. If a woman didn't marry by age twenty-nine, she never married. Ninety-one percent dated men. The average age for first same-sex sexual experience for women who never married was twenty-one and for women who did marry was thirty; for both age cohorts it was twenty-five years old.

Emotional fulfillment was rare from husbands and was far more often provided by a woman lover during the marriage. Ten women had affairs with women during their marriages and one had sex with several different women in swinging clubs but not in relationships. Over and over again I heard that the married relationship lacked emotional intimacy, something which other women offered. Divorces were generally painful, sometimes nasty, and overwhelmingly instituted by the narrator.

The younger women had larger families than did the older women and larger families than they grew up in generally. The older group of narrators averaged 2.20 children, and the younger narrators averaged 2.46 children. More of the Whistling Women were single moms and more were working moms than their own moms had been.

Sixty-seven percent of the married younger women were married for at least seventeen years versus 17 percent of the older women. All but one older narrator ended her marriage after thirteen years. Whistling Women even persevered longer in their marriages than do "heterosexual women" in general. The average length of first marriage for a heterosexual couple in the United States in 1998 was eleven years but was 13.41 years for these twenty-two lesbians while the average of all marriages in the United States is 7.2 years and 12.64 years for the Whistling Women.

Divorce failed to change appreciably the economic status of women who were already in the lower classes or who were working or recently educated at the time of divorce. It did significantly affect those women who had three or more children and were marginally employed. As for socioeconomic class during the working years, it seems that a job did just as much for a woman as did a husband.

But I wasn't really of sound mind. These other people I got mixed up with—it wouldn't have happened if I'd have had a good mind. But when I was away from my first husband a year or two, your mind begins to heal itself, once you're away from the situation. (Sandy)

Chapter 4

Lesbian Relationships

She was the ball player. When I couldn't tell men from women playing softball, I didn't feel comfortable there. (Gigi)

Some of the women in this project had expansive social worlds and some seem to have minimal contact with family and co-workers. In Chapter 3 there is a sense of the lives lived by married women, all of whom are still involved with their children and, in some cases, grandchildren. Of course relationships are primarily based on verbal interactions, and I explore their world of words in Chapter 7.

In this chapter I wish to tour the issues of coming out, and relationships with lovers. The sample is too large to spend much time exploring specific relationships, but some commonalties among relationships offer points of comparison. Sexual activity is, of course, the defining characteristic of being lesbian for these women, and some information is presented here. Butch and fem practices are explored in depth and argued to be role playing, gender performance for a bar subculture, and not a lower class or working class phenomenon. Using the information in the narratives, it is also possible to examine the longevity of relationships and compare them to heterosexual behavior. I conclude that lesbian relationships may well be more stable than heterosexual ones. Information on relationships with parents, siblings, and children round out the relationships section of the chapter. No evidence here suggests that these lesbians were sociopathic, neurotic, or marred by their sexuality or their change in sexuality.

The final section of the chapter delves into the conventional politics of the Whistling Women—party affiliation, political activities, political concerns—and their degree of feminism. In fact, few of them consider themselves to be feminists. Although many feel a debt to gay activists, many do not, and few are aware of gay rights politics or a national gay community.

Since the reader may not be aware of gay history, I begin the chapter with my particular perception of the sequence of events and then place each woman in the half decade she began a lesbian lifestyle. Throughout the chapter there is historical information that I am hopeful will give context for their lives and relationships.

OVERVIEW OF LESBIAN HISTORY IN THE UNITED STATES

Classical thinkers attributed sexual and gender differences, as well as intellectual differences, to body heat. Heat expended excessively made men thin. Greater heat in men increased the blood supply to the brain, explaining its greater size in men and their greater intelligence (Schiebinger 1989). Body heat also explained sexual ambiguities. Classical thinkers told stories of women being changed into men by too much heat or misdirected heat; these women sprouted penises, and their wombs shriveled. While rejecting some of these stories, writers of the early 1600s defined hermaphrodites as either male or female, depending on the amount of body heat (Schiebinger 1989). A manly woman had excessive heat and, consequently, excessive intellect. The intelligent woman, then, was physically abnormal, was masculine, was sick.

The Nineteenth Century

In the early part of the nineteenth century, women of the United States were told that if they became educated and assertive, they would turn into men; either their genitalia would change, or everyone would perceive them as men. Intellectual women unsexed themselves. Those who sought education were "semi-women" or "mental hermaphrodites," warned both male and female writers and speakers (Faderman 1981, p. 235). Medical doctors soon "discovered" that education endangered a woman's health; specifically, the brain used up the blood needed for menstruation, leading to deficiencies that resulted in everything from nervousness to mental breakdown to organ failure.

Dr. Edward H. Clarke, a Harvard professor, was "probably the most influential spokesman for the continued subordination of women," arguing that "the only thing the female could not do" if she were to remain healthy "was to be educated on the pattern or model of man" (Bullough and Bullough 1977, p. 124). The body could not simultaneously do two things well, and females aged twelve to twenty were encouraged to concentrate on developing their reproductive system. During the menstrual period it was thought to be crucial that the female allow her physiological processes to be unrestricted. Mental activity interfered with ovulation and menstruation (Bullough and Bullough 1977). Clarke maintained that the education of women created a class of sexless humans. Similarly, Dr. Ralph W. Parsons, writing in the *New York Medical Journal* in 1907, explained that "educated women neglected to cultivate refined speech, had loud voices, laughed with gusto, and sometimes even used slang and profanity (Bullough and Bullough 1977, p. 130).

By the middle and late nineteenth century, women were agitating more loudly and in greater numbers for women's rights. They achieved gains that fed national anxieties about a collapse in gender distinctions. If women achieved their goals, what would induce them to marry? Women were not yet knighted with sexual appetites so the worry led to a woman's need for companionship and a home. With no barriers to income, jobs, or rights, what would stop women from turning to each other for companionship and home? Romantic friendships had in fact been widely tolerated in the English-speaking world prior to this period of gender trouble, but these romantic friendships soon became threatening and the subject of unflattering literature and medical research. It was not just the English-speaking world that identified women in romantic friendships as sirens. "French anxiety about the potentials of female alliances rose to a fever pitch by the end of the nineteenth century" as well (Faderman 1981, p. 238).

The sociology of sport literature reviews turn-of-the-century attitudes about physical exertion and its effects on women, particularly the notion of play. The physical exertion of thinking was thought to be enough to destroy the health of a woman, and any sustained athletic endeavor could modify the secondary sex characteristics of a woman. Many parents, young girls, and potential husbands believed this cause-and-effect relationship so that education and physical exercise were long and widely believed to modify either the actual sexual characteristics of a woman or people's perception of a woman's womanliness. It was enough to discourage women from entering the more physically demanding professions that developed between 1880 and 1930, such as archaeology (Claassen 2000).

The medical profession, with much help from a single figure, Sigmund Freud, created in the late 1800s a category of personality, two personalities actually, the homosexual and the heterosexual (Halperin 1995; Foucault 1988). Whereas before in history and religious thinking, anyone was capable of same-sex acts, seductions, sins, by 1900 the Western world came to view these acts as the behavior of a particular type of girl, the lesbian. The tomboy who got educated was a lesbian, forever destined to fight her affliction or give in to it. There were individuals, a minority, who struggled with same-sex desire. Parents and neighbors could spot them, doctors could predict them, and cures were prepared for them.

The abnormality of women loving women was brought vividly to light in 1892 when Alice Mitchell murdered her lover Freda Ward in Tennessee. The story was carried by all the major newspapers and stimulated at least three novels by 1895 (Faderman 1991, p. 5). In the decades that followed the Ward murder, lesbian novels flourished even as romantic friendships seeped out of view. The most widely read of these novels was *The Well of Loneliness,* published in 1928 and authored by Radclyffe Hall. Twenty-five of the Whistling Women have read this book, most of them before they were twenty-five years old.

While the attack was on to criminalize and medicalize the homosexual, homosexuals themselves in this same period, 1869 to 1930, were organizing. In Germany from 1869 to 1871, the legislature considered and passed a law—paragraph 175—which made male homosexual acts criminal. In response, several groups formed there, the first being the Scientific Humanitarian Committee founded by Hirschfeld, whose aim was the abolishment of Paragraph 175 and the dissemination of the message that homosexuals were part man and part woman, a harmless third sex. In 1914 the British Society for the Study of Sex Psychology, which stressed education over politics, was founded by Havelock Ellis and Edward Carpenter. In 1924 the first U.S. group formed, the Chicago Society for Human Rights. They too saw the homosexual as mentally and psychically abnormal and advocated legal relief from abuse.

The Twentieth Century

After the patriotism and work of women carried the United States through World War I, women's rights efforts were stepped up. The association between feminism—the catchall word for all political and natural inclinations toward nonpassivity—and lesbianism in the United States began in psychiatric circles in 1901 (Faderman 1981). Freudian theories of female homosexuality were offered to "explain" those women who did not want to accept a life of passivity and servitude. Uppity women were depicted as abnormal, not women, lesbian. One writer in 1927 proclaimed that the women's movement was led by "men women" who seduced the normal young women in the movement and spread lesbianism. The young woman's education "must preserve her femininity and discourage any masculinizing influence" (Eberhard, quoted in Faderman 1981, p. 336).

The association of lesbianism and feminism soon moved from a discussion of individuals to an attack on women's colleges. In those locations, women engaged in athletics and developed boyish figures, executive skills, and masculine feelings, all of which threatened to modify the secondary sexual characteristics to the point that lesbianism, as medically recognized, was inevitable. In 1932, William Carlos Williams wrote that lesbianism was "the 'knife of the times,' and it was killing women and castrating men" (Williams, quoted in Faderman 1981, p. 339).

World War II took millions of young people from their homes and families and moved them into cities and onto bases, put them in the company of other single people, gave them incomes and a purpose. Bars in port cities thrived, and when they were discharged and when the war was over, thousands of gay people stayed in those port cities.

The Chicago Society was succeeded by the formation in Los Angeles of the Mattachine Foundation in 1951. In 1953 they began publishing *ONE Magazine,* with the purpose of fostering a homosexual group identity but with two differing opinions on the role of the organization—to fight for rights or to assimilate. The Daughters of Bilitis (DOB) soon formed in 1955, a Los Angeles-based lesbian social group who rejected the butch/fem scene and bar life. Within a year they had become a political group stressing a positive image of lesbians and publishing a magazine called *The Ladder.* Ultimately there were DOB chapters in several large cities in the United States.

Bar raids are commonly referred to in telling gay history, and they seem to have been more prevalent in New York City than elsewhere. The only raids the narrators were caught in were in Detroit, in Boston, and in New York City. On a night in June 1969, in Greenwich Village's Stonewall Inn, a police raid sparked the fury of over 200 patrons who staged a riot that lasted two days and nights, the first of its kind to have entered history. Claire and Jean alone reported hearing about this event. But its effects were positive and benefited all the narrators. The American Psychiatric Association reversed its opinion on homosexuality in 1973, removing it from its list of disorders.

Gay Liberation

The Kinsey report of 1953 threatened the stability of the medical understanding of a personality type called homosexual when it revealed that a shockingly large percentage of women and men in the United States had had same-sex sexual activity yet were passing and functioning as heterosexuals. The Kinsey Report, combined with feminism, was urging women to take back control of their bodies and to view women as allies. Combined with the free-love movement and its sentiments, "love the one you're with," "love without strings attached," the direction was set for the new gay movement after Stonewall. That direction was gay liberation, an unmistakable return to the pre-1880 understanding of sex, that anyone was capable of any sexual desire, including same-sex sexual desire. We all should explore sexuality and this way of experiencing another person. Women should cultivate the manly elements in themselves, should cultivate sex as an expressive realm, should bond with women sexually. Only a woman knew how to please a woman. A lesbian experience would prepare a woman for sex with a man, helping to ensure her satisfaction.

The politics of gay liberation were (1) that countless numbers of people, in fact all people, were implicated, (2) that the sexual behavior harmed no one, and (3) that the behavior was a healthy expression of human capabilities. Clearly, then, repressive social and legal practices were unwarranted and inappropriate, as were the fears of heterosexual individuals. Everyone was capable of same-sex love. It was a hard message to sell.

By 1980, gay liberation morphed into gay rights, a return to the idea that gay people are a biological minority and cannot change their condition. Like blacks or Hispanics, homosexuals deserve legal protection and need all homosexuals to band together to build the group identity and political strength. Of course, some believe the cause of legal protection is threatened by the inclusion of groups such as transsexuals. The movement toward Queer and queer identity politics promises to be a more inclusive identity group that is fighting to protect difference, rather than conformity. The women in this study, although not particularly politically active or aware, have lived lives of conformity and occasionally express displeasure with the more radical factions of the homosexual and transsexual world. They are who the gay rights movement hopes to appeal to.

Mary1 remembers discovering a gay bookstore in Phoenix in the 1970s and then the Metropolitan Community Church (MCC) congregation in Los Angeles beginning in 1975 or 1976. She joined Daughters of Bilitis in the 1950s and read their publication *The Ladder,* then tried to start a DOB in Florida in the early 1980s. She discovered Olivia Records through the Phoenix bookstore. "If we had had these things in the 1950s how different life would be for a lot of people. But we had to pave the way."

If we'd had an Ellen DeGeneres back when I was a teenager . . . I mean, you don't know how many kids I've had that killed themselves 'cause they were gay—blew their heads off in high school. The pain that came through thinking that you were the only person in the world like that. It permeated your entire being; you lived the lie every single day of your life. You put on a mask to the world and it took a toll. (Mary Lou)

COMING TO RECOGNITION

And on this trip we ended up in Greenwich Village in New York City on a Saturday night. And we were in a bar and it was the first time I had ever seen gay people. They were gay. They were women that were dressed like men and I heard my father or one of the other guys that was in our group say, "Well, there's a couple." And I didn't know what they were talking about. It struck me then—damn, this is odd, women dressed like men. I could understand that but I'd never seen it. So that was my first exposure. Then when I had my first relationship, I realized I was "one of them" and that almost devastated me 'cause I didn't want to be "one of them" dressed like a man. (Gigi)

We didn't know what to do. It was like, okay, I love you, now what do we do? It was, in a way, coming home, feeling whole, feeling yes, this is really what I need to do in my life; this is where I belong. I'd been in the closet of marrlage and this was coming out of that closet for me. It was a very self-af-firming thing. So I knew that whatever it was, I'd figure it out and it would be right. I just didn't know what to do. And, as I said, I was always afraid of being a lesbian because I thought I had to be either a butch or a fem and I thought I had to use a dildo. So I just shied away from anything that even said "lesbian" because I didn't realize that it was about relationship. Being a lesbian was about loving somebody on this intimate level. In retrospect, when I came to my lesbianism, it felt right. That was the reason why I couldn't love my husband on that intimate level, aside from the abuse that I had from my husband. The sex just didn't feel right and I knew it then. But I had never had any little inklings before because I'd never let myself think about it, I never let myself act on it. (Edie)

BARBARA: I said, "I feel that I am going to have a relationship with this woman." She said, "How would you know?" I said, "I don't know, I just know. I met her once. I just know that I'm going to end up having a relationship with her and I believe she's gay." She said, "How do you know that?" I said, "I don't know how I know—I just know." And I did know.

CHERYL: Did your heart stop when you say the word gay to this person? You're not having situational difficulty?

BARBARA: Not at all, ever. I've heard that people do and I'm sure they do. But it was never that way for me. It was, wow, look at this, life is really opening up for me.

After I got out of high school and was working. I flirted with this woman who was a divorcée and she flirted back, by gum. I was very surprised. I think, you know, how that kind of thing comes about, that's when we started to kiss and fondle and that kind of thing. And I believe she wanted more from me, but I didn't know how to do that. (Cam)

CYNTHIA: I think I read it someplace. And I thought, I think that's what I am. But the connotation of being homosexual was so bad, I didn't want to be that.

CHERYL: Was that the word, you think?

CYNTHIA: Yes. I didn't really want to be that and I was in denial.

CHERYL: Give me an age when you first read it?

CYNTHIA: Probably twelve to thirteen years old, maybe a little older.

CHERYL: How did you proceed from there? Did you try to follow up on this word homosexual and get other information?

CYNTHIA: I would try to find all the information that I could get and I would hide and read it. And then I started reading—my ambition. . . . I started reading about Greenwich Village in New York and we'd hear stuff about it. And I wanted to go there so bad. And it seemed like such a faraway land to me. I was about fifteen to sixteen years old. . . . I think that's when I started thinking that's definitely what I was. But I could not be openly gay anyway, there was no way. I knew I had to leave there.

I never heard the word "lesbian." I heard about her hot, torrid lovemaking and the things they were doing in very indiscreet places. But no, I never had a word put on it. . . . But it seemed like at that point I started to fall in love with Shirley as a possible playmate. She really opened my eyes. I was raised such a strict Catholic. (Ellen)

In 1977, my son was already away at college and my daughter was a senior in high school . . . and I realized that I needed some friends to fill the emptiness that was about to get even more empty. So actually my husband was in the hospital awaiting minor surgery and I asked a friend at work out to the movies and I knew she was a lesbian. The movie we wanted to see wasn't playing, so I had her back to my house and we sat and talked and just talked and talked and talked. And I knew she was interested in me as a friend. In fact she had some of those books—adult astrology—where you can just thumb through and get somebody's sign, so that's what we talked about all evening. And when I took her back home in my car, she got out and she kissed me on the cheek and it was like fire. So the lesbian relationship developed from that and by July I decided that I would move out from my husband and get my own apartment. (Marilyn)

COMING OUT

Both age groups have had to grapple with the meaning of homosexuality and with coming out. Thirty-eight of these women identified their homoeroticism prior to 1969 (see Table 4.1), the date of the Stonewall Riots and the symbolic start of the gay liberation/gay rights movements, when being homosexual still meant having a private sexual attraction. Everyone understood the need to be discreet in public, and to develop other, public, aspects of herself.

Since 1970, however, when six of the women in this sample were discovering their erotic proclivity, "homosexual," "lesbian," or "gay person" has been marketed as a public persona that required "coming out" to maintain a healthy social adjustment. As should be predictable, not all of these women were convinced by the logic of gay liberation or gay rights even though they may acknowledge that in 2004 it is easier to be gay. Nine of these women do not consider themselves to be out and three of those are in the oldest age cohort. This topic is explored in depth in Chapter 7, "Words and Us."

Negotiating straight society has been fraught with worry and danger for most of these narrators, and it was general knowledge that only fools broadcast their homosexuality. Fear, of course, is the rea-

TABLE 4.1. The Half Decade When Narrators Began a Long-Term Lesbian Lifestyle

Decade	Younger	Older
1935-1939		Roberta, Mary2
1940-1944		Carolyn
1945-1949	Mary Lou, Nancy, Chris, Cynthia	Claire, Kay M, Cam, Addy, Sheri
1950-1954	Judy, Mitch, Joyce, Bobbie, Rose, Gigi	Diane
1955-1959	Jackie, Pat N, Mary1, Jan, Janet	Joanna
1960-1964	Pat M	Amelia, Gloria, Kay, Bing
1965-1969	Nan, Ruth	
1970-1974	Edie, Dorothy, Marilyn	
1975-1979	Barbara, Kate, Sappho, Ellen	
1980-1984	Liz, Pauline	Vera
1985-1989	Sandy	
1990-1995	Dawn	

son, fear that they would lose their parents' love and home, be cut off from their families, and lose their careers, jobs, housing, fear of dishonorable discharge, fear of physical harm, fear of losing their lovers. So all this bad stuff we all imagined and dreaded—how often did it happen?

Parental Punishment

Gigi was kicked out of the house at age eighteen for lesbianism: "I came home and my clothing was outside. I said, Okay. So that's when I moved in with Marilyn." Diane says, "Well, my family locked me up and all that usual stuff, but I got away." Addy's father gave her his tux and said, "Get out." Jan's father threw her out of the house but she refused to go.

Kicked Out of School

Diane was expelled for lesbianism in school.

Loss of Housing

Roberta was kicked out of her rental apartment because her land-lady found love letters, in the middle of the night, 1941.

Loss of Job

Diane lost a university teaching position because of suspected les-bianism, 1974.

Military Harassment

They were following us. OSI was really on my case and trying to get me out of the service. What got people in trouble was they were always willing to squeal on who turned them in. Like I had one woman who did turn me in. She was a cute, little, teeny thing. And she was very nice but I just wasn't inter-ested. I guess I was going out with someone or something. She asked me if I had seen some picture which she had hung over her bed. It was there and I was here and it was small and so I went with her to look at it, God knows why. And I leaned over this way and the next thing I knew she grabbed me and she was all over me. I'd gone out with her once, but I just wasn't interested. I just grabbed her and I shook her and I said, "What part of no don't you un-derstand?" She turned me in to OSI that I was gay. And they are not sup-posed to tell you who turned you in. So they had gotten on me and followed me and they knew I went to these bars and I was a pretty heavy drinker at the time. But I could drink. My mom and dad went out every Friday and Saturday and they have five, six, seven drinks and I never saw them drunk in my life. We can just drink, our family is that way. So if OSI saw me drink three or four drinks, then for all intentional purposes, I was drunk. But I wasn't. I was doing the driving also. But, anyway OSI grilled me and grilled me and grilled me until I was just exhausted. They kept me there four or five hours, six hours, didn't care. And one of the questions was, "Why do all gay people like to wear pinkie rings?" I said, "I don't know. Why don't you ask them?" You had to be sharp because almost everything you were going to answer was going to be incriminating. So finally they sent me back home. . . .

Then I met with the gals and told them everything. The best people they had were all gay and they're going to get them out of the service. No matter what they tell you, do not blame another person. Anyhow, the outcome of the whole thing, the upshot was that the only person they threw out of the ser-vice after that whole thing was the person that turned me in, because she had to incriminate herself which she did and none of us did. And that was that. I had a commanding officer I thought was marvelous. He was really a great guy, came out to the stable and rode horses and what have you. He was a colonel, but he got busted to major for taking a woman up to his room. He came up to me one day and said, "You stupid bitch, they have so much evidence on you." He said, "I'm not asking whether you're gay or not, but the OSI has so much evidence on you, if you move one crooked foot, they will have you. Good day, ma'am." (Mitch)

Caught in a Police Raid

And then they let us all go. When we got to court, the bailiff came up as we were being checked in and said, "That policewoman is really out to get you." But apparently Billy's had a good lawyer and we were all dismissed. What happened was in those days the people in the neighborhood probably complained or else they didn't pay up. It was all a payoff scheme. And so they either missed a payment or the neighborhood was putting pressure on them and so they had to set up a night. (Mary2)

And then, of course, I lived through the days of Anita Bryant too. I was in Miami at the time and it was dreadful. The bars were raided and we had a mayor, at that time, whose daughter was gay and he went on a vendetta about gays. He even had raids at the gay beach where he had both ends to that beach cordoned off and had the police cars come in there and the police were even running into the ocean to try to pick up mostly the fellows. It was terrible. And you wouldn't go to a gay bar without worrying to death that you were going to be raided. (Roberta)

I was once in Boston [in a house party raid]. But they didn't find me, I was hiding in the shower. They used to raid houses all the time on Beacon Hill. (Mary1)

Yeah. This time the lights didn't only blink, they blinked, blinked, blinked; they kept blinking. Well, when I come into a bar, I always notice where the back door is. I didn't know, by the way, all these travels I was doing, OSI was following me from the base. But this time I don't know if they were or not. But there was no back door. So I went into the ladies room and there was a window there and it was not too far a drop to the bottom. . . . And this raid, it wasn't the normal come in, look around, make sure nobody was doing whatever. I don't know. They came in to collect their money, that was about it. But this one looked like it was going to be a real raid. It was a black bar and we're white. But we wanted to hear the music and that's why we went there. (Mitch)

Loss of Child Custody

I heard so many times this word at the [custody] trial—dyke. They tried to get me to admit that I was dyke. I think I said at one time, "I don't know what a dyke is." (Kate)

My Children Will Reject Me

Sandy has been rejected by one daughter.

My Lover Will Leave Me

Mary1, Cam, Jackie, Bobbie all had lovers leave them after coming out.

Marge was mad. And then I entered a stained-glass exhibition that was the first arts and crafts show for the gay community in Phoenix. And I entered that, she had a fit because I was coming out. I was finally coming out. (Mary1)

Well, we grew apart. I wanted to be out more and more, be more and more social and she just needed to be in a closet. Also, she became more and more obsessive-compulsive. It would take 15 minutes to check and re-check the house just to go out somewhere. It got to be pretty bad. (Barbara)

Conclusion

Those bad things did happen but not as often as we were prepared for. There are uncomfortable relationships with parents, siblings, and children in the narrations. Although fear was ever present in most of these women's life stories, today most of them feel much freer and worry only about petty vandalism. Their jobs are over, their parents are dead, their children are savvy or dumb, they have friends, they have books, movies, and activities that support their lifestyle (see Chapter 6). More discussion of coming out is found in Chapter 7.

NARRATORS' TALES OF COMING OUT

She was staring at me all evening in this sort of way that made me a little uncomfortable. Later I found out the word for it was I was being cruised. But I didn't know it at the time. I can't believe that I was ever that innocent. Somehow something got started and it was totally wild. I was out of my gourd. I mean I didn't think about anything else. I just sort of flipped my lid over this young woman. She was a little younger than me. But at any rate, I'm telling you about her, not because she figured importantly in my life, but because, in a way she did because she introduced . . . I came out literally with her. I had been living a gay life all this time, a lesbian life, but I had not been to a gay bar and I had no circle of gay friends and I never talked about it. So, she took me to my first gay bar. (Nancy)

Never came out to my family before. But when I bought my house in Provincetown, I thought they all know, you know. But I was surprised, they're in denial. My sister calls and she said to me, "Your brother and his wife want to come up because they've never been to the Cape." I said, "Well you know Carmen, this is a gay town. Most of the people in this town are gay. If they don't mind that, they're more than welcome."

So I said to my sister-in-law, "Let's take my brother out." We took him out to dinner. I said, "Drink anything you want. You don't have to pay for anything." So we went to this bar and there were these two old drag queens, full drag, sitting right in front of us. And I said to him, "Those two are guys. I know that." So, okay. He didn't seem to care. And so he gets up and goes to the john and I said to my sister-in-law, "You knew I was gay didn't you?" And she said, "Yeah, I tried to tell your sister that years ago and oh she got so mad at me for even mentioning that." I said, "I can't believe after all those years they didn't know it." I just assumed they did and just didn't talk about it, not in front of me anyway. (Cynthia)

And I've had some of their employees come over and ask me, "Do you know so and so and is she gay?" I said, "No they're not. I would lie about it 'cause I know what can happen. And just because people are gay doesn't make them all nice. Some of them can be little bitches. And sometimes their complaints are frivolous. Yeah, I could understand. If we want to get someplace and we want to get some rights and we want to get power, we have to have women in higher places and you're not going to get them in higher places by tearing them down. So you have to be very careful about that. And gay women tend to be jealous of other gay women and this is just human nature. It happened to me. I remember one time there were a few gay women that wanted to take a petition to have me deported. They said, "All these foreigners come into this country and they make all the money." (Cynthia)

I put an ad in *Psychology Today,* woman looking for woman. That was when *Psychology Today* was taking personal ads. So I put an ad in there and you should have seen the responses I got. I took out a post office box, of course, I didn't want to get caught doing this. And I got such support. See I was living in a straight area—couples area. I didn't know a soul. I got supportive letters. I even got letters from women in prison, which scared the crap out of me. But a couple of responses, I started writing back to. And what it did for me, it told me there were other people out. I met a lot of women through this ad. (Ellen)

We were talking about somebody else and I said, "What do you mean, gay?" I didn't know that word. That's how naïve I was. But I was a practicing lesbian. So they said, "Oh, we've got to take you to a gay bar." I said, "What the hell are you talking about?" So we all went to Cleveland to a gay bar.

[Talking about now] Well, I never said anything. If you're accepted, why go into issues? If I'm invited somewhere, I'd say, "Oh yeah, I'm bringing so and so." They say, "Fine, bring her." (Gigi)

I just have many, many straight friends and I don't think it's necessary. If they know, fine; if they assume, fine. But I have no need—probably a lot to do with age, you know. (Janet)

I guess . . . I got brought out. Because one of the women just said one morning, "How long have you two been together?" And it was like, "Thank you God." And from then on I just came out gradually more and more, though not anywhere near what I needed to and it was always because I was protecting my partner who had such anxiety about it. The reasons that she gave were, you know, very valid for her because she was still living in the community that she'd been brought up in, that her grandfather had lived in, that everybody knew, she had this big extended family and they all seemed like okay reasons to me, that I would be hurting her. I didn't take a look at what I was doing to my-self in the process. And we were together for twenty-two years.

And then simultaneously, because I was out and meeting people, I found that there were some projects going on that I could get involved with through the lesbian/gay coalition of New Jersey. I got on this committee that was do-ing workshops for teachers and parents and anyone else that was inter-ested, sensitizing them to the needs of lesbian/gay adolescents. And then my name started to be out all over the place and it was like wonderful. . . . What I was missing [for twenty-two years] was community. (Jackie)

And at that point too, my father was already dead, but I'd come out to my mother and she was totally shocked. My mother was a gym teacher as a young woman, so of course she knew about this stuff. So, I said I had a new friend. She said, "Is she a lesbian?" I said, "No, she's a librarian. (Marilyn)

My dad knew. We walked into a gay bar one night and [my dad] was there. I told him who she was and he said, "Fine—if you're going to do it, do it right." My dad was kind of like me. And we left. He'd always ask about her after that. If I was talking to him, he'd ask, "How's Robbie doing? Have you seen her or have you been out again?" (Pat M)

Coming Out to Kids

That's the one thing we didn't do early in our relationship. Two of her boys were foster kids from the Jewish Childcare Association. We thought that if we were out at all, those kids would be taken away. They had already been in eight other homes and she wanted to see them through high school and into college to make sure that those kids got what they deserved in life. So we didn't come out to the kids and we didn't come out to anybody in the school system. We were both afraid of losing our jobs. Whatever we wanted to do together, we'd go off on the weekends and we'd do it. Sometimes at different retreats we'd go to, there would be these workshops about the coming-out stories and how to tell your parents. It was funny because we were now in our forties and the coming-out stories were, how were we going to come out to the kids, not how were we going to come out to our parents. So we always kind of felt in this kind of weird place because most of the women were much younger than we were.

We always said that if the kids asked, we'd tell them. And that's what hap-pened. When my oldest was nineteen, he took me out for a Mother's Day dinner and he said to me, "Mom, I want to ask you what the relationship between you and Doreen is." And I said, "It's a love relationship, and since you've asked, I now will tell you. But I'm going to ask you also not to talk to your brothers for a full week and let us have time to tell everybody our own way." So we went through the kids one by one during that week. (Edie)

He was twenty-one by the time we got divorced, so no, it was no problem. And I never actually told him and we never talk about it, but he knows. (Joanna)

My husband said I couldn't do that, that he didn't want them to know. But then . . . my husband said okay—two or three years after our separation. (Marilyn)

It came about through my first girlfriend. She told her daughter when she had come out. And it seems that my son was friendly with her daughter and they went for lunch or something one time and she just happened to talk about it. And she talked about me too. And he found out about it. We just talked about it very briefly. And that was it, I didn't add to the conversation too much. I just didn't want to go into this whole thing. There's nothing you can do about it, you can't change anything. He'll have to deal with his emotions like I had to deal with my emotions. I can't make it better. My daughter is fine with it. (Kate)

And I said, "Yes [I'm gay]." I've thought so many times since then that I should have lied to her, but I didn't. I didn't lie to her. I told her, "Yes, Roberta and I are a couple" and the whole thing. Well you know, she turned against me. You hear about parents not accepting their children. You never hear anything about children not accepting their parents. (Sandy)

You know, the funniest thing about the gay and lesbian community is, they think that all the heterosexual people are stupid. They particularly think parents are stupid. And I always told all the young people when I did rap sessions and even when I speak at conferences, "You have the responsibility of making the effort to share with your family members. It may not work out the way you want it to, but it's your responsibility to make the effort to share. Because if you don't, you're cheating yourself of a great emotional support and a relationship that you could have. You never know unless you try." (Vera)

RELATIONSHIPS

In this subsection of "Lesbian Relationships," I wish to explore the nature of these women's relationships with the world around them and with each other. I present information from the interviews on longevity of lesbian relationships and matrimonial unions, butch/fem, and sexuality, and summary information about relations with parents, siblings, and children. The topic of lovers is very difficult to summarize in any useful way. I offer information on longevity of relationships, and, at the end of the chapter, I compile some of the sociological information contained in the interviews about dozens of other women. Here is where it would have been most useful just to copy stories verbatim, but snippets of stories will have to suffice.

Relationships with Lovers

Most of the narrators considered a proper relationship to involve living together, sexual activity, and monogamy. For some speakers it seems that a small group of friends sufficed, that excessive drinking was frequently a problem with a lover when younger, and that supporting the lover financially (discussed in Chapter 5) was done in a few cases. I will begin this section by discussing sexual activity.

Sexual Activity

Sexual activity with another woman was the defining attribute of a lesbian in the decades 1930 to 1970, when most of these narrators had their first homosexual experience. If family and co-workers thought a couple were simply best friends or roommates or sisters or mother and daughter, then the couple was safe. Women engaged in many tricks to keep themselves out of the category "lesbian," at least to their satisfaction. Faderman points out that many women who had same-sex sexual experiences were able to exempt themselves from the label "lesbian" because neither was their behavior neurotic, nor their appearance mannish. She reminds us that Emma Goldman, who "had held another woman to her 'unconfined bosom' and shared her 'love juice' with her" (Faderman 1991, p. 34), exempted herself from the lesbians, because she did not hate men. One of the narrators specified another strategy—if she didn't let a woman touch her below the waist, then she wasn't a lesbian. Other versions of this logic are that oral sex isn't "making love," and that if I don't make love to her then I am not being unfaithful.

I mailed each woman a sexuality questionnaire rather than ask questions that might impede the interview by making one or both of us uncomfortable. Questions were asked about abuse, about butch/fem, about preferences and practices. Twenty questionnaires were returned (45 percent), in the manner outlined in Chapter 1. Not every woman answered every question. I go now to the results.

Masturbation is enjoyed by fourteen women, seldom by one woman, and never by three women. Most of the respondents began masturbating as teenagers.

All but one woman reported liking sex and all but two thought reciprocity of attention during sex was important. Nineteen prefer to have sex naked and only two preferred the room to be dark. The type of foreplay named was kissing (eleven), petting (nine), touching (six), talking (four), hugging (four), sucking (one). Three women have used soft porn for stimulation, and no one admitted to using hard porn. Having sex to the point of an orgasm was unimportant for three women and important for fourteen women. Bringing a partner to orgasm was important to nineteen women.

Oral sex is one method of sexual stimulation used by several of the women. Twelve women enjoy receiving stimulation orally, five do not. Thirteen like using their tongues, three do not, and one woman has never tried it. Most women had their first oral sex as young adults, only six waiting until after 1970.

In contrast, only four women report liking anal penetration. Twelve like vaginal penetration. Sex toys have been used by twelve respondents. Two women had been in a mixed-gender threesome and no one had had sex with more than two other people in one setting. However, one woman discussed going to swinging groups with her husband during the interview.

The frequency of their sexual activity was solicited for the 1970s and the 1990s. For the 1970s, when these informants were between the ages of thirty-two and sixty-two, twelve women said they had sex one to three times a week, two said rarely, and one was having sex with men. In the 1990s, when these women were between the ages of fifty-two and eight-two, only five women said they were still having sex one to three times a week. Five said once a month, three said rarely, and three said never. Whether or not they are, or were, partnered has much to do with the frequency of sex. One woman admitted to having paid for sex with another woman sometime in her fifties.

The final question I asked about their sex lives was how they would characterize those sex lives. I offered them the following choices: prudish, conservative, harmful, innovative, wild. Two women wrote in "none of the above" and another respondent wrote in "normal." Ten checked "conservative," none chose harmful, four chose innovative, two "wild" (with qualifiers "sometimes," "at times"), and none checked prudish. In retrospect, writers of the late 1990s characterize lesbian sex of the 1970s as prudish, but these women would not agree.

These women were also asked to comment on sadomasochism in the lesbian community. Chris characterized it as circus fare. Sappho knows one woman into S&M and says it's okay for others. Jan knows a few women into S&M. Barbara knew of some teenagers in the early 1980s into S&M. A group of St. Pete Beach/Gulfport women attended a lesbian night at a local S&M bar in 2001. Jan remarked, "I didn't like what I was seeing the other night. I was uncomfortable with this beautiful young woman wanting to be tied up and wanting to be beaten. It was really uncomfortable."

Abusive relationships seem to be equally unusual. Gloria had a woman lover who was physically abusive as did Pat N and Mary Lou.

Kennedy and Davis (1993) contrast the sexual activity information they got from working class lesbians in Buffalo with that reported by Kinsey (1953). In Buffalo, in the 1930s to 1960s, oral sex was uncommon and friction was the preferred method. However, Kinsey reported that 78 percent of the lesbians surveyed used oral stimulation of genitalia. This difference led Kennedy and Davis to conclude that there is a class difference in sexual activities that I have not been able to explore.

Prostitution was another sexual activity identified by Kennedy and Davis in Buffalo. They heard from their narrators that it was common for prostitutes to work a circuit of towns in Pennsylvania, Ohio, the District of Columbia, and West Virginia. These women worked in a different "house" each week and had the week of their menstruation off. Tricking occurred in lesbian bars between straight men who wandered in off the street and fems. I asked many of the Whistling Women if they knew of lesbian prostitutes, with only two positive answers. Pat N went to a party given by woman who was a prostitute, but lesbian. She also had an affair with a German girl from a bar in Hamburg who had a drawer full of paraphernalia for clients. Claire had some information:

I knew some prostitutes. Not out of the bar, but I knew some lesbian prostitutes. They were prostitutes with men. These two gals had a lavender Thunderbird. . . . they ran a circuit from somewhere on the West Coast. I think it was Los Angeles, Cleveland, and New York and when they were in Cleveland, they were very attractive girls. They would come to the parties and that was their living. When things got a little warm in Cleveland as far as the authorities were concerned, they'd go on to wherever else. (Claire)

Butch and Fem

Much that has been written about butch and fem has struggled with whether it should be viewed as performance, an alternative gender, or the fossilization of male/female genders among lesbians. The writing has also struggled with issues of class, some writers arguing that butch/fem was a product of and situated in working class bar communities, others claiming that it was more widespread than just working class and just bars. The comments recorded from these forty-four narrators can help to enlighten and perhaps further this discussion. Similar opinions on this controversy were stated by Sandy and Mitch during their interview:

I know people that are [into butch or fem]. But really I think it's just the way they happen to be. I don't think it's a role. I think it's just the way they are. (Sandy)

No, to me it's a personality thing. It's a head thing; it's got to be in your head. I can be butch and yet as helpless as a son of a bitch when it comes to the house as far as nailing things together. It has nothing to do with being butch. It's not that. It has nothing to do with being dressed in pants. 'Cause I love shorts. I wore shorts the better part of my life and bikini bathing suits are my thing because the less I have on, the happier I am when I'm in the sun. On the other hand, I am a bit shy so therefore when Fire Island went topless, I didn't. And unfortunately the women there knew I was kind of shy. I'd walk down the beach every morning, get the newspaper, get a cup of coffee, have breakfast, and come back up the beach. I never walked the boards because I liked splashing through the water. And I had friends there that would be on the beach, run up to me with their shorts on only, and I would talk to them like this, almost looking through the part on their head, not at their eyes and certainly I wasn't going to look any lower. They knew it and they did it to tease me. And it was funny, and here again it's a head thing, if you were butch and you ran up to me on the beach, it would not bother me one bit. I could care less that they were topless or pantless, it wouldn't have bothered me. If you were fem, it blew my mind. I didn't know where to look and got very uptight about the whole thing. And yet, both were women. Another thing, fems were more aggressive. (Mitch)

Eight narrators (18 percent) considered themselves butch at some point in their lives, two (6 percent) fem, and thirty-four (77 percent) did not relate to these labels. As is apparently usual in studies of butch/fem, there are far more narrators who consider themselves to be butch than to be fem. I have often wondered about the mathematics of this social phenomenon and think that fems must leave a gay identity more frequently than do butches, although there was probably always a numerical imbalance in favor of butches. The one woman in this study who no longer identifies as gay, Pat N, was an avid fem in the 1960s in New York City. I also think that fems are less likely to identify with butch/fem yet to be identified by others as fem.

There are no transgendered women in this study. Only one woman expressed a desire to be a man. When asked to pick an identifier for herself she uttered "gentleman," then "soft butch." Instead of wanting to change genders, several women adamantly stated they had no desire to be men, even those who had had an active butch phase, and that butch/fem is what turned them away from lesbian bars.

I am surprised at how few women adopted these labels/identities, given the impression created by studies such as *Boots of Leather, Slippers of Gold* (Kennedy and Davis 1993), and *Odd Girls and Twilight Lovers* (Faderman 1991), that most women were into butch and fem in the period from the 1940s to the mid-1960s. I think the important ingredient missing from our understanding of butch/fem is the gay or lesbian bar. For women who sought and found community in the bars of the era, butch or fem were to be chosen. But for women who did not frequent bars, there was little knowledge of and little incentive for the institution of butch/fem. I will return to this bar ingredient later.

As was mentioned earlier, several social theories "explain" butch/fem. Gagnon and Simon (1973) believe that butch/fem is a class phenomenon, specifically lower class, and involves mimicry. These theories involve issues of class, education, gender, performance. Each of these topics will be addressed in turn.

In order to address issues of class background for butches, fems, and nonparticipants, I have compiled several tables. Table 4.2 is a look at the number of women in each half decade they began a lesbian lifestyle and their butch, fem, or unaffiliated position. The reader can see that no woman reported adopting a butch/fem identity after 1959. This fact would suggest that the second wave of the women's movement did not bring an end to butch/fem but that end began a decade earlier.

TABŁE 4.2. Count of Butch/Fem/Unaffiliated Women by the Half Decade They Began Their Lesbian Lifestyle

Half Decade	Butch	Fem	Unaffiliated
1935-1939	1		1
1940-1944			1
1945-1949	4		5
1950-1954	1		6
1955-1959	2	2	2
1960-1964			5
1965-1969			2
1970-1974			3
1975-1979			4
1980-1984			3
1985-1989			1
1990-1994			0
1995-1999			1

Table 4.3 reveals the birth class of each woman who began a lesbian lifestyle in the era 1935 to 1995. Table 4.4 looks at the class at birth of each woman who assumed a butch/fem identity.

Looking at Table 4.4, we see that 50 percent of the women born to upper-class families came to identify as butch at midcentury (but not now), 12.5 percent of the upper-middle-class women, 22 percent of the middle-class women, none of the lower-middle class, and 22 percent of the lower-class women. This distribution does not support the notion that butch/fem was a working-class phenomenon.

A slightly different question can be asked: what percentage of the women who claimed a butch or fem affiliation, or were unaffiliated, were upper-class born, etc. (Table 4.5)? Of the eight women who identified as butches from 1935 to 1959, four (50 percent) were born middle class, two (25 percent) lower class, one upper class, and one upper-middle class. The two fems came equally from middle-class and lower-class family situations. The unaffiliateds came most heavily from the middle class and lower-middle class, again decrying the notion that butch/fem is a working-class construct.

TABLE 4.3. Class at Birth and Identity of Women Who Began Lesbian Lifestyle Each Half Decade

Half Decade	Butch	Fem	Unaffiliated
1935-1939	m		Lm
1940-1944			m
1945-1949	um, 2m, L		L, 3m, um
1950-1954	u		L, 2Lm, 2m, um
1955-1959	m, L	m, L	Lm, m
1960-1964			L, Lm, 2m, um
1965-1969			m, um
1970-1974			2L, m,
1975-1979			2m, 2um
1980-1984			L, Lm, m
1985-1989			Lm
1990-1994			
1995-1999			u

L = lower
Lm = lower middle
m = middle
um = upper middle
u = upper

TABLE 4.4. Percentage of Women in Each Birth Class Who Assumed a Butch/Fem Identity

Class	Butch	Fem	Unaffiliated	Total
Upper (n = 2)	50	0	50	100
Upper middle (8)	13	0	87	100
Middle (n = 18)	22	6	78	100
Lower middle (n = 7)	0	0	100	100
Lower (n = 9)	22	11	66	99

Nor does age correlate strongly with butch/fem participation. Four of the fifteen women in the older cohort did identify as butch, or 27 percent, and none as fems, which is slightly more than did among the younger women. Seventy-three percent had no affiliation. Among

TABLE 4.5. Percentage of Butch/Fem from Each Class—Viewed by Affiliation

Class	Butch (n = 8)	Fem (n = 2)	Unaffiliated (n = 34)
Upper	13	0	3
Upper middle	13	0	17
Middle	50	50	47
Lower middle	0	0	23
Lower	25	50	13
Total	101	100	101

the younger women, six, or 21 percent, took on a role and 79 percent did not.

In Table 4.6 the educational level of butches and fems is presented for the era 1935 to 1964. Four of the butches either were in college or had finished college when they began their butch identity, one went to a two-year program, three completed only high school, and one dropped out of high school. Among the fems, one completed high school and the other one had graduated college when the identity was adopted. Of the ten women who identified as butch or fem, 50 percent were college students or graduates, more than any other educational level represented among butch/fems. Lesser education is not a predictor of butch/fem participation.

Was butch/fem performance? I think I have observed what Sandy alludes to among these women who are older than I am and were lesbians before I was. The women I would label "butch" attending the activities and parties that I have gone to in the Tampa Bay area have been "manly" all their lives. They are "manly" or "butchy" at home, during the day, at the grocery store, at the property owners' association, at the MCC meeting, in short, all the time. They are not performing at this point in their lives, if they ever did. The gender performance among the sixty-plus group that I have seen occurred at two New Year's Eve parties, 1996 and 1999. On those occasions women who always have the butch demeanor dressed in tuxes, but even some women who appear the normative feminine 364 days of the year dressed in tuxes. Defying conventional wisdom on the topic, both members of one couple dressed in tuxes. We have all heard of butch/fem and figured out where we would fit, but many of us never

TABLE 4.6. Corresponding Educational Level with Butch/Fem Affiliation

Half Decade	Butch	Fem
1935-1939	college	
1940-1944		
1945-1949	no hs, two-year college, college	
1950-1954	college	
1955-1959	hs, hs	hs, college

participated with name, appearance, or exaggerated behavior, and many of us have openly resisted those labels.

Having said that I do not think all (and today not even most) butchy women are performing butch, I do think that butch/fem is primarily a gay bar performance, a lesbian public theater. Women who found their community in the mixed and lesbian bars of the 1930s to 1960s either joined or resisted this gender parade, but they did have to deal with it. Body type and personality made it easier for viewers to determine a woman's role than it was for the woman herself in many cases. The bars became stages and any woman entering that space in those decades was faced with exploring the edges and core of her behavior and desires. Did she look "manly," walk like a man, think like a man? Who were the most likely subjects for her sexual interests—were there patterns?

To support the claim that butch/fem was a bar phenomenon and thus a performance, rather than a class phenomenon, Table 4.7 presents the bar attendance records of narrators according to their "role" affiliation. There appear to be only two categories of bar goers, frequent and rare.

With the exception of one butch, who referred to herself in 1999 as "a gentleman," all of the other butches and fems were active bar goers. All nine women frequented bars when they adopted the identity. I find it interesting that the one woman who owned a lesbian bar did not adopt a role and the one woman who managed at least two lesbian bars was butch only in her young adulthood.

Several quotes also make it seem that women were performing for a bar audience/community and doing so consciously.

CHERYL: As a butch, then, were you acting this out mostly in bar settings?
ADDY: Oh sure.

TABLE 4.7. Narrators' Mixed and Lesbian Bar Attendance and Butch/Fem Affiliation (%)

Frequented Bars	Butch/Fem	Unaffiliated
Rarely	2 Butch	26
Frequently	6 Butch, 2 Fem	8

CHERYL: So you spent a lot of time going to bars?

ADDY: Oh, there was one particular one in New York that was really fantastic and that was The Bagatelle. That was a great place—it really was. First of all, we were all protected, so that was really nice to be there. And, yes, I lead when I dance.

CHERYL: Were your friends other butches?

ADDY: Both. I think a lot of my friends are butch.

CHERYL: Were you slicking your hair back and wearing tuxedos?

ADDY: No, no. This is funny. When I was singing in California, I used to sing at a club called The Continental and that was very funny because I would dress masculine. I wore a bow tie, I had a key chain, the whole thing. When you're young, believe me, you do things you don't do when you're older. But I would never cut my hair and my hair was long. I don't know why, but I didn't.

CHERYL: Were you a part of butch/fem?

CHRIS: Yeah, in the good old days.

CHERYL: And you were which role?

CHRIS: Always butch. I tried to be fem once for some butch and it really didn't work out. I wasn't comfortable.

CHERYL: Did you dress differently? I would assume that you're playing this out in a bar setting.

CHRIS: Yeah.

CHERYL: So did you have daytime clothing and bar time clothing?

CHRIS: Hopefully yes. If I went to work, I would wear the tailored suit anyway.

CHERYL: With a skirt?

CHRIS: Always. We didn't have the pants; pants didn't come to work until the 1970s. Then you got into your dungarees, dressy dungarees.

CHERYL: Did you slick back your hair? Grease back your hair?

CHRIS: When I was on vacation, I did.

CHERYL: That would be Provincetown or Fire Island?

CHRIS: Yeah, the grease, that was when you bought your tube of grease.

CHERYL: Did you ever pass as male or was that ever a goal for you?

CHRIS: Oh, I loved it. Even now I pass as male, if I don't put [on] any lipstick and earrings and all that stuff. Like down here at the Museum of Art, I went in one day, had to go to the bathroom, right? Story of my life, I'm more in the bathroom than any place. I went in there. I'm in there minding my own business and the cop is outside the door. I didn't know it was a cop and he knocked. I said, "I'll be out in a minute." So then I come out and he looks at me. And he said, oh something, I got the message right away. And I said, "Oh, it's only me, and I walked on by."

I try to go for fems, otherwise we call them kikis. That's sad. I've heard of the others [stone butches] and I can't picture that, no way. If a woman or a man look at me in any way or anything like that, I'm uncomfortable. But if I go to a dance and I have a chance to wear my tuxedo, I'm comfortable. Whenever I have a chance, like the dances, to go real butchy, you know, or at the MCC, you know, your tie and your shirt and all that. But to get out of my house with all of this, you've got the raincoat on, no rain. The raincoat is on, you're covered up and I don't like to do that. What am I hiding here? I haven't killed anyone. Why am I sneaking out of the house and sneaking back into the house like nobody knows? I'm sure the neighbors, some of them, must know. They've got to get an idea after a while.

CHERYL: So you still feel like you've got to sneak around?

CHRIS: Yeah. When I moved down here I was a little more comfortable with that. That is redneck country. But I look the other way, I just pretend I don't hear it. Nobody's come out and said anything to me. I've seen a few women look at me, the way I dressed, you know, real sloppy at times just going shopping or something. When I wear the lipstick or the earrings, believe it or not, when I go to the OLOC [Older Lesbians Organizing for Change] luncheon I do that because I'm going into a straight restaurant. See, when something is predominantly one thing. You know, when in Rome. So I float in with that.

CHERYL: So you wear lipstick and earrings when you're going into a heterosexual situation?

CHRIS: Yeah, to mass, if I had to go to mass, yeah. When I don't have to, I don't.

CHERYL: You also mentioned MCC. Do you go to that?

CHRIS: I haven't been there in months. But when I go there, I get my shirt and tie on and jacket, dress up. I'm comfortable. Around gay boys, I'm comfortable if I'm dressed as a man.

Pat N played up fem when she went to bars in New York City and in Germany. She wore tight form-fitting pants, perfume, and lipstick, looking for a butch. Twice she met stone butches.

CLAIRE: Well, I was a butch. I was attracted to feminine women. There were some exceptions, you know. But largely that was the case. I'm trying to think when it was permissible to pull out from that. At the same time though, I always liked very strong-minded women and always have. I think it was safe to pull out of that in the 1960s—late 1960s. It was permissible.

CHERYL: Do you feel like you were forced out of it?

CLAIRE: No. I was much more comfortable. I always felt this was a lot of put on. But I always admired women who dressed as men and still looked feminine or dressed in a mannish way or a tomboyish way and yet looked feminine. That was always an attraction. Now, I feel, I would not have said that then. But I felt that.

CHERYL: But they always had a feminine side to them too?

CLAIRE: Oh yes. They were obviously women, obviously female.

CHERYL: And the females or fems that you are attracted to, they probably weren't playing a role. They were simply conforming to what it was to be female at that time, is that right?

CLAIRE: I think that they were putting on as well as the butches, of course. They were putting on to a certain extent, many of them that I knew were very strong women. But they did the cute kitteny stuff, which was baloney. That wasn't true.

JAN: What I remember most and what struck me the most is I wore slacks to work at the theater but I went out in skirts. And then as I became more comfortable in the bars, I started to go out by myself. And the first time out I'm wearing a skirt and somebody said, "Jan, you are dressed incorrectly here." And so I went to slacks and pointed patent shoes because I like shiny shoes.

CHERYL: And this was in the 1950s. Was butch/fem important in the bars you were going to?

JAN: Very important.

CHERYL: And for you, did you adopt a role?

JAN: Yes, as butch.

CHERYL: And did you slick your hair back?

JAN: Yes, I did—into a DA.

CHERYL: But this was just a nighttime appearance?

JAN: Just nighttime. But that was not a real long time that that was happening. That was a year. Then I got hired in the summer theater in Cleveland and ran into more gay people and was hanging around with those gay people, men and women. They were more closeted though, but I became more comfortable.

CHERYL: Did you date fems or were you attracted to fems?

JAN: I was, and only fems.

CHERYL: Because you've learned this butch role?

JAN: Sure. And only fems would respond to me.

CHERYL: Were you able to go back and forth? Did you ever try to be fem or were you ever considered fem?

JAN: No. I don't feel fem. I feel like I'm probably in the middle somewhere, but I don't feel fem at all. But I am sometimes attracted to butchy women, yeah. It doesn't matter to me now.

Back in the 1950s, they had these really wild colored men's pants. Of course, you couldn't wear a fly front either then; that was definitely telling. And so they were pink and green and blue and I got one of every color, brought them to a tailor and had them take out the zipper, sew them up and it was kind of like a pistol pocket. See I couldn't fit in women's pants anyhow; I didn't have the hips. And every damn time you went out and bought a size eight or ten or whatever, the hips were like this, which did not fit me. So I got in the habit of buying men's jeans, men's pants. I'd wore Levi's all my life as a kid when women weren't even wearing jeans. But I was riding horses, so that's how I got into that. And I would wear a shirt, just a regular short-sleeve or long-sleeve shirt and just try to keep it nongender. (Mitch)

CHERYL: Did you get involved in butch/fem?

DOROTHY: Yeah, because I guess I've always thought of myself as fem and I've always been attracted to butchy-looking women. Yeah, I guess I was involved. But that just seemed sort of natural. I know that there was a lot of stigma in those days that we don't see now, that women had to do that kind of thing. But I don't think there's much of that now. It's so much more "lipstick lesbian," that you don't really know anymore. But I think it's what people want to do. If you get dressed up and you want to go out to dinner, you wear what you want to wear. If it happens to be casual and sporty looking, then you're liable to get a label. On the other hand, I don't wear a lot of frills and ruffles either.

CHERYL: In the 1950s, did you dress the fem part?

DOROTHY: Yeah, because there were certain things that you did when you went out. And, yeah, I did dress the fem part. But I loved my slacks and my blazer jackets and that kind of thing and I wear those as well. I pretty much dressed the way I felt. And then once slacks came in and were acceptable, then we just wore slacks all the time.

KAY M: Butch and fem were big in those days when we first started.

CHERYL: Did you participate in that?

KAY M: Oh yes, absolutely. In Chicago I went with this dancer. She was kind of a stripper, but she called herself an exotic dancer. (That was another [woman] that I was going with when I was living with Nan.) I would go to her nightclub on Madison Avenue nearly every evening, toward the end of the night, to take her back to her apartment. I had two different Pendleton jackets that I thought were hot stuff. I would wear these Pendleton jackets and my slacks. She told them there at the club, "When my girlfriend comes in, I want her at this table," which had been set aside, and I would be there at night during her dance. She was fem, very petite.

CHERYL: Was she consciously fem?

KAY M: Absolutely, by the way she dressed, by the way she wore her hair, her makeup.

CHERYL: She was fully cognizant of butch/fem?

KAY M: Absolutely. When we played ball, people were butch or fem.

CHERYL: So fems played ball too.

KAY M: Oh yes. There were a few that were fem. There was one that I liked a lot and I went around with her for a while.

CHERYL: Were there certain positions that a fem would never play?

KAY M: No.

CHERYL: So you could have a fem catcher?

KAY M: Well, it seems to me they were always out in the field. I think that's a good point.

CHERYL: Were there some fems who were really good hitters?

KAY M: Yeah, there were a few.

MITCH: No, there was the kiki thing. I did a research study one time myself and this was asking every single one that I knew that was this kiki thing, I was so confused; I didn't know about it. It would appear that if two of them got together, the relationship lasted a while. But if that mixture got in with a butch or a fem, it didn't work. This was a personality thing, maybe personality matches didn't work based on needs. Which for me, the butch and the fem worked just perfectly fine if you had a true fem and a true butch. If you had two fems who decided one was butch, that was not going to work. I really did spend time trying to figure this out. And the whole thing was it was a need for this other individual. It's almost like if you see a straight couple where the man is this little thing—a lot of stereotype English men would fit that bill—with this overpowering masculine woman. It works perfectly. Because there you've got your roles reversed, but it's the needs that are being filled. And that's what was wrong with this kiki thing. Two of them together was fine if you had truly that. But if you didn't, it was not going to last.

CHERYL: So did you always date a fem?

MITCH: Yes. And I used to have a lot of butches knocking on the door constantly. I wasn't a dykey looking butch and I didn't want to be. I was kind of butchy to begin with but not compared to what was out there then.

The strongest message exuding from these narrators is that a minority of women who were living a lesbian lifestyle in the 1930s, 1940s, 1950s, and 1960s were attending bars, and were situating themselves in butch/fem roles. As the quotes above reveal, not even those who were adopting a role stuck to it. It is curious that no one admitted to being "kiki," sometimes butch, sometimes fem, perhaps reflective of the disdain associated with it in the bar culture as expressed by Mitch.

In fact, most of the narrators in this project were turned off by butch/fem and by butchy women.

We're talking about a total denial of the female—total denial of the female body. I mean they went beyond rejecting gender roles. They went beyond all of this and simply rejected everything female. Well, one woman that I chanced to come in contact with actually wore men's undergarments. And to me this was grotesque, frankly. So there was no group for me to join that I could see. (Claire)

Bobbie didn't feel like she was either fem or butch but everyone else at the bars had a persona. Her friends were equally uninvolved in the b/f scene.

CHERYL: Did you only run into butch/fem in bar settings?

BOBBIE: Yes.

CHERYL: So if you stayed away from the bars you didn't have to?

BOBBIE: Right. Teachers and people that I ran around with were just kind of normal-looking like I was.

CHERYL: Didn't have secret lives where they would go to different towns where they could be butch on the weekends?

BOBBIE: No, we weren't that inventive.

GIGI: Yes, [butch/fem is] what I objected to. That's what offended me in Cleveland. And that's what offended me in Greenwich Village. That's what offends me today. I wore a uniform my whole entire career up until fifteen years ago.

CHERYL: With a skirt?

GIGI: Yeah. It was totally different. The gay women were manly, so that they really didn't care what people thought and that offended me. There's no reason to be like that. You can love women and not have to be like that. So that's why I had a controversy with the gay issue.

CHERYL: What about butch/fem?

CYNTHIA: Oh, very much so. In the old days, it was real . . .

CHERYL: When would you say that faded out?

CYNTHIA: You know when I got my second bar in the 1970s, in my bar in the clientele you didn't see that at all. Mostly young collegiate type, mostly very athletic-looking women coming in with ponytails and they all look alike—blue jeans and T-shirts. The girls used to say Dykes on Bikes; there was a motorcycle crew. We had all kinds. Then would come the disco queens—you know, with the big hair and the makeup and the heels and the dresses—would come into the bar and I'd call them Dykes on Spikes.

CHERYL: Did you participate in butch/fem? In that role-playing?

CYNTHIA: I think I'm very butch.

CHERYL: But did you dress the part?

CYNTHIA: No, no.

CHERYL: Even in the 1950s?

CYNTHIA: No, not even in the 1950s. I don't like to go out with a woman and she's dressed very feminine and I'm dressed, you know, I don't like that at all.

CHERYL: You never tried to pass as male?

CYNTHIA: Oh no.

CHERYL: You didn't have your butch name?

CYNTHIA: No. I don't do that. I don't want to be a guy. I'm not a guy, I don't want to be a guy. I would never have a sex change or anything like that. But I am attracted to very feminine women. Other than that, I don't do roles like I don't cook and I don't do dishes. When I lived with Gloria, she did all of it mostly because I was so busy. But when I retired from that and she was sick and I took care of her, I did a lot. It's not something that I can't do or I don't want to do or I don't think it's my job.

So, it would seem that at least in this group of narrators, butch/fem was not a class or age related phenomenon but a bar phenomenon and, I think, a role playing phenomenon at that.

I think several points are significant in this examination of butch/fem and deserve specifying given the current research interest on butch/fem.

1. Not every woman who frequented bars adopted these roles. In fact, as many did as didn't—eight butch/fems and eight un-affiliateds.
2. The women who rarely went to bars did not affiliate.
3. Many lesbians of the 1940s, 1950s, and 1960s were repulsed by butch/fem.
4. Other types of lesbian communities existed where butch/fem labels were not adopted.
5. Many women had no lesbian community.
6. Most of the women who did participate in butch/fem did think of themselves as performing.

Unexplored in the discussions of butch/fem have been two literary events that I think should not go unmentioned. These two literary events are the 1892 murder of Freda Ward by her lover Alice Mitchell and subsequent books based on it, and the tremendous popularity of *The Well of Loneliness.*

The Ward murder in Tennessee was an act of passion by an older woman afraid her lover would marry.

The medical journals described Alice Mitchell in terms out of Krafft-Ebing's and Havelock Ellis' work: as a child she preferred playing boy's games; she liked to ride bareback on a horse "as a boy would"; her family regarded her as "a regular tomboy." Alice planned to wear men's clothes and have her hair cut like a man's so that she might marry Frieda Ward and support her by working at a man's job. She killed her lover because she feared that Freda would marry a real man instead of her. (Faderman 1991, p. 56)

The case was covered in dozens of city newspapers and in *The New York Times.*

In May 1892, *The [New York] Times* report of Alice Mitchell's murder of her once-beloved Freda Ward referred to nothing more scandalous than Mitchell's statement that she "loved Freda desperately" and had wanted to marry her. In striking contrast were those medical journal reports of the same case which headlined it "Lesbian Love and Murder" and referred to intense love relations between women. The national newspaper publicity in the Mitchell-Ward case probably marked a major shift in the public awareness of a suspect potential in the love relations of women. (Katz 1983, p. 165)

This medical literature, and the nationwide newspaper reports of the case, made it one of the major incidents in the public history of lesbianism in the United States, comparable to the publication in 1929 of *The Well of Loneliness.* (Katz 1983, p. 223)

In 1895 three novels appeared which built on this real-life murder. According to Faderman, these books were Mary Wilkins Freeman's "The Long Arm," in which a mannish businesswoman kills the man who is seducing her lover Mary; Mary Hatch's The *Strange Disappearance of Eugene Comstock,* wherein a lesbian, passing as a man, murders a man and then marries a woman, and John Carhart's *Norma Trist; of Pure Carbon: A Story of the Inversion of the Sexes.* Norma is a tomboy in youth, gets an education, and then wishes to marry a woman whom she kills when the woman gets engaged.

Faderman points out that once the lesbian image took root in the American imagination it did so as a mannish person. "Lesbianism and masculinity became so closely tied in the public imagination that it was believed that only a masculine woman could be the genuine article" (1991, p. 57).

Radclyffe Hall's book, *The Well of Loneliness,* did for the 1930s to 1960s what the murder did for the 1880s-1910s. It reinforced the idea of a manly homosexual woman—Stephen—attracted to a feminine heterosexual (thus nonhomosexual) woman—Angela.

> *New York Times* reports of the censorship of Radclyffe Hall's *The Well of Loneliness* in England, and later *Times* reports of the attempt to censor that novel in the United States, helped make the book an international cause celebre and best seller. The complex, contradictory impact of Hall's novel, intended as a defense of the female congenital invert, is only now beginning to be understood; this impact is apparent in scattered references in several documents. (Katz 1983, p. 161)

Twenty-five of the narrators specifically mentioned having read *The Well of Loneliness.* Twelve read it as teenagers. It is surprising that Gagnon and Simon (1973) had only one of twenty narrators who read this book. Carolyn was given the book at age fourteen, by a married woman librarian; Gigi was given it by her father at age fourteen. Three women read it in college and three read it in the 1970s. Nan was given the book by her male therapist. Four Whistling Women said they had never read the book.

One woman who played at being butch said she didn't relate at all to Stephen and Angela, while the gentleman said she wanted to be like Stephen. For several of the readers, it was their first realization that another couple had experienced the same feelings, a realization also quoted in the Gagnon and Simon study. I explore the Whistling Women's reactions to the book in more depth in Chapter 7.

A masculine woman obsessed with a more typically feminine woman was strongly implanted in the minds of many Americans by the 1940s through this literature and through real women who came to those expectations either naturally or through mimicry. Popular culture perpetrated and created these images, placing butch/fem in the realm of performance. That literature and the medical information about mannish neurotics would have filtered further, faster among the reading population, the upper through middle classes, and created negative stereotypes rejected by a number of the narrators. It is important to note, however, that butchy, dykey, or manly women are also the product of genetics and many of those women easily dubbed "butch" had/have no conscious part in butch/fem acting.

Longevity of Love Relationships

Monogamy and longevity of relationships were verbally valued by most narrators. Cotten (1975), too, found that lesbians have few sexual partners and exclusivity is usually practiced when they are involved. "Patterns of overt sexual behavior on the part of homosexual females tend to resemble closely those of heterosexual females," said Gagnon and Simon in 1973 (1973, p. 180). The same seems to be true thirty years later.

At least twelve of the narrators have had a union or commitment ceremony and two other narrators married legally in Vermont. Among the unions, three were private ceremonies, one was a Unitarian ceremony, two were MCC ceremonies (one in 1975), and one couple married at the 1993 March on Washington in the group ceremony. One woman has had two ceremonies, and one woman has been through a palimony lawsuit.

These forty-three women named 183 lovers and thirty-one lesbian friends (no names mentioned by one woman), for an average of four lovers, probably not unlike the heterosexual population. Kinsey wrote in 1953 that only 29 percent of lesbians had had sex with three or more women. That our number is higher would seem to indicate possibly that the greater visibility of lesbians since the Kinsey report has resulted in a slightly higher average number of lovers. Kinsey (1953) also reported that only 4 percent had had ten or more partners, a situation that was not quantified in this project but would seem to be only slightly higher now. Gagnon and Simon in 1973 believed these figures to be nearly identical to those for heterosexual women. I think the low number of lesbian friends named underscores the isolation of many of these women. Three women have had only one woman lover. Several women said during their interviews that lesbians change partners frequently, flirt with coupled women, and generally misbehave in a group. One woman said she wouldn't go on an Olivia Cruise or a lesbian group trip because of the flirting. So how impermanent are the relationships?

Unfortunately, length of relationship often was not specified. Of the 183 lovers referred to, I have longevity information on 118 of them (64 percent). Seventy-five of these relationships lasted five years or fewer (64 percent). Nineteen lasted seven to ten years (16 percent), 5 percent lasted eleven to fifteen years (N = 6), nine (8 percent) sixteen to twenty years, and eight persevered for seventeen to thirty-two years (7 percent) (Table 4.8). Taken together, forty-two (36 percent) of these relationships lasted more than five years. The longevity of relationships when these women were younger is quite different now when only three relationships have been in existence for fewer than six years (18 percent), and 82 percent have been in place for five to thirty-two years, 76 percent for twelve years or longer. Gay men fifty-one-plus who have been married averaged fourteen years in those relationships (Cahill et al. 2000). The reader should remember that in Chapter 3 the following facts were presented: The average length of first marriage for a heterosexual couple in the United States in 1998 was eleven years but was 13.41 years for these twenty-two lesbians, while the average of all marriages in the United States is 7.2 years but 12.64 years for the Whistling Women. Looking at the narrators' heterosexual marriages (Chapter 3), 12 percent lasted fewer than six years and 88 percent lasted longer, 59 percent for twelve years or longer. As a group, the narrators are staying committed to women partners longer than they did to male partners.

It may not be appropriate to compare these lesbian cohabitation relationships to the legal marriage relationships. In several studies and Web sites on cohabitation statistics for the United States, one can read that 40 percent of cohabiting couples break up within five years. In light of this figure, 62 percent of the relationships among this group of lesbians lasting five years or less would seem to be high—but not necessarily. Again, the figures are for cohabiting couples, which many of the relationships mentioned by the narrators may not have been.

Fifty percent of cohabitors either marry within two years of starting to live together or break up. The percentage who break up is not specified, but half of them seems a conservative figure. Thirty relationships mentioned in the interviews lasted one or two years or less, 30 percent, which may indicate longer relationships among these les-

TABLE 4.8. Duration of Lesbian Lover Relationships (Number of Relationships)

Years	Current Relationship (Number)	Past Relationships (Number)
1		15
2		23
3		6
4	1	12
5	2	18
6	1	
7		4
8		7
9		2
10		6
11		1
12	1	
13		2
14	5	2
15		1
16		1
17		4
18		1
19	1	
20		3
21	2	
22		1
23		2
24		1
25		1
26		
27	1	1
28		
29	1	
30	2	

bians. Furthermore, 20 percent of heterosexual cohabitors stay together more than five years. It is unspecified how many of the couples opt to marry at five years, so one can't conclude that the cohabiting relationships that don't last five years end in separation. They may end in marriage. Nevertheless, finding that 39 percent of the past lesbian relationships lasted more than five years and that 82 percent of the current relationships have lasted longer than five years probably indicates greater stability of lesbian relationships than of heterosexual ones.

The cohabitation data brought to light several interesting points. Lower-income heterosexuals are more likely to cohabit than marry, and people who have divorced are more likely to cohabit in future relationships. Women who cohabit for more than two years have significantly less likelihood of marrying. Cohabitors are the least committed to marriage and the most accepting of divorce (www. clasp.org/pubs/familyformation/cohab.html). Could it be that some women are in lesbian relationships because they offer sexual pleasure without pregnancy issues and because there is no pressure for a legal commitment? When lesbians do have shorter relationships than their heterosexual counterparts, is it because they have less commitment to marriage and more tolerance of divorce?

It is also interesting that "Full-time employment of the male reduces the odds of separating in a cohabiting union by about 40 percent" (www.clasp.org/pubs/amilyformation/cohab.html). Education and income of male strongly influence the decision to marry. I suspect that higher education and income of one partner strongly influence the decision of that person to stay in a lesbian relationship as well.

Relationships with Parents, Siblings, and Children

Although the medical professions from 1880 to 1970 managed to convince many people that lesbians were neurotic and sociopathic, it is clear from the narrations of these forty-four women, from the work of Franzen and Kehoe, as well as that of Gagnon and Simon (1973), that lesbians are rarely either.

Good or excellent relationships were reported by twenty narrators with twenty-nine of their parents. Sixteen of these parents were mothers and thirteen were fathers. Bad or weak relationships with fathers were mentioned by four narrators (two older, two younger) and with mothers by seven women (two older and five younger). Four more reported lukewarm relationships, three with mothers and one with a father. One woman said she had a dutiful relationship with her parents. Seven said they had no relationships whatsoever with their parents (four older, three younger). This amounts to twenty-nine of the eighty or so parents involved in the lives of these women. Gagnon and Simon (1973) found that preference for male or female parent was equally divided among their twenty informants, a situation much like this one and belying the notion that affiliation with the father makes for a lesbian daughter. (For ten women I couldn't tell the nature of their relationships.)

With respect to relationships with siblings, thirteen women are only children, leaving thirty-one with siblings. Cynthia and Kay M had ten and seven siblings respectively, and the interview did not go into the relationships with each one. Seven women did not mention the nature of their relationships. Of the twenty-two women remaining, three women reported bad relationships with brothers, and three spoke of nonexistent relationships with brothers and three with sisters. Only Rose claimed an excellent relationship—with her brother. Okay relationships were reported by two women with sisters and one with a brother. Good relationships with nine sisters are reported by seven women and with seven brothers by six women. There is a hint here of more problems with brothers than with sisters. Kehoe (1989, p. 30) said of siblings that "Half of the respondents who have non-gay brothers report 'seldom' or 'never' having any contact with them, while those with married or non-supportive sisters communicate with them somewhat more often."

Bad relationships were registered by five mothers with two sons and three daughters, and weak relationships with two sons and one daughter of one woman.

Far more mothers have good or excellent relationships with their children—fourteen in fact. These relationships include sixteen sons and five daughters. Three women have adequate relationships with one son and three daughters.

Of the twenty-nine sons and thirteen daughters birthed by this group of eighteen women, the women report bad or weak relations with 14 percent of the sons and 31 percent of the daughters. They enjoy good or excellent relationships with 55 percent of their sons and

38 percent of their daughters. Relations with daughters seem to be the most difficult in this group of lesbian moms. There is even a hint of greater trouble in relations with their own mothers, as stated previously. Kehoe's sample reported more difficulty with sons than daughters (1989).

Race/Ethnicity

The reader may recall that only one narrator is not white in this project. That is Vera, an African-American woman. The narrators' stories do not include much information about race. I usually asked about the racial mixture in the bars of the 1950s to 1970s, and in their friendship groups then and now, but I rarely heard of any diversity. Vera had a lover in 1958-1960 and friends in Los Angeles who were Japanese. Mary1 was involved with a Japanese woman in the early 1960s. Gigi partied with many Filipinos in her hospital. A bit more about ethnic diversity will appear in Chapters 6 and 8.

That was really the first time I had got into any kind of a . . . even friendship with black people, was when I went to New York. Well, some of [the black women] came to the bars and some of them we just met at home. One was in the Navy at the time, so she didn't get out and about very much. One of the other nurses was also in the military and also black. (Pat M)

[The Detroit lesbian community] was very ethnically diverse. There were at least two black gals in our group, a couple of Jewish gals, and certainly the run-of-the-mill English and Irish background. We had a couple of Ukrainian women. (Dorothy)

Chris had this to say about diversity issues:

CHRIS: No, she doesn't have to be Catholic. It would be nice, but it doesn't have to be. I've known a lot of Protestants in my lifetime. And I've gone with a Jewish woman and I've gone with a woman under almost every sign of the zodiac. But that was years ago.

CHERYL: Have women of other ethnic groups ever been much of a part of your social life or sexual life?

CHRIS: No.

CHERYL: Just didn't run into them? They didn't go to the bars?

CHRIS: I met them, Negroes like that. Yes, I could have had my chance with a Negro woman I guess, if I'd pushed my luck.

CHERYL: Just didn't care for her?

CHRIS: She was gorgeous. That just wasn't my thing. I would just be embarrassed going any place with a black woman. Or a Chinese or some[one] like that. I'm not into that.

AMELIA: One of my very best friends had lived with this black woman for many years. That was the first time I had come across this and I didn't agree with it. I still don't like it.

CHERYL: She's white and she's living with a black woman?

AMELIA: Yes, and they've gotten along thirty years at least. But way back in the back of my brain or something, I just don't think white and black should be together. Be together socially, but not marriage. Maybe lovers if you want, but not marriage.

CHERYL: So was she the only nonwhite person moving in these two circles?

AMELIA: Yes.

CHERYL: And how do you think she was received?

AMELIA: Oh, everybody loved her.

JAN: No, no blacks in the bar. They were not allowed in the bars. And a dear friend of mine, a white woman, was coupled with a black woman and they were not allowed in the bars. The group that I hung with finally organized and protested that and we were able to get that couple into the bar. That was in 1955. 'Cause then I went off to Cleveland, so it was before I went to Cleveland. And I was in Cleveland in 1956. We were able to get that couple into the bar, but I don't know that we made much of an impact because at that time blacks were not in the bars. And we were discriminating among ourselves and that was awful, I thought. I did fuss about that pretty much.

CHERYL: Were there some black gay bars or some black bars that had a lot of gay clientele?

JAN: Not that I know of; I don't think so. I don't know where the black folk went, but I know through this one woman we connected with other blacks and we were able to get other blacks into the bars, so it started a little bit.

CHERYL: Can you remember how you phrased the argument with the bar owner?

JAN: We just stood outside and protested, first of all.

CHERYL: Not with signs . . .

JAN: Yes, we did. And said, we won't come in, we just won't come in and they were losing their clients, unless you allow these folks in, these people in.

CHERYL: And this was an exclusively gay bar?

JAN: Yes. Well, it was open to the street.

You know we didn't have that many blacks [in Syracuse bar]. Maybe we had one in a great while. Blacks are a minority, gays are a minority. In the blacks, it's like double minority and so in gay life there's not that many blacks unless there's some parts of town. But that wouldn't be in Syracuse; we only had óne bar. I feel sorry for especially gay women. I think that gay men have a little bit more freedom in the blacks. But the gay black women, I think especially in those days, had double whammy. Because not only were they discriminated against from everybody, but they were discriminated against within their own. (Cynthia)

POLITICS

Lesbian politics arise at several levels—party politics and the politics of rights movements. I will explore the political thinking of the narrators now using both of these subdivisions.

Considering first party politics, the narrators were asked how they were registered when they first voted and how they were registered when they last voted. When the older women first registered to vote from 1935 to 1947, ten of the fifteen (67 percent) registered as Democrats, four (27 percent) as Republicans, and one is unknown to me. When the younger women first registered to vote, from 1948 to 1956, eighteen of the twenty-nine (62 percent) registered as Democrats, five (17 percent) as Republicans, two as Liberals, one (3 percent) as an Independent, and three (10 percent) didn't remember how they first affiliated.

Upon last voting (for most women that is between 1998 and 2001), thirty-five of the forty-four (84 percent) women were registered as Democrats. One woman still considers herself Liberal, one says she now swings between parties, four were registered as Republicans (9 percent), and one was of unknown affiliation (2 percent). Only two women (4.5 percent) have switched affiliations from Democrat to Republican over their lifetime, while six have switched from Republican to Democrat (13.6 percent) and one Republican sometimes now votes Democratic.

They are as a group and in their age cohorts, overwhelmingly registered now as Democrats and have been Democrats throughout their lives. Democratic party affiliation is the norm for gays and lesbians in the United States in 2004.

Large majorities of GLB voters supported Democratic Congressional candidates (65.1 percent in 1998; 72 percent in 1996; 73 percent in 1994; 77 percent in 1992; and 61 percent in 1990). The GLB vote constitutes a clear and strong component of the remaining House Democratic voter base; indeed GLB voters identify as and vote Democratic in far higher proportion than non-GLB voters. (Bailey 2000, p. 9)

Meanwhile, gay, lesbian, and bisexual (GLB) voters have been increasingly switching over to Republican party affiliation, although this is not the case among these older voters.

In the 1992 election 23 percent of GLB voters cast their ballots for Republican House candidates. In 1994, 26 percent voted Republican and in 1996 28 percent cast their ballots for Republicans. This trend continued in 1998 with 32 percent of GLB voters voting Republican—approaching the documented high mark of GLB voter support for Republicans of 39 percent in 1990. (Bailey 2000, p. 9)

GLB voters over forty years old amounted to 4.3 percent of the exiting voters in 1996 (Bailey 2000). In the 1992 exit polls for Congressional elections, 47 percent of GLB voters were women (Bailey 2000). Lesbians and bisexual women supported the Democrat House candidates in the proportions of 53 percent in 1990, 82 percent in 1994, and 63 percent in 1998, while 53 percent of heterosexual women voted for Democrat House candidates in 1994. On the other hand, lesbians showed less favor (67 percent) than did homosexual men (72 percent) for Clinton in 1998 (Bailey 2000).

In 1996, 5.1 percent of the voters surveyed as they exited the polls identified as gay, lesbian, or bisexual (GLB). The only larger voting subgroup/bloc that year was African Americans at 10.1 percent of the exiting voters. More readily recognized subgroups than GLB were smaller: Latino voters amounted to 4.5 percent and Jewish voters 3.4 percent (Tafel 2000).

The 1998 exit poll data found that about 67 percent of GLB voters had incomes below $50,000 while only 53 percent of heterosexual voters have incomes below $50,000 (Bailey 2000).

Several of the narrators are or were greatly involved in local, union, or state level party politics. Bing was quite active in Republican politics at the state level. She ran for public office but lost and then organized the visit of Reagan to her county. Addy is quite active in her town politics but so far has resisted suggestions that she run for an office. She has an appointed office. Dawn, who had ceased to vote for a time, ran for city council and won in 2001. Claire was very active in her teachers' union mid-century as was Mary2, and Vera was quite active in Los Angeles County politics and union politics. A few women mentioned membership in the League of Women Voters.

Assuming that the narrators would be attuned to gay rights issues and active supporters of gay rights candidates, I asked each woman about her political activities. The following are the questions and the positive responders.

1. Do you consider yourself to be or have been an activist for gay rights? Yes: Edie, Jackie (including picket), Marilyn, Sappho, Rose, Kay M (attended National Lesbian Organizing convention in Atlanta, 1992), Vera

2. Have you ever been an organizer for lesbian or gay issues? Yes: Edie, Jackie, Sappho, Vera

3. Have you attended/watched a gay rights/pride march/conference? Yes: Edie and Jackie (1993 March on Washington), Sappho (one New York City march), Pat M (Key West, Golden Threads, Atlanta 1992), Gigi (Tampa), Marilyn (1979 DC, Cincinnati), Vera (many plus 1993 March on Washington, annual OLOC conferences, two Texas Lesbian confabs), Joanna (two marches in Washington)

4. Have you worked for or contributed money to an openly gay candidate? Yes: Claire, Jackie, Kate, Cynthia, Jan, Vera

5. Do you belong to any gay rights organizations/subscribe to media/contribute to causes? Claire mentions OLOC, NGLTF, Silver Threads; Edie and Jackie OLOC and many local groups; Ruth and Barbara contribute to Human Rights Campaign (HRC), Lesbian Defense Fund, and Center for Gay Youth; Marilyn joined OLOC, many in the 1980s; Sappho HRC, Silver Threads; Carolyn HRC; Dorothy OLOC; Cynthia (Syracuse WEB); Jan OLOC and Silver Threads; Vera Senior Action in a Gay Environment (SAGE), OLOC, Mazer Archives for Lesbians, Peace and Tolerance, sent mail, faxes, e-mail, letters; presented at the G/L National Journalist Association Conference

6. Have you ever boycotted a product because of antigay policies? Cam (Shell Gas, store items); Gloria, Pat M, Dorothy, Roberta, and Amelia (Cracker Barrel); Kate and Roberta (orange juice); Sandy (Coke); Diane (you're damn right I have); Cynthia and Gigi (Miller beer); Edie, Jackie, Nancy, Ellen, Jan, Bobbie, Vera (unspecified products)

7. Do you actively seek out gay-owned businesses/credit card? Dawn (member of a gay business bureau), Nancy, Kate, Diane, Dorothy, Roberta

8. Do you have any gay insignia, clothing, stickers on your car? Mary1, Cam, Kay M, Dorothy, Roberta

9. Have you ever spoken up about gay rights at work or in your marriage, maybe to defend a co-worker or to give your child another perspective, corrected someone's language? Yes: Edie

10. Have you attended a lesbian music event, gone to a gay Mecca, been on an Olivia tour? Claire, Kay, Carolyn (Olivia tours); Claire, Kay, Kay M, Nan, Marilyn (concerts); Dawn (Gay Fair in Tampa); Barbara and Kate (Provincetown, Fire Island, Cherry Grove); Jackie and Dorothy (Provincetown); Edie (Provincetown, Key West, Michigan Womyn's Music Festival [8 times]); Mary Lou (Fire Island, Key West); Joanna (N. Virginia music festivals, Provincetown); Sappho (music festival, Cherry Grove, Provincetown), Jan (twenty years to Michigan Womyn's Music Festival)

11. What do you think about gay marriage?
    unnecessary: Nan
    needed/great: Kate (for medical benefits, financial benefits), Diane, Ellen
    married in Vermont: (Edie and Jackie)

Issues of rights for homosexuals at voting time generally did elicit a positive response. Gigi and several other women have only recently become attuned to gay rights at the polls. Kate and Liz said they would not vote for someone espousing an antigay stance. Jan remarked that while she gives gay rights issues some serious thought before voting, she cannot get her other gay friends to consider the topic.

Claire pointed out that there was no way to work for gay issues before NOW, the National Organization for Women, formed in 1966. Currently she belongs to the Civil Liberties Union, the Gay and Lesbian Task Force, and OLOC, Older Lesbians Organizing for Change. While few narrators spoke strongly about any political activities or need for them (also discussed in Chapter 7), Claire probably represents a few more narrators when she said, "I have voted properly, and worked for candidates."

The following subset of comments from the interviews are revealing of the diversity of opinion about gay issues among these forty-four narrators:

I really didn't give two damns about gay life or gay rights. I protect me and mine first—still. (Mitch)

We haven't come far enough. I think it's a disgrace that gays are treated the way they are . . . but I've never been an activist about gay rights. I'm very pleased to see progress that's been made and I think the situation is ultimately going to be settled in the courts. (Roberta)

Race, class, gender, sexual orientation—all are connected. There is no separation for me as far as oppression . . . Not gay rights—I call myself lesbian. I have a different lifestyle than what gay people live—that's a heterosexual type lifestyle. . . . We realized that the minute you create a women's bookstore—it makes you political whether you want to be or not. (Edie)

We are a straight married couple who are lesbian. (Ruth)

We have gone out of our way to make it better for the gay society and I think [Gay Pride marches] go out of their way to tear it down. . . . We also spent a lot of our lives trying to make it better for the upcoming generation. I think we were making a great deal of progress until the AIDS situation. (Joyce)

I think a national gay group is wonderful, great. If I were born now, I would be part of every group available and probably marching in parades and all kinds of different things. (Kate)

A couple of years ago down here, getting involved on the computer, a lot of gay rights things come up and I think that helped politically. And of course getting involved in MCC again and meeting some gay political activists, people that are in politics and that really shook my tree. When Clinton came in and it was at that time I started getting involved in politics, or the political aspect of gay rights. I was corresponding with several people in California and they kind of opened my eyes too about the gay rights that are not out there [in California], that everybody thinks are there. (Gigi)

Two women objected to the political activities of MCC (Metropolitan Community Church), but many more particularly liked the political activism of the MCC church and their own politicization that had occurred through their membership.

Being a lesbian has never had a political component to it for Nan. Nor had it for Gigi until the Clinton era.

Liberalism is totally outdated, declared Claire. She likes OLOC because it makes demands. "Lesbians and gays need to organize" and are failing to do so, she thinks, but OLOC is such a group. Sappho understands the role of previous activism in her own freedom to be gay, as do Dorothy and Kate:

And the consensus with our group anyway, and I think mine personally, is that I will probably never walk in a parade and carry a placard. However, I feel very special that I have gotten a lot of benefits because so many people have done that. I feel very grateful to them. I feel sort of bad that I can't do it myself. But we did talk about that; that is something that we weren't sure that we could do. But, hey, somewhere along the line it's going to benefit us. And it has; it really has. (Dorothy)

CHERYL: Is it important to you that there is sort of a national gay group?

KATE: I think it's wonderful. I think it's great. And I think if I was born at this time, I would be part of every group available and probably marching in parades and all kinds of different things. But at the time that I was born and when I came out, it was completely different. I'm sort of like structured already. I think that what you're brought up with at any given time is really what you carry on with you.

Barbara expressed a concern that some others may share, that the government is keeping tabs on all this political activity. This certainly was the impression they lived with in the 1950s and 1960s.

BARBARA: I do have one little fear. I have a Big Brother complex I think to some extent. I don't feel that I want the government to know anything about my personal life. Because I do feel that the government knows a great deal more about us than we would like them to. Everything, since the computer age, is right out there. So I don't like to set myself up to be labeled as anything in particular, particularly gay or anything else. I just want to kind of blend in and do my own thing.

CHERYL: Do you think that there's somebody keeping track of Web sites you visit on the Internet?

BARBARA: Yes, I think that's a good possibility. I'm not paranoid about it and I don't think about it daily. But I do think there's a good possibility. And the more I read, the more I believe it. I just think the government knows a whole lot more about us than we might like them to.

Feminism

Feminism has appealed to several of these narrators. Situating themselves explicitly as feminists are Joanna, Mary1, Nancy, Claire, Ruth, Barbara, Edie, Jackie, Kate, Sappho, Judy, and Ellen. Interestingly, Carolyn dropped out of NOW when lesbian rights became part of the platform. Cam says she is 75 percent feminist—Diane might concur. Edie discovered feminism through the peace movement of the 1980s. Those narrators who mentioned NOW membership were Claire, Joanna, and Carolyn of the older cohort, and Ruth, Judy, Jackie, Marilyn, and Sheri of the younger cohort.

I started out belonging to NOW and I dropped out when it became an almost overwhelmingly lesbian organization [1973?] because I didn't think that was its proper role. And I think they turned away many, many, many women, some of them lesbians, because they were emphasizing that lifestyle and how it should be accepted by everyone, which is a fine goal. But I didn't think the National Organization for Women should be so narrow. (Carolyn)

I'm more interested in seeing women's rights and women's movements than I am being segregated as a lesbian because I am a woman first prior to any other choices in my life. I care about how women do businesswise and that women deserve just as much of a chance as men, minorities deserve a chance, for the whole of the population I don't like to see segregation of women, men, races, religions. I feel that the age we're at is a very spiritual age and that people should be pushing those damn walls down and joining together. (Nan)

I'm not a bra burning, man hating, not one of those real radical ones, but I would say I'm in favor of issues that will protect women. (Diane)

I'd joined the NOW organization earlier and I was surprised at the lesbians when I went to Lily's open house [in DC in 1973]. When I went to her open house and met all the women there, I thought they would all be real feminists, but they weren't. In fact most of them weren't interested at all. (Joanna)

Yes, but not a real feminist compared to what the feminist feminists are. But like in my little school, I was the radical feminist. It didn't take much. (Sappho)

Nan's first criterion in choice of political candidates is support for women's rights, particularly abortion. Nan prefers woman-owned businesses to gay-owned businesses. While patronizing gay businesses, Nancy, Pat N, and Marilyn give preference to woman-owned businesses. Joanna is more supportive of feminist than gay candidates. Pat N was quite active as a feminist, organizing self-defense classes, book displays, and self-help groups and being the base liaison on women's issues on military bases, but as a straight woman at that time.

Other women found it impractical to separate themselves into woman or lesbian. Bing considers herself to be equally interested in gay and women's politics, and Dawn said she can't separate gay from woman.

Rejecting feminism and labels in general are at least Gigi, Gloria, Pat M, Barbara, and Sheri.

Absolutely not [a feminist]. I used to go to the NOW meetings and I'd argue with those women up one side and down the other. I got into more trouble. (Gigi)

No, I haven't [considered myself a feminist]. Mainly because some of the first people I ever saw that were feminists, I felt that it was a good excuse to go without a bra and a bath. They were just dirty, sloppy-looking people. As I said earlier, I don't like labels. I think that the feminist work ethic and salaries and things like that, yes, I think that women should be paid the same as men if they're doing the same job. And I think that women have been downtrodden a lot, but a lot of it they ask for themselves. (Pat M)

I've listened to a lot of the yakkety yak and when they get on their soapbox I think, I was born free, nobody dictated what I had to be or do. What are these people so upset about? If they want to put themselves in a box and close the lid, that's their problem, not mine. I never felt restricted. I never felt put down. I never felt stymied by anything. I did what I wanted to do. I just think sometimes they make a big hullabaloo about nothing just to get attention. (Sheri)

I think of myself as beyond woman. I don't think about being gay. I'm a soul. . . . It's funny how when you talk about it, I don't really identify myself in terms of gay or woman. It's interesting to find that out. I really don't. (Barbara)

Gloria says something very similar to Barbara: "I am a spirit. I've never been primarily a lesbian. I felt primarily female but I was never an activist." Gloria says she supports causes financially and in prayer and will.

A number of issues of concern to feminists are of concern to these women, mothers, workers, aging, lesbians, even if they rejected the label "feminist" or "activist." For Mitch and Nan abortion rights is their number-one political issue; Ruth will not support a right-to-life candidate either.

Other groups with political activism as part of their charter or causes that these women mentioned belonging to are (one to three narrators each) Planned Parenthood, the American Civil Liberties Union (ACLU), HRC, NJ Women and AIDS Network, Syracuse Web, Women's Energy Bank (St. Petersburg), various groups in the

1970s and 1980s, trade unions in the 1960s, animal welfare, sexual harassment, recording women's history. Membership fees become harder to justify and maintain as one ages and one's income shrinks.

Well, those [marches] were back in the 1960s for racial and feminist justice, open housing, peace in Vietnam. As far as specifically gay and lesbian, oh yes, just this last spring we marched in front of city hall to have our city clerk rehired. This was in St. Pete Beach. The issue was sexual harassment. (Claire)

Two groups that are particularly important for their political activity and that affect the lives of a number of these narrators are the Women's Energy Bank (WEB)/Salon of St. Petersburg, Florida, and OLOC, a national organization. Both groups are discussed in Chapter 6.

Between us we had seven children and two husbands. . . . We didn't know anything different than a heterosexual model until we began to see how other people did it. Our relationship was more egalitarian in that one wasn't butch and one wasn't fem. We could both pass so we didn't have that kind of butch/fem dynamic. The power issues were mostly with money since she made much more money than I did. So the power issues were also with her work which in the beginning of our relationship took much more time. So I was the "wife." We still had these seven kids. We didn't live all together. We waited until most of them were in college.

We didn't live together for three years and then by that time five of our kids were in college or working. That is when we moved in together. You know how kids are when they're in college—they're home even though they're away at college. So there were a lot of times when I'd say we had banquets every night because there were all these people around the dinner table. I had more time to cook and do those kinds of jobs. But then when we moved to Florida there were just the two of us and the jobs totally switched because then she was retired and I was going to school and working as a nurse at night. We had a lot of trouble in our relationship then in switching over those roles. But then we began to learn about shared responsibility, shared roles. We developed a lifestyle where we didn't have so much of that heterosexual model. (Edie)

SUMMARY

The women in this study, while not particularly politically active or aware, have lived lives of conformity and occasionally express displeasure with the more radical factions of the homosexual and transsexual world. When the Whistling Women are politically interested it is in sympathy with a gay rights movement, while the call for a more inclusive queer nation, has failed.

Thirty-eight of these women identified their homoeroticism prior to the Stonewall Riots. After 1970, the gay liberation movement and the gay rights movement proclaimed that one needed to "come out" publicly. As should be predictable, not all of these women were convinced by the logic of gay liberation or gay rights even though they may acknowledge that in 2004 it is easier to be gay. Nine of these women do not consider themselves to be out and six of those are in the youngest age cohort. When the lesbianism of these women was discovered or a woman chose to out herself, rarely did the horrible things happen that we all dread. Three women were kicked out of their natal homes, three fought custody battles, one was taken to a police station in a raid, one lost a job, one was kicked out of school, one has been rejected by a child, and perhaps, unexpectedly, four had lovers leave them.

Five women say they were still having sex one to three times a week, five said once a month, three said rarely, and three said never. Writers of the late 1990s characterize lesbian sex of the 1970s as prudish but these women would not agree.

Eight narrators considered themselves butch at some point in their lives, two fem, and 34 (77 percent) did not relate to these labels. I think the important ingredient missing from our understanding of butch/fem is the gay or lesbian bar. For women who sought and found community in the bars of the era, butch or fem identities were to be chosen. But for women who did not frequent bars, there was little knowledge of and little incentive for the adoption of butch/fem. No woman reported adopting a butch/fem identity after 1959. This fact would suggest that the second wave of the women's movement did not bring an end to butch/fem but that the end began a decade earlier.

Neither age, nor education correlate strongly with butch/fem identity. Fifty percent of the women born upper class came to identify as butch. It is my conclusion that butch/fem activities were role-playing, performance, not a lower class or working-class phenomenon. In fact, most of the narrators in this project were turned off by butch/fem and by butchy women. Twenty-five of the Whistling Women have read *The Well of Loneliness*.

These forty-three women named 183 lovers for an average of four lovers. Seventy-five of these relationships lasted five years or fewer

(64 percent). The longevity of relationships when these women were younger is quite different from now, when only three relationships have been in existence for fewer than six years (18 percent), and 76 percent for twelve years or longer. The Whistling Women are staying committed to women partners longer than they were to male partners.

The narrators have slightly more relationship problems with their brothers than their sisters and significantly more problems with their daughters than their sons.

Few of the narrators call themselves feminists. When they are interested in women's issues it is typically abortion rights. Over 80 percent of them are Democrats. They expressed little interest in a national lesbian-gay rights movement, and few have ever fought or marched for lesbian rights although several have boycotted products or companies and consider the gay rights stand of political candidates.

Twice that first day, as I was walking around the campus, some student would say, "Good morning, Miss Baker." I thought, *Who the hell is Miss Baker?* I hadn't met Miss Baker; I didn't know who she was. So when I went to Dotty's house for dinner, I said, "By the way, a couple of people have called me Miss Baker. How come? Does she look like me?" And Dotty said to me, "Well, she's gay too." Well, I could have dropped over, "She's gay too." I was so flustered; I had no idea that anything like this was going to happen. And she said, "Oh, I've known from the beginning, when I met you that night. I knew that you were gay and I knew that I was going to get together with you somehow." So, I did not go home that night, nor the whole weekend. She had a little Karmann Ghia automobile, which I think was the only one in town. Sometimes she would park on the street a block away, because we didn't want to advertise. This was 1962 and she was a professor at the college. Back in those days, you had to be a little more careful, and I was just starting there. But we were together every night. We went out on weekends up to the mountains, up to the Poconos. We were together a lot, all of the next twenty-eight years. (Kay M)

Chapter 5

Work and Money

The lesbian must learn a whole set of instrumental tasks which are only learned to a very limited extent by other women. (Gagnon and Simon 1973, p. 200)

When the idea for this study first came to me in 1997, it was in the context of a brunch held at my house. My partner and I had invited a number of year-round residents, mostly employed by the local university, and second-home owners in northwestern North Carolina, primarily retired and living half the year in Florida. "Retired" and "lesbian" were my group labels for these women, and I found their ability to support themselves in an upper-middle and even upper-class manner fascinating and educational for me, once the details began to be explained. Feminist scholarship and claims about life before the second wave of feminism had led me to think that women had little to no economic savvy before 1970, when many of these women were in their forties. Many of these lesbians had been married (and thus should be ignorant of worldly finance) yet now had handsome homes and cars, lives of leisure, and no husbands. Their stories indicated stock market experience, sophisticated understandings of legal documents and protections, estate planning, insurance instruments, real estate expertise, and salaried lives. I had begun learning about the stock market and actively putting salary money and savings into stocks in 1995, primarily through the example set by my partner. In addition to an academic interest in life histories and gay studies, these women could teach me much about the financial world.

This research project began with the question, How could adult women living in the 1940s, 1950s, and 1960s support themselves without husbands and educate themselves about finances when women stereotypically were dependent upon husbands for all their financial needs? Many of these women, in their seventies, now enjoy a higher standard of living than many men and widowed women in the general U.S. population. Several women have more income in retirement than they did when working.

Several topics are addressed in this chapter: education beyond college, types of employment, work during marriage, sequence of jobs, financial education/planning, class status in this period of life, home ownership and investment properties, and financial arrangements with partners.

WOMEN, MONEY, AND MEN

It was conventional wisdom in the 1930s, 1940s, and 1950s that women needed men—specifically husbands—for financial reasons and for household income and retirement benefits, even if they themselves had jobs. As Gagnon and Simon (1973, p. 200) put it, a woman "needed a man to manage the relationship between her and the demands of the external world."

In no profession or job did women earn the same amount of money as men. For instance, in 1947 a female laundry worker in Illinois made 55¢/hour while a man made $1.10, and women in retail stores in 1951 earned only 48¢ to a man's dollar (Chafe 1972). At the end of World War II, women, it was argued on numerous fronts, needed to return to the home to stem juvenile delinquency, to prevent a recession caused by massive unemployment, to restore the American institution, the family, and to perpetuate the sharp division between men and women. "Men were expected to earn a living and to make the big decisions, while women were expected to take care of the home" (Chafe 1972, p. 178).

In 1910, the proportion of all women holding jobs was 25.2 percent. In 1920 it had fallen to 23.3 percent, 24.3 percent in 1930, and 25.7 percent in 1940, a growth rate of only 0.5 percent in thirty years (Chafe 1972). By 1940, 45 percent of women workers were doing "nonmanual" work, particularly stenography and typing, the third most common job by 1930 (Chafe 1972). The expansion in clerical jobs allowed the middle-class woman to do work thought to be more fitting to her class than the manual work that was engaged in by immigrant, working-class women.

Although the typewriter started out as a machine used by men, by the 1920s it was primarily a machine for women. Chafe comments on how the rise of typist/secretary positions for women created jobs with which middle-class young women and their parents were comfortable. I have been surprised in this study that only three women mentioned going to a business school after college, which my own mother, born in 1917, had done.

Over and over again Chafe found that women's suffrage in the United States did not benefit women economically. Ten years later, the Depression worsened women's economic position. Most of the available work was domestic, part-time, seasonal, or marginal. By the end of the Depression more women than men were out of work.

> The deepening economic crisis proved especially damaging to college women interested in entering business or the professions. Teaching jobs almost disappeared from the market because of an oversupply of applicants and the number of teachers who were women fell from 85 percent in 1920 to 78 percent in 1940. (Chafe 1972, p. 59)

> Married women joined the labor force at a rate five times faster than that of other females and comprised 35 percent of all women employed in 1940, in contrast to 15 percent in 1900. . . . In 1940, only 5.6 percent of married women held jobs if their husbands earned over $3,000 a year, but 24.2 percent were employed if their husbands received less than $400. (Chafe 1972, pp. 56, 57)

In 1938, over 80 percent of Americans opposed the idea of working wives, but by 1943 over 60 percent voiced approval (Chafe 1972). None of the women in this project were both married and working in 1940. Today, over half of people seventy years or older think that a wife should help her husband's career rather than have her own career (Yutema 1997) while half of people fifty to fifty-nine years old had working moms and approved of mothers working.

"From 1925 to 1945 American medical schools placed a quota of 5 percent on female admissions. . . . As late as 1937 the New York City Bar Association excluded prospective female members" (Chafe 1972, p. 60). Women received almost 33 percent of all graduate degrees during the era but secured only 7.9 percent of the professorships in the country's colleges. Instead of being professors, lawyers, or doctors, as had been many women from 1900 to 1920, 75 percent of women professionals were either teachers or nurses. None of the women in this sample were doctors, lawyers, dentists, or architects.

The immediate postwar years saw a new prosperity in the United States, and with it came jobs for women. By 1950, 32 percent of women worked, up from 25.7 percent in 1940. Participation in heavy industry grew from 9 percent to 13 percent, and the female labor force had increased by over 5.25 million. Severe shortages of typists, stenographers, nurses, and teachers were commonplace (Chafe 1972). The greatest gain in employment figures in the United States was among married women. In 1950, seven narrators were married and five of them were working. By 1960, the tide had turned and only one of the thirteen married Whistling Women was working.

CAREERS AND JOBS

Most of the Whistling Women prepared themselves to work and to take care of themselves. Those women who did not go to college immediately after high school found employment primarily as typists. Carolyn worked in a publications company as a typist, Mitch got a typing job, Dorothy was a secretary, and Pat N also worked as a secretary. Pat N tells of her workplace recruiting high school women to work as secretaries upon graduation. She signed on. Mary1 and Addy did factory work, and Cynthia did manual labor. Vera, the only woman of color in this study, got a job with Los Angeles County as a messenger clerk in 1946. Chris was a secretary at an insurance company. Factory jobs and manual labor jobs were considered the fare for lower-class/working-class women, which includes Mary1, Addy, Vera, and Cynthia, particularly immigrants and black women (Cynthia and Vera), and, I would add, orphans/wards of the state, a status which includes Addy and Vera. Addy, Vera, Cynthia, Carolyn, and Pat N live comfortably today, all having made careers for themselves, four of them gaining county, corporate, or federal pensions. Chris and Mary1 have the fewest resources among the Whistling Women.

When I went to work for the county in 1946, I went to work as a temporary employee and eventually I became a permanent employee. And I was going to school and taking exams and getting promoted and working my way up through the system. I've quit because I would get so provoked at the power pits of county government and I just quit. Well the rule was, if you quit, if you came back within a year, you got reinstated with all benefits. So I would always go back at the end of the tenth month. In the meantime while I was gone, I was out there working in private industry and I would go out and learn all these good things that they had out in private industry and then when I went back to my county job, I was so confident it was ridiculous. Because they have a way of crippling you when you work in civil service. They have tremendous control and I would go out there and I would learn all this good stuff about data processing and how to be totally independent and how to design program cards and do all this stuff. This was before the age of computers as we know it now. And then when I'd go back, well I knew all this stuff which made me very valuable. I worked for the county for thirty-six years. During those years, I worked for thirteen different departments. (Vera)

It is clear from the review by Chafe and the degrees earned by these narrators what the career options were for women from 1940 until these women began retiring in the 1980s. It is urban folklore that lesbians are concentrated in the fields of nursing, library science, and primary and secondary teaching —but so were heterosexual women— those were the professions favored by all women. No one said she sought out the military or a specific career because of the company of women or probable company of lesbians.

The narrators actually show more variety in their careers than the surveys of the era would suggest. (Could it be that lesbians choose a greater variety of careers than do the straight women those surveys supposedly sample?) The eight narrators who completed four-year college degrees by 1951 earned degrees in history, English, math, social work, education, nursing, and journalism. Two other women earned a certificate or two-year degree in nursing and medical assistantship.

An even greater variety of degrees is represented among the younger women who began earning their degrees in 1952 to 1970. Three women took degrees in education, two in art, two in music, and one each in engineering, English literature, business/economics, and drama. From the medical field two women obtained degrees. Nursing credentials were earned by five women.

To compete in the tighter job market of the 1940s and 1950s, women were encouraged to obtain advanced degrees. "A graduate education became essential for a female student desiring a decent position" (Chafe 1972, p. 59) and schools such as Smith told graduates that it would be impossible to get a job without one. Joanna said her corporation recruited women to study engineering then work for them. She signed on and all of the recruits who completed the training got at least three job offers.

Six of fifteen women in the older cohort (40 percent) got master's degrees, as did sixteen of twenty-nine of the younger women (55 percent), clearly demonstrating the greater job pressure in more recent times (Table 5.1) and perhaps other factors as well. These degrees were earned in education (five), music (two), library science (three), and in art, social work, counseling, psychology, journalism, social science, ESL, biochemistry, nursing, and health/PE.

Doctorate degrees were equal in percentage between the two groups: two of the older women (13 percent) and four of the younger women (14 percent) made that step. Three of the doctorates were in education fields (education, communication, ESL), one was in divinity, one in psychology, and one was in a medical field. One woman took the necessary coursework for a library science doctorate but never wrote the dissertation (older cohort).

TABLE 5.1. Advanced Degrees Earned by the Narrators

Decade	Older Cohort	Younger Cohort
Master's degrees		
1940s	0	0
1950s	4	3
1960s	2	5
1970s	0	5
1980s	0	2
1990s	0	0
?		1
percentage	40%	55%
PhD degrees		
1940s	0	0
1950s	0	0
1960s	incompl	2
1970s	1	1
1980s	1	0
1990s	0	1
percentage	13%	14%

Methods of obtaining master's degrees seem to vary between the two cohorts. For the younger women, going back to school was spread out over three decades, while all the older women obtained advanced schooling in the 1950s, fairly quickly on the heels of their undergraduate degrees (Table 5.1). Given that more of the younger women than the older women married, it could be that schooling was delayed until children were a certain age or divorce was eminent or past. However, it may be that while the older women were prepared for teaching and nursing jobs with just the bachelor's degrees, the younger women had to graduate and face the job market to be convinced that they needed advanced degrees.

Comparative statistics are a little difficult to find. In the *Statistical Record of Women Worldwide* (Schmittroth 1991) one can read that in 1978, when four narrators had earned PhDs, 34 percent of the PhDs awarded to women were in education, 22 percent in social sciences, 19 percent in humanities, 14 percent in life sciences, 5 percent in physical sciences, 4 percent in professions, and 1 percent in engineering. By 1988, when two more women gained that degree, those figures had changed slightly such that 30 percent were in education fields, 22 percent in social sciences, 19 percent in life sciences, and 13 percent in humanities.

In 1973, 42 percent of lesbians in a study based in Richmond, Virginia (Albro and Tully 1979), were working in the fields of psychology, social work, nursing, sociology, anthropology, or criminal justice, reflecting the degree programs popular at the University of Virginia. It is interesting that primary and secondary education are not in this list, nor does the list suggest that the Virginia women would be making their livings the same way these narrators were. In the 1984 study of West Coast lesbians, careers were not quantified (Kehoe 1989). Seventy-three women had had professional careers, eight checked "clerical," four "the trades," and three "domestic."

Nine Whistling Women were nurses (20 percent), eight primary or secondary schoolteachers (18 percent), six professors (14 percent), three librarians (7 percent), three musicians (7 percent), two social workers, and two researchers. Many other jobs were quite unique. Some women had a variety of jobs or different settings for their job, such as working for a city park department and then teaching physical education in a school, or being a singer and teaching music at a public school. They are double counted. Other jobs include travel agent, dog grooming/breeding, driving delivery trucks and ferry boats, insurance sales, realtor, minister, cook, psychologist, engineer, magazine/newspaper writing/design, computer programmer, systems analyst, acting, and secretary.

It is also possible to pinpoint the occupations among the 183 lovers, available in seventy-nine cases. Fifteen of these women were teachers, nine were nurses, and five were librarians, supporting the stereotype that lesbians abound in these professions. However, the following careers had three women each: social work, hospital work, church work, psychologists, and waitresses. Other lovers were professional golfer, musician, camp director, house cleaner, electrician, artist, secretary, writer, singer, showgirl, stripper, insurance agent, graphic designer, stewardess, professor, bartender, bookkeeper, antique seller, airport manager, chef, hotel staff, factory worker. Several lovers were supported by a narrator and thus not in the workforce.

It was only after my little guy was in school that I decided that I would go back. I was a painter earlier and I did sculpting, as a teenager and into my adult life. As a matter of fact, I used to show my paintings in Greenwich Village and it was real fun. Then I went back to school, to college. I got a bachelors at that time, medical biology. I became licensed as a medical tech and I ran the health insurance plan, medical center, the medical laboratory up in New York. I ran that for several years. Then I got tired of blood and people's urine and I decided I wanted to be with people. So I went back to school again and I got a master's degree in psychology and a minor in medical technology. I then went on later to get my doctorate; it was much later actually. (Barbara)

At that time if you had really declared yourself homosexual, I'm not certain that you could have gotten a degree in the school of journalism at {}. In fact there was one man who was ousted from the program but it wasn't necessarily because he was homosexual. It was because he was having a relationship with a younger boy in the school of journalism building. [I]f he had been more discreet in terms of his situation, I don't think he would have been ousted, but the dean did oust him because of the nature of the behavior. But one certainly would not have talked about homosexuality at that time in terms of the school of journalism, even though it existed all over the place at {}.

I was the second woman to get a doctorate at the school of journalism at {}. The first woman was a nun. (Judy)

JANET: I did mostly industrial and commercial buildings, stayed away from bridges and highways. I wanted to do highways and had a job with highway department out of college. And at that time [1958-1960] they were one of the only Equal Opportunity employers, being a government group.

They would hire a woman. But I had some medical problem, I had a blocked kidney and had to go to surgery and the doctor wouldn't release me. But finally I went to Cleveland, being closer to home. And I had to wheel and deal to get that job, a man fortunately really wanted me and took my picture off my application and changed my name and talked the personnel manager into hiring me. That's how I got my first job. It was tough; they didn't want women. They felt they would spend a lot in training you and you'd just quit and get married and leave. You would disturb the organization, you would bother the men, and all sorts of crazy things.

I was, of course, the only woman engineer in the company and realized that to be good, I needed field experience and I was not allowed in the field. And three of the largest construction companies in the United States were doing the civilian work in Vietnam. And you could go there for eighteen months, come back with $34,000 in the bank, if you made it back, and I would be able to be out in the field. So I interviewed for that. They had every excuse in the book.

CHERYL: Do you consider yourself a feminist?

JANET: I don't think so. Little things bother me a little more than they used to. It was my goal to be an excellent, an outstanding engineer and make it easier for the next woman that followed.

CHERYL: Do you think you succeeded?

JANET: I believe so. I was respected and got along beautifully with the men I worked with. I ended up mostly in management.

I decided I didn't want to stay in the company and I realized you, first of all had to have a college education. But being a woman, it wasn't going to do you a damn bit of good anyhow. Because I looked around, the company wasn't that big. It's the fourth or fifth biggest in the nation right now. But maybe 100 people or so at the time were working there. Not one woman officer. I always knew what I wanted and I'd do whatever I had to do to get it and that was that and I'd get it. And I said, "I'm not going to get very far here." So I sat and thought about it and no matter what I investigated, you weren't going to get far no matter what. You could be twice as good as the man and you were going to be working for him. Now it started to aggravate me. (Mitch)

And then I didn't like teaching school so I decided I was going to be a school bus driver. So I did that for a year. Then I didn't like that so much, so Karen and I opened a ceramics shop and we were both very good. (Amelia)

I thought, *Well, I've got to open a chiropractic office. That's what I'm supposed to do.* So I went back to Shreveport where my home was. My mother had wanted me to come back. She owned an apartment building and half of her lot was empty. My brother-in-law was a builder. Mother said, "We'll build you an apartment building if you'll come home and live." All I had to pay for was a note every month. I didn't have to buy the house or anything. So I said, "Okay." I opened my chiropractic office in my apartment. But that was when chiropractors were not licensed in the state of Louisiana, [and shortly the law changed requiring a license]. So there I was—I couldn't practice [legally].

You had to hide it; you couldn't put out a sign or anything like that. So that business was not successful for me.

I decided to go back to college. I went to Northwestern State University in Louisiana and I majored in elementary education and I minored in library science which wasn't much at that time. It took about three years for me to get my degree. When I got through, I got a job teaching the fifth grade. . . . I didn't teach very long because integration reared its ugly head. The principal called us in and said, "I want all of you to sign a statement that you'll not advocate integration." I said, "When anybody tells me what I have to believe or what I'm going to do, I'm out of here."

I was teaching in Lake Charles, the fifth grade. So when I went back home, I went by the library where I had gone to college and this man, Dr. Watson, was the library director. I told him I had quit my teaching job and he said, "Well, what are you going to do?" I said, "Well, I haven't decided yet what I'm going to do." He said, "Why don't you go to library school?" I said, "Oh, I don't want to be a librarian." The next day he called me on the phone and said that he had a fellowship for me at University of Denver to go to library school. The fellowship would pay me just about what I was making teaching and I hadn't lived in Denver so my dad helped me buy a car and off I went to Denver—1956. (Kay M)

GIGI: And I was in real estate and had my little tax business. Then one of the hospitals calls me again and I said, well, I'll come back part time, and that turned out to be another full-time job. And this was a little hospital and everybody there was gay. And then from there, after four years, I started my own business—designed and staffed laboratories or clinics and doctors' offices . . .

Maybe I was caught up in my own self too much to know—I don't know [if gays were discriminated against]. And they accepted us socially. Even in my hospital environment, I was always with a woman. It was always accepted. So I was never worried about my job. But I was always the head of something. I never worried about my position.

CHERYL: Did you ever think there might have been employees of yours or people who you were hiring who were afraid of losing their job if you knew that they were gay?

GIGI: No, because I knew by then who was gay and who wasn't. It was just accepted.

CHERYL: Pretty common in nursing.

GIGI: Oh yeah, in medical technology, yeah. In fact at my second job, I met my best friend who was gay and her friend. I hired her to work in my lab and her friend worked in X-ray and she was a boater and we all got together. So there were two more gay people. The personnel manager was gay and I was dating her. You talk about a real complicated situation in the hospital, hell, I'd stay at her house and we'd drive in to work together in her car. I said, "Are you sure you want this?" She said, "Sure."

CHERYL: Did you ever know of people losing a job because they were gay?

GIGI: No. I don't know of gay bashing or anybody losing anything because they were gay.

I was doing contracting, that was when I was in the house that I owned with my ex-husband. I was doing contracting there with two fellows. We were doing work with designers and decorators and things like that. But I gave that up when I sold the house. I did that for about four years. And then I had income from the restaurant when I sold it. I sold it right after I got my divorce.

Well, I had a job working as a general manager for a real estate company. I was there about six years. And I managed apartments, about 500 apartments. Then after that, while I was doing that, two years after we bought our house, I got very friendly with this fellow who put the alarm system into our house. And he was looking for a partner. So I went in with him into the alarm business. And then we decided we wanted to go to Florida, so we sold the house and I sold my share of the business to my partner. And we came down to Florida. And then after that, we formed a corporation and we did several things within the corporation. We were doing telephone and electric audits. We were finding mistakes and getting refunds for the customers and we got 50 percent of whatever we found.

And then after that, we were getting refunds from the federal government for clients. I contacted all the different municipalities in the states and major companies all over the United States and I would make calls telling them that they were due refunds from the federal government and did they know about it? And everyone said no. I said, "Well, we would like to help you file for these refunds and to me it looks very sizable." You're talking about $10,000, $15,000. One company we got back $65,000 and then we would get a percentage of that. I did this for four years.

And now I've found something else that I'm doing. See, in between all this, I do the options and stocks and stuff. But now what I'm doing is fixing people's credit. Like if you've got bad credit and you want a mortgage and you can't get a mortgage because you've got a lot of various negatives on your credit reports. We can fix it.

It's not so much the accounts. But what would happen was that I would go through a mortgage company, and what happens is that they check the person's credit and the credit is no good. They don't qualify. So if they tell the person they don't qualify, they've lost a customer. They've lost a mortgage customer and that customer goes out the door. So this way they say to them, look, we can have your credit fixed. If we don't have it fixed, you get back 110 percent of your money. It costs like $399 to do this. So the company has never given back a guarantee yet. (Kate)

I was always involved with some type of investing [even when I was married and not working]. It was real estate. It wasn't land. I'd buy contracts, I'd buy discounted mortgages. I had a triplex that I sold and I was holding the mortgage on it. There was $50,000 owing on it and the worst thing that could have happened was me getting the triplex back because I didn't live in the area anymore. So I sold the mortgage at a discount, I sold for $35,000 and took a discount on the mortgage of $15,000. But I used to buy mortgages when I was younger.

It was very interesting times and remember I had my real estate to fall back on. I had several apartment buildings by the time I divorced and I had these real estate contracts. But I had that for backup. I got involved in a couple of businesses before I got involved in real estate. The businesses weren't big businesses, they were more of a physical nature, like owning vending machines. (Nan)

Military Employment

Fewer than 300,000 women enlisted during World War II, for the reasons given in Chapter 2 no doubt—they didn't want to leave a lover or job or home, had no friends to go with, or weren't sure what life was like in the service. Three of the fifteen narrators in the oldest age cohort were in the military (20 percent) while only two of twenty-nine in the younger cohort were (7 percent). As we will see in Chapter 6, the younger women enrolled in the military at the same rate as presumably heterosexual women while the older lesbians were more eager to serve than other women in their cohort.

Roberta went into the service as a WAAC (Women's Army Auxiliary Corps) in 1942 for one year where she taught driving (2.5 ton trucks). Bing was in the Navy Waves during World War II for a total of eight years and came out there. She says that they were some of the best years of her life. When she left the service she took the civil service test and sent in her naval papers as part of a job application. Her first name had a typically male spelling and with her Navy service, she got a score of 100 on the test and got a job as a social worker. Today she uses the VA hospital.

Mitch also went into a branch of the military.

Lackland, Texas, first, then Cheyenne, Wyoming. Then I went to communications school in Wyoming as part of the service. There, again, I got bored and so I volunteered to work in my spare time, when I wasn't in school, and I picked—again you can see this mind of mine—shipping and receiving. Now that meant that I could choose where I wanted to go and be stationed the rest of my career. I volunteered a lot for things. I was always volunteering to prepare for my next move.

Oh yes, I was having a grand time. I loved it. We had the greatest parties. I noticed some of the older women—they were career people, staff sergeants, master sergeants—and I looked at them and I thought, do I want my life to be at this level when I'm that age. 'Cause I loved it and I could have re-enlisted and I knew how to handle them now. I had passed all my tests as far as I was concerned. And I thought, *You never grow up.* And I had always felt I had a Peter Pan syndrome, that was my life really. I thought, but surely, I don't really have to grow up but I think I better do something a little more than I'm doing now, like partying every night. And that's when I decided not to re-enlist. And also I kept volunteering to go overseas and to go to this war and that war. And they wouldn't take women. So they had nothing more to offer me and I sure wasn't going to offer them anything. So I did get out of the service then.

Oh, I ran a business on the side, I had a horse stable. I was bored and I was running horses over the Canadian border illegally. I was buying the good, young workhorses at the slaughterhouse. I swear to God, I know we helped that situation up there because Canada was still using work horses. We were killing all of ours. We were making a run two ways. Going up they allowed us to bring them up without quarantine. They let us bring them to a certain veterinarian in the area. And we were selling them and buying riding horses and bringing them back. I had a big farm, the guy who signed all the papers for me had a big farm and we were partners in the business. (Mitch)

My former partner, she went in for two years to the Air Force. And when she finished her two years, she decided she didn't want to stay in there. [S]he loved the Air Force, but they had this thing about gay people, so she didn't want to stay. (Joanna)

Sappho taught on a German Air Force base for one year, but Pat N is the only narrator who actually had a career in the military. She signed on as a civilian in the Army and stayed in that status from 1968 through 1982, when she retired with a federal pension. In the 1970s she was actively creating programs for women. She was base liaison for several women's issues. While she was lesbian before and in the beginning of her military career (never had an affair with a military woman), she went through a heterosexual period and then a celibate period in the military. She married a few years after retirement from the U.S. Army Corps of Engineers, her stateside placement after each tour in Europe.

Socioeconomic Class While Working

The narrators were asked to pinpoint their socioeconomic class while they were working. This is of course a very subjective evaluation and is not directly comparable from woman to woman, but it is an estimate of how they placed themselves with respect to the people they saw around them.

Fifteen women consider themselves to have maintained the same class standing they were born into as working adults. Typically this is the sentiment of women who were born into upper-middle-class families. Twenty-one women assess their socioeconomic class status to have been higher when they were working than when they were children, while five women say they dropped in class standing as working adults. Identification as a lesbian or practicing lesbian sexuality did not result in dysfunction for these women when considered as a group. Altogether, four women selected upper class, eleven women upper-middle class, 22 women middle class, one woman lower-middle and one woman lower class for their standing while working. (Two women did not support themselves by working at wage labor so reported only on their married class standing, and one woman did not reveal her class standing.) Their educations, their self-dependence, their motivations, their family backgrounds, led these women to be productive members of their communities and to make economic achievements comparable to those of men.

Working Histories of Whistling Women

> Addy: factory worker, fruit picker, music industry—recording artist, artist manager, dog groomer
>
> Amelia: teacher, school bus driver, ceramics store
>
> Barbara: painter, medical technician/running health insurance plan, psychological clinical director, private practice psychologist
>
> Bing: military, social worker, insurance agency owner/agent, sorority house mom
>
> Bobbie: schoolteacher
>
> Chris: secretarial
>
> Claire: schoolteacher, landlord
>
> Cynthia: factory work, electronics department, bar owner, house restorations
>
> Dawn: stewardess, antique shop owner, officer in family corporation, city council person
>
> Diane: hospital nurse, nursing teacher, psychiatric nurse, writer for nursing magazine, nursing instructor and needs assessment for foreign country
>
> Dorothy: schoolteacher, coin laundry, substitute schoolteacher
>
> Edie: wife, mother of three, teacher aide, hospital nurse, traveling nurse, home health nurse, nonviolent activist

Ellen: wife

Gigi: instructor of medical technology, supervisor, raised chinchillas, real estate, apartment owner, tax consultant, designed and staffed laboratories, clinics, and doctors' offices

Jackie: psychiatric social worker, college faculty, public school system

Jan: acting, occupational therapy, pottery teacher, sleep technician

Janet: engineer

Joanna: federal government researcher, Pentagon contractor, computer programmer

Joyce: singer, clerical, public school music teacher, travel agent

Judy: high school teacher, university professor

Kate: contractor, restaurant owner, general manager for real estate company, apartment manager, partner in an alarm business, independent telephone and electric company audit/refunds, credit fixer, options trader

Kay: schoolteacher

Kay M: car parts store, chiropractor, teacher, college librarian

Mary1: magazine sales, roller derby, Los Angeles County employee, county hospital employee, computer person at community care for elderly agency

Mary2: PE teacher, city park employee, park supervisor, math teacher

Mary Lou: YWCA camp director (five years), school counselor

Mitch: military, horse boarding, bank employee, insurance agent, typing teacher, school counselor, assistant principal

Nan: buying/selling mortgages, realtor

Nancy: university instructor, private music teacher

Pat M: bartender, secretary, cook, riverboat cook, minister

Pat N: secretary, elementary schoolteacher, librarian—civilian and military

Pauline: nurse, writer

Roberta: military, Penn Railroad, ferry boat driver, dairy sales representative, diaper delivery service, annuities salesperson

Rose: nurse anesthetist, vendor at craft shows

Ruth: prep school teaching, university professor

Sandy: secretary, nursing, boarded men, dog breeder, gold mining, Habitat for Humanity staff, nursing, GTE yellow pages,
elderly sitting/housework
Sheri: driver's ed instructor, teaching, guidance counselor, air-
craft charter service (financed with lover)
Vera: Los Angeles County, various supervisory positions

And when I tell you I didn't work long enough to get a teacher's pension,
I worked in Detroit for three years and there was no lock-in. Barbara and I
came to Florida because [the student population dropped] and we only had
three years into the system. So we came down here and bought a small coin
laundry and dry cleaners and ran that for five years. Then when we sold that,
I wanted to get back into teaching. I wanted the freedom of substituting, even
though I knew I was going to be taking a position for a whole semester. So I
substituted for twelve years which was a mistake, because I realized, who
wants to pay your own health insurance. And I picked up a full-time contract,
then I was unable to work to lock in retirement. So I retired when I was sixty-
five with eight-and-one-half-years years with the county. (Dorothy)

CHERYL: Did you get another secretarial job down here?
CHRIS: Yeah, for a while I did. It wasn't that long. I tried a couple of things. But
then you get disgusted. Between the pension money, which wasn't even
$200 after nineteen years, I lived on that. And then when the money just
ran out, then I had to go to St. Vincent and all this sort of stuff. I managed
and then when I was sixty-two, then right away I picked up my social security. I had to, I couldn't get a job. Funny how you say things when you're
young and it actually happens. The first chance I get, even if I have to eat
dog food, well that was it. I didn't get to the dog food yet.
    I don't want to work now. If I had to, I don't know what I'd do. Then I was
thinking, *Well, maybe if you go in a couple of days during the week and go
over to Public's and bag the groceries and you don't exert yourself—God
forbid you should exert yourself.* But even when I was working, I'd take a
day off a month just to rest. I was falling asleep. I'd get to bed, you know,
and I'd get up early and I'd be going all day long and I was doing all this
wonderful exercise and getting with it. And then I'd come home and that's
it. You wouldn't be good for anything. So then once a month I'd try to take
a day off. I was sick, I'd call it, and then I'd just stay off the whole day. It did-
n't do me any good because I'd worry that I'd lose my job. But I had to
catch up on some of my sleep. If I went to bed at 8 o'clock once a week or
8:30, I had the best next day. I was right there. And then I'd go, how long is
this going to go on? You know, your middle fifties, your late fifties, I mean,
you've been working. I could have gone to college and everything. No, I
knew everything. And I could have had a good big job—who knows—decent money coming in. But I was working since I was eighteen really. So
here it was over forty years working and you're a little tired of it.

FINANCIAL EDUCATION

So where did the majority of these women learn to deal with money and to capitalize on resources, since most of them were not married during the last decade of their working lives? How did they learn about the world of finance?

Financial education for these women came in many forms—successful parents and/or financial support from parents, childhood lessons about money and saving, house ownership, loans, friends and spouses who understood or wanted to understand the stock market, jobs with retirement clinics, handling accounts, and sometimes dumb luck, sometimes bad luck. In some cases they learned along with husbands, or learned from husbands; in other cases they learned from male friends, particularly gay male friends. But not every woman has had success with real estate or the stock market or even pensions nor feels that she can make decisions and investments on her own. Sappho says that she can't absorb financialese, although she does know how to read the stock tables in the newspaper.

Childhood Lessons with Money

Childhood lessons about money, particularly the behavior of parents with money, do influence children. In fact, Harvard University in the 1970s required parents of graduate students who did not receive aid to fill out financial profiles. This was not to check up on the parents' ability to pay but to predict how the student might treat scholarship and grant monies. Frugal parents probably would mean a frugal student, while indebted parents would probably mean a fiscally irresponsible student. Overt lessons about money are rare in any era, but those lessons are often remembered by the adult child.

Barbara's father was a bank VP and an investor. She read a book at age twelve called *Banking Studies*. Gloria said that her mother was a terrific saver. Cynthia's parents were terrible models. Cynthia did learn something about saving money from her uncle, however.

I had an uncle [and] I used to go play cards with him and his wife when they needed a fourth player and they would call me. And he would always say to me, "You know, to save the first thousand is the hardest." And I kind of remembered that a little bit.

We always lived in rented places and never had anything, just barely lived: We were dirt poor. All I know is my mother used to say to me, when I got older a little bit—I don't remember this—but she said I'd stand with my hand on my hip and I'd say, "When I get old, I'm not going to be poor." That must have been from hating being poor so much I think. It may be the motivator. (Cynthia)

See, I was a product of the Depression, so I was always concerned about how I was going to get along financially, and I was interested in security. (Claire)

I've never worried about money. It's always been there. I was reared in the Depression, but even during the Depression we never lacked for anything, even though my father only worked a couple days a week. Mother was a terrific saver. She managed incredibly well and I always knew that whatever I needed would be there. (Gloria)

I didn't have a very good [lesson about money] because my father was very frugal. The money we got for necessities, that's it, period. His responsibility was to make sure he clothed and fed and had a roof over our heads. And then the other thing was, I think that my mother and father got into the stock market and my father bought a lot of Insul and the company went belly up and so he lost heavily in that. And the other one he bought was Tucker. That was a very revolutionary car that my father believed was just the thing, and it was. But the big conglomerates blocked it. So he lost money on that. So I kind of shied away from the stock market. I remember those two things. Now my mother invested and she invested wisely. She invested in things like Walgreens and things like that. But I think we heard more about Insul and Tucker than we did about Walgreens and some of the ones that she had that were doing fine. (Mary2)

Nobody ever talked to me about finances. I never knew what my father made. He did all of the usual stuff and my mother spent it. I was never aware. They were just sort of protecting me I guess from the nitty-gritty, but it was a disservice. I think parents do a disservice to their children when they don't let them know what's happening, especially by the time they are in their teens. These are the facts, and these are things you need to think about, so I was unprepared for anything fiscal. (Nancy)

Savings accounts were common childhood lessons and are common among this crowd, now and in the past. Dorothy said she saved 10 percent of every paycheck, something she learned to do as a child. Janet started saving the day she started working.

I've always had a savings account, since I was a kid. I can remember in the 1950s when I graduated from high school and I went to New York to make my way in the big city. I modeled coats in July. My $42.50 take home pay, I took out $10 of that and put it in my drawer and that was my savings. And then when I wanted something extra special, then I would use it. I did open up an account finally. But basically it was just like my money set aside. (Edie)

My mom really taught me the value of money when I was a youngster. She gave me a quarter allowance, which was a lot of money. But she wouldn't give it to me as a quarter. She would give a dime, two nickels, and pennies. I had a bank which was a brass monkey and mother said when you put money into the bank and fed that monkey, he would smile. I never argued with her, but I watched and watched and watched and I never did see him smile. Anyway, she'd give me this quarter and wanted to know how much I was putting in the monkey. So I would take a penny and she would say, "No, that's not enough." But she had me put in at least a nickel. And whenever I got my allowance, she said, "There's one thing you should always remember: you pay yourself first." And she made me open a little bank account and when you saved up a dollar, you took it to the bank and so forth and so on. And, of course, it was highly motivating. Not at first, I didn't want to give up the nickel and I didn't want to give it to somebody else to hold, you know, it was out of my control and I liked to control my life. It doesn't always happen that way so you roll with the punches. She taught me that and from then on, even my very first job when I couldn't afford to save anything, I did. I would have to juggle things to get that savings. Because naturally, like everyone else, I was living beyond my means. (Mitch)

And this is my first lesson. He sits me down and he says, "Now, this is $100. You only gave me $75. The rest of that is interest and that interest means money you don't have to work for—that's what interest means." He didn't get into Economics 101 or anything like that. He just said, "This is money you didn't have to work for." Now I didn't know much about the concept of work either, but I do remember he said that. It stayed with me. And once you get the foundation, you begin to notice things. You don't notice it otherwise, it passes right over your head.

When I say I can't afford to do this and I can't afford to do that, I hear my mother's voice in the background. And I used to say things like that to my mother and she would say, "You mean not that you can't afford it, but that you don't want to spend it." So there's a difference. (Sandy)

On the other hand, not everyone saved. Kate says she was never told to keep a savings account and was a spender—everything she earned or received as allowance went straight into her pocket. Her parents had a business that they grew very well. She first worked for her father and received a very nice salary.

Roberta's grandmother was very involved in the stock market, living off of dividends, but Roberta took no interest in the market. This grandmother supported Roberta into her forties when Roberta got her first checking and savings accounts.

Home Ownership

Home ownership is probably the single biggest investment that any woman in this group has made. It is also considered to be the foundation of economic health and of a portfolio. Most Americans have their wealth primarily in their homes and with time, in most markets, those houses appreciate in value. Owning a home in New York in the 1990s, selling it, and then buying another home in Florida or North Carolina often left the owner with a significant sum of cash and a new, grand house.

At least thirty-six of the narrators own or co-own their current home, while three rent. Home ownership prior to retirement is not a guarantee of financial comfort in retirement but it has a close correlation. Of the three poorest women in this study, two of them have never owned a house while one of them owned two at one time. Conversely, the most wealthy women in this project made their money in real estate, buying, improving or building, and selling houses.

Addy and Joyce, together for forty-four years, have had three houses in their history. Addy bought a house in coastal California in 1965 using the $5,000 she had inherited from her father. They jointly sold it and shared the profit. They returned to New York City, rented while looking for a property they could afford and then bought a house with half cash and half mortgage. When they decided to move to Florida, near Addy's mother, the mother carried the loan and died, leaving them without mortgage requirements.

Mary Lou bought her first house in 1957 at age twenty-six, also using $5,000. She got three friends to move in and let them pay rents equal to the mortgage so that she lived rent free. Nancy and a lover bought a house in Brooklyn in 1970 with three floors. They rented out the top and bottom floors and lived there themselves rent free.

House purchases were completed in two ways. Friends or family loaned down payment money or bought the houses outright, and banks made loans. Both methods had their pros and cons, as is evident in the following.

And I was heartbroken about Mary and I said to Daddy, if you put a down payment on a house for me, I will move down here, take care of you and make the payments on the house if the house will be mine. And he said fine. (Cam)

It had to be 1960s. I bought a house. This was a little Cape Cod and the windows were broken and some of the shingles were missing and there was holes in the walls. After the closing, I went over there and I stood in the street and I was looking at that. And I came from a family that never owned their own place and I thought it was like wow, this is mine. The first time in my life that I was living in a place that I owned. And you know I've owned $300,000 homes and I've never felt that since. After the first time, the thrill is gone; after that it was business. (Cynthia)

When I went to buy the house, I had a rich ex-patient in Washington, DC. And I got her to put up a second mortgage. So then I went to the bank and got a first mortgage. From then on it's been all right because I've kept good credit; I paid my mortgages and so forth. I've been a good person. (Diane)

Dottie and I bought a condo which was very expensive, in Daytona. I lost about $30,000 in equity. The manufactured house I had here, I paid $55,000 and sold it for $32,000. Up north, the first house I paid $19,000 for and sold it for $35,000. The second one I paid about $35,000 and sold it for $55,000. The first one in Florida, twenty years ago, cost $55,000 and we kept it for about ten years and then we sold it for $75,000, so I always made a little money until I went into condos and manufactured houses. They are very difficult to sell. (Kay M)

I left New York in 1987. [W]e got a motor home and we went traveling around the country for a year prior to settling in Florida. I didn't tell you. We rented that house for almost a year and then we bought a house. And we lived there for five years together. It was a lovely house. It had a great heated swimming pool. We bought that together. We bought the motor home first and then we sold the house. We sold the house and then traveled. So we had some money, which we invested, and bought the motor home and then took off. (Barbara)

In 1981 we bought our lot in Florida and in 1982 we put our home on it and started renting it out, mostly to relatives and friends. And it was paid for by the time we retired and moved down there in 1988. (Carolyn)

A sequence of buying and selling homes at a profit is typical of the majority of the narrators. Three women, however, abandoned homes they had bought in order to get out of a distasteful relationship. Two women (one of those who abandoned a house) declared bankruptcy during their working lives, and thus lost their properties. Both of them own homes once again today. Two other woman bought their first homes near the end of their working days, in their late fifties. One woman has never owned a house.

The wealthiest women in this project own several houses or house and condo simultaneously and live part of the year in one state and the other part of the year in another state. Two women currently own four houses, with two being investment properties.

Investment Property

A few of the narrators have bought investment properties, a move that has proved profitable for all of them. Dawn owns several business properties in the St. Petersburg area that she leases, and she once had a store in her home. Kate owned a restaurant for three years and sold it, at a profit, when she divorced, to raise cash for life as a single parent. Owning duplexes, triplexes, or apartment buildings was a successful strategy for everyone who has done it—Roberta, Kay M, and Nan.

[My dividend income] was about $250 a month at that time, which was good money in those days. And I took all those securities and I liquidated them and I bought real estate. I guess probably about 1952. I bought some apartments in 1954. I bought a duplex and I had another apartment built for me next to it [that I got rents from]. (Roberta)

Purchasing investment property with pooled money of friends served several narrators well. Kate, Barbara, and Mary Lou jointly purchased a house in 1981 and rented it out until selling it at a profit in 1989. Claire, her lover, and another lesbian couple together bought a twenty-two-acre resort in 1956.

It was an old, old Finnish couple selling it and I think we paid—of course now we're talking about 1956, I think . . . but we paid $50,000. And there was a house on the mainland with a sauna, then nine cottages, each of them on a quarter acre, plus I think there were twenty-some lots. And of course we ran the resort for one hectic summer. And then we subdivided; we sold off the cottages, individually—they were two- and three-bedroom—and sold the lodge. We sold them off as residences. [T]hen we sold off the house on the mainland and we had a long strip of land going out to the highway and we gave everybody a parking spot. We made nothing but money. And we financed some of the loan ourselves. [T]hat was back when loans—people— were paying 12 percent for money. And then we sold off the lots. We were still getting paid off seven years after we were out of that place. (Claire)

Kay and Mary2 have rental properties from which they derive some income. Rose owns a rental house. Barbara and Kate have bought and sold two rental properties. Amelia inherited a rental house but she never realized a profit from that house. Roberta got involved in real estate in the late 1940s into the 1960s.

Mary Lou, Claire, Nan, Mary2, and Cynthia have been the most aggressive in buying investment properties. Claire, now a retired school teacher, has continued to buy rental properties since the days of the resort, several of which she vacations in, always sells them at a profit. Mary Lou, a school guidance counselor, made her money for retirement by buying, renovating, and selling homes in St. Thomas, Key West, the Pines, Gulfport (Florida), and Tampa, or building and selling houses in Boone. Cynthia has bought, renovated, and sold over a dozen houses in the Eastern United States. Joanna and Rose are also buying and remodeling a series of houses in their retirement.

CYNTHIA: And I was into remodeling and I was into running this bar and bought a lot of houses in my life. I bought so many houses and remodeled so many houses, made a ton of money. Not in the bar business, but mostly in remodeling homes. The bar business was all right, had a lot of people, but you really don't make that much money.

CHERYL: So you would say the money you're living on today is coming primarily from remodeling?

CYNTHIA: Yes. In the 1970s and early 1980s, you could do that a lot then. Early 1990s it died out and luckily I had liquidated everything I owned, just about, except the home I lived in when everything went flat. And then I waited and just lived in my house. Since then I have sold—well, just in the last five years, I bought in Provincetown. I owned a house on the East Coast that I sold. I bought a house in Florida on the water that I sold. Sold my house in Provincetown. I own a condo and I own this house [in North Carolina]. That's just since I've been retired.

The one we built turned out to be a real good investment. I've always come out okay on houses, but that's because the housing market has always been increasing. I'm buying houses. I enjoy doing that. I like fixing houses. (Joanna)

Although Kay M made a profit on the sale of all three houses, she lost money on a condo and a manufactured home. Time shares are also popular among this crowd but not usually profitable. Cam has two time shares and Mary Lou received seven in lieu of a debt.

Undeveloped land has been invested in less frequently than housing, and has returned less than house investments. Buying and selling undeveloped land served Cam and Mary2 well, while Claire and Mary Lou have had mixed success.

Yes, I own land. In fact, that's basically where I made my money— in real estate. In my early years, I didn't have much money when I was growing up so as soon as I got a little money in my pocket, I was eager to spend it. Until I guess I grew up a little bit and realized that I probably need to save. But basically I saved through buying property because I had to make a payment. I bought a lot that I paid about $8,000 for and within not too long a period of time, I sold it for $22,000. If I had it today, I could have sold it for maybe $200,000. My mother always said, if you're going to buy land, buy it on water. But I didn't exactly follow her recommendations completely. Then I bought a place and sold that. I have one that I'll never get my money out of probably and the other one I probably will. (Mary2)

From the perspective of 2004, property has been the best investment these women made. That statement would not have been true when this research project began, when the stock market was vastly outperforming all other types of investments. Their interaction with the stock market will be explored shortly.

NAN: The way that you make money is that you use other people's money— you don't use your own. That's when you go to banks and you establish credit lines; never be afraid to do that.

CHERYL: So the bank is funding you?

NAN: Sure. That's how businesses work. Like income-producing property during your income years, I would never buy anything unless it was a fourplex or more. And what I would do is that the income that was produced from these rental properties would pay for the mortgage and the taxes and maybe there'd be some left over for me. So that's what I was working for.

Loans

Given the impression from 1970s feminist literature that women could not get loans on their own then or in earlier decades, I have been shocked at the few incidences of loan trouble these women-without-men and women couples experienced. In fact, there are many cases of two women buying property jointly since 1946, but only seven had trouble getting loans. Reasons given by banks for refusing loans included being single, needing to sign a paper promising they wouldn't get pregnant, "being female," and not having a credit history.

Roberta applied for an FHA loan in 1949 in Miami but was rejected since they didn't lend to single women. She bought the house with money from her grandmother. Mary Lou's father had to sign the mortgage papers on her first house in 1957. Sheri and her partner had trouble getting a loan in 1956 in New York and used the nine acres they had bought with cash as collateral to get a loan to build a house. Carolyn bought a house in Baltimore with her partner in 1960 and also had loan trouble, as did Jan in 1970.

We had a hard time getting a mortgage. As a matter of fact, we didn't get a mortgage. At the last minute when we were still trying to find a bank that would lend money to two women, her parents came forward. [T]hey had some savings money in a 5 percent account and we'd [have] had to pay six to six-and-one-half so they said they'd give us the mortgage for five and one-half percent, which was just another tie to them. It was a convenience but not a favor to me. (Carolyn)

Oh sure, and both names were on the mortgage. But we didn't have any problem because of being two women. We had a problem because it was way out in the country and at that time, in 1956, it was not easy to get a mortgage for anybody. We had tried the city banks because Jane felt that one of those city banks would be bigger and more likely to lend money. But actually the little bank in Ontario—little privately owned bank—was where we got our mortgage. (Sheri)

We were rejected by many money lenders. We may have looked gay when we asked because I always dressed butch. One lender wanted us to sign a paper promising that neither of us would be pregnant and be out of work. It had nothing to do with gay. But that we would be out of work, therefore missing payments. That was an FHA loan officer. We ended up borrowing money from my lover's sister. She offered the money at the going rate of interest. And a few years later she resented that, because the interest rate had changed and she wanted more money from us. And I said, "No way, you signed a paper; you signed the agreement for what we were doing." This was 1970 and we did have lots of trouble being rejected. (Jan)

Ruth and Judy co-bought a two-family house in Long Island and had two banks reject them. Funding for Cynthia's first bar presented a problem. Again, friends stepped in with money:

I was looking for some kind of business to get into [1972-1973]. And it just took so long, especially for women it was so hard. Would you believe the first bar I had, I was with this bank for ten to twelve years and I asked them for a small loan of about $9,000 and I was coming up with the rest of the money. And they wouldn't give it to me. The people that sold me on the bar, they gave me the loan. [But the building I leased had a renter.] I had to wait to open until his lease was up. Well as it was, my bank that refused me had lent this very guy the money to go in business [in the first location]. And he was an old drunk, a bum, and they refused me and that really pissed me off. I wanted to get him out of there—he wasn't paying his electric bill. So I called the electric company and I said, "You know, I'm not responsible for his electric. But if you shut his electric off, he can't operate. And if he can't operate, he's out of there, [and] I'll pay the bill." So that's what they did.

And they called over there for him and he was long gone. And I was operating in my bar. And [the bank] said, "Well, this man owes us $8,000." It was a lot of money at the time. And I said, "Well, I'm sorry for your loss, but you know who I am and you people refused me a loan. I'm as solid as a rock and you people refused me a loan strictly because I'm a woman. And you give this old bum and drunk a loan without asking any questions." I should have said, "You deserve to lose it." And then they came back and said, terribly sorry, if I ever need any money to operate or for remodeling or anything, please call. I changed banks. (Cynthia)

Cynthia's problems did not end with the financing. To obtain her first liquor license, in 1970, Cynthia had to have a male cosign the application.

Ellen has no credit history. The lack of a credit history cost Janet, an engineer, a mortgage.

I tried to buy [1971] and couldn't get a loan. I had no credit. Yes, I had a problem. In fact, I couldn't get a mortgage. Well, I talked to two banks and they were scared—single woman. I don't have any background of paying because I had many savings accounts. One was to buy the car, so I never bought a car on credit. When I collected enough, then I'd go buy a car. I saved to go to Hawaii; that was my dream, one of my goals. After it was up twice as high as I needed, I couldn't stand to think I had worked that many years to just go spend it. So I put that as a third on the house, my mother loaned me a third and her bank took her farm as collateral and gave me a third on a seven-and-one-half-year note. So I paid the bank off, paid my mother. Then I changed jobs and moved and got a mortgage because I think I put two-thirds or three-quarters down on the house. The mortgage was something like $120 a month or something. (Janet)

Mitch found a way to trick the bank that was treating her unfairly:

I went to the bank. And they said, "Well, what kind of credit do you have?" I didn't have any credit. Argued back and forth, how much money are you going to put down and on and on. If I am a man, I have to put down $1,500. If I am a woman, I have to put down $3,000. Legal, that was what the banks were doing to us. I do not like people to be unfair and of course life is unfair. I had $1,500 because the real estate man had told me how much money I was going to have to have to put down. He told me what a man would have to put down, not thinking. So I went to another bank and said, "Can I make a loan here?" They said, "Do you have a good enough job? Do you have any loans outstanding?" He said, "We can't say you have it or don't have it; we have to let you know." Oh, I had bought a vacuum cleaner. That was my only credit. I had all the money for the vacuum cleaner. It was an expensive vacuum cleaner. It was like three or four hundred dollars and back then that was a lot for a vacuum cleaner. I had all the money. I paid $100 down as a down payment and the next payment was due and I paid it all off. So I had excellent credit. I did it only for that purpose 'cause I did have the money for the vacuum cleaner. But I went into two banks at the same time ultimately, took two loans out for $1,500. I told them I did not have any outstanding loans. I get $3,000 in my hand, closed for the house. Lied all the way, it was the only way to do it because they were not treating me fair so I treated them in kind. (Mitch)

In spite of these stories, most women reported no loan trouble in buying a home either as a single woman or as a pair of women. One explanation for this success was that the women were teachers, obviously employed, and earning a known amount of money. Mary2 bought two homes in the 1950s with another woman, incurring no problem. Addy used personal money to buy a house in California in 1965, but she and Joyce had no trouble buying together and getting a loan in New York City in the 1970s. Nor did Diane in the 1960s or Nancy and her partner in 1970. Claire, Kay, and Janet had no problem in south Chicago in 1964 and 1972 respectively.

No. That's another thing, business-wise, insurance-wise, I have never had any trouble with another woman. (Gigi)

CLAIRE: We did know a number of women who did own their homes together.

MARILYN: Was it thought automatically that you were a couple if you bought a home together?

CLAIRE: Oh no. In fact, the only worry they had when we first bought the house in 1964 was that we might be fronting for a black couple. That was the worry they had then, that we were going to integrate Glen Oak Acres. They said, "You know, it would be all right to do that but we'd like to know; we'd like to prepare the way." Now whether that's true or not, I don't know.

JOYCE: We both loved [the house] and we bought it for cash and a mortgage.

CHERYL: Any trouble getting a mortgage?

JOYCE: No.

CHERYL: Both names?

JOYCE: Yes. I was a teacher and she had a steady job. I was working, teaching out on the island, driving in snow and rain and everything at 5 o'clock every morning. And we tried and we saved money.

It was very easy to get mortgages in that area of Brooklyn because Robert F. Kennedy had promised a rejuvenation. It was not a part of the large black area in Brooklyn, but it was sort of on the fringes and so they were looking for people to give money to in that area to help lift the level. There were·about seven or eight banks that pooled mortgage money for that area. But there was no problem getting it. (Nancy)

Barbara had no trouble buying with her partner in 1979 in New York State, Gigi never encountered trouble using two women's names in Ohio, nor Dorothy and her lover in 1978 in Florida.

Stock Market

Extra cash often got invested in real estate, in individual stocks, mutual funds, bonds, or annuities. The proceeds from the sale of Barbara and her partner's home went partially to purchase a motor home and the rest into investments.

BARBARA: We got some stocks and various different kinds of investments. We had maybe one mutual fund. We varied our investments. My father was a banker. Remember I said he was a bank manager when I was about five. He ended up Vice President of Banker's Trust Company. And so he was an investor himself for many years. And I knew a lot about investments. And my partner also knew a lot about investments.

[We used our broker's guidance and made our own decisions.] I remember we were sitting down at the table in the kitchen and she gave us some information. I bought some McDonald's and Kodak overseas and some stocks. We made a lot, we lost a lot [in 2000].

CHERYL: So you got the house sale in 1987 and the market is going to crash in October.

BARBARA: Isn't that amazing? And we sold the house; we moved out in September.

CHERYL: Had you invested it before this October crash?

BARBARA: We had invested it before the October crash, but not necessarily in stocks. We had that house money. We never would have gotten that kind of money had it been later.

CHERYL: When did you buy your first stock?

BOBBIE: Probably not soon enough—1980s probably. I should have gone into it sooner and I should have put more into it. But you never have enough money, you know. And you just better put it away anyway. I just treasure this being free so much and I'm glad I went to Europe every year when I did because I don't think I could afford to go now.

It is interesting to hear how these women learned about these investment vehicles. This usually involved tutelage by a man. Barbara specifically sought out information on the stock market from a male friend when she gained excess cash from a house sale. Claire didn't know much about investing outside of real estate before 1985, although she did know how to read the stock ticker tape and had purchased stocks, mutual funds, and an annuity before then. A male friend taught Cynthia about the stock market.

There were other routes for education about the stock market. Schools and universities offered workshops for employees, for instance. Carolyn, a federal employee, took workshops on stocks while working, as did Bobbie, a schoolteacher.

Dawn learned about the stock market from her sister, who knows a lot about financial planning, funds, and investing.

CYNTHIA: I had bought stocks in AT&T and they tripled in about two years. So I had a nice little nest egg. I went with it for two years. I bought stocks. But there wasn't much money left to live on, so I got rid of my car. I took a bus to work. I would take a bus to get groceries and stuff and live very tight for about two years. [T]hen it split and I kind of had a good idea that it was going to and then that would give me a little chunk of money. And I bought my first house.

CHERYL: So you sold your stock after the split?

CYNTHIA: Yes, and bought my first house and I remodeled it, all of it, physically everything. I was there three years and I doubled my money.

CHERYL: How did you educate yourself about these different instruments?

JANET: I went to night school, adult education night school, probably in 1959, soon after I graduated from college.

CHERYL: What was the subject?

JANET: Stocks, investing. I took two classes and started at that time what they called a monthly investment plan, where you could pay just a small amount per month, select your stocks, and buy quarter shares or whatever. And I bought property soon after I started working, lake property, just vacant land.

CHERYL: Where you getting the money to buy the property? Is this out of the savings account?

JANET: My salary. Stocks were maybe twenty dollars a month and I had the land, the people that sold it held the mortgage and it was like forty dollars a month.

CHERYL: And you were making at least $120 a month or something?

JANET: Not a lot. I started out I think at fifty cents an hour and I soon went up to seventy-five. And to pay off, say college bills, etc., I worked weekends pumping gas at a filling station.

After her divorce, Ellen took the money from the house sale and went to six different brokerage firms asking what to do to protect it. Four of the six advised her to put it into annuities, which she did.

Joyce knew a male math teacher in California in 1968 who was very interested in the stock market and especially in gold. He was buying gold stocks when gold was thirty-two dollars an ounce and predicted that it would go to four hundred and thirty-two dollars an ounce. Joyce and Addy took a chance on gold and Joyce began stock market research on Sunday mornings, making decisions on what to buy each week. She says they have a very conservative portfolio now.

Although Roberta sold annuities in the 1970s, she says she knows nothing about the stock market.

ROBERTA: Yes, [my boss] left the diaper service; I can't remember exactly when. And he went to Merrill Lynch then originally. Now Smith-Barney. He still handles my money. 'Cause I know zip about the stock market. And if I didn't have him, I'd have to get out of it.

CHERYL: So what gave you the confidence to go back into the stock market?

ROBERTA: He did because he knew what he was doing. And I also told him that if anything happens, I told him to never put me in a position where I have to go back to work. And if the bottom dropped out, he has to support me. He's been very, very good to me. We're very dear friends.

CHERYL: So you put just the sale of the house money into the stock market?

ROBERTA: Yeah.

Kate says she learned the hard way about the stock market.

My ex-husband used to invest in the market. We had a lot of friends that invested in the market and I would hear that they made a fortune by buying this stock and that stock and what they did with it. I had a certain amount of money put aside for investing. I was listening to brokers, what they'd tell me to do and how to invest my money and things like that. And over a period of about five years, six years, I found that I had much less than I started with, much, much less. Of course I was able to deduct it as losses. But I didn't like that. I wanted more control.

Then when I got a divorce, I got involved with this group of men. There were about thirty of them. They were from all walks of life, doctors, lawyers, accountants, every profession that you could possibly think of and they were very, very wealthy. And all of them said that they made it in the market. And they were doing all kinds of different things. They were trading with different trading programs. Myself and this other girl, plus these thirty men, were the whole group.

I think I learned the hard way. I listened to brokers and I lost an awful lot of money listening to brokers. And I decided when I got to be a certain age that I was going to do it myself and that's basically it. I do all my finances myself. I do all my stock trading myself. I do all kinds of various things with options and things like that. (Kate)

A gay male friend of Mary Lou's taught her about the stock market. "He told me what he bought, I started learning how to read symbols, and getting *The Wall Street Journal* in 1988." A gay man also talked with Dorothy about buying stocks. The son of a neighbor taught Joyce and her partner about the market.

JOYCE: He, at the age of forty, resigned from his job as a controller of a real estate company, not an agency, and he just makes a living on the stock market. And I said to him once, I said, "Hal, how do you do it? How can you live and support your family and in this kind of a house?" He said, "Well, if you're really interested, I'll tell you." And we sat down one day and he showed me how you can get an income from bonds and stocks and how you play the market.

CHERYL: But you had already educated yourself about the stock market?

JOYCE: Yes. But I wanted to have something that brought in an income because we weren't working anymore. So I had to go very conservatively into the market. You know regular stocks pay very little dividends. So we were careful and as we went on these last years, we've built a very nice portfolio which we still worry about. I guess you wanted to know how we prepared for retirement; that's how.

My friend's friend worked in the stock market and I talked to him a couple of times. And he said, "Just use your head. Read the business page of the newspaper, listen to the news at night and see what you think is going to go." It's just like technology is so hot. Well, it doesn't take very many smarts to know that, and the phone company is hot. Well, people are getting two and three lines in their house because of the fax machines and the computers. So he said, "This is the way the country is going to go and everybody knows it. So, you go with it." (Dorothy)

Sandy educated herself about the market.

SANDY: Mother gave the kids' money to me before she died—it wasn't really in a will—and I set up separate accounts for these kids—investment accounts for them, and I increased that money quite a lot for the kids. And it bothered me to see what happened to it after I had worked with it, but anyway. She bought them each a new car and she bought me a car too when I got married the last time in the 1970s. When she died, she had the house, which I sold for $47,000 and there was probably about $100,000 other money in CDs and things like that. So that was the foundation that I had. My father always said, "It takes money to make money." Now I had it to work with. And I began to invest it.

CHERYL: When do you think you figured out how to read the stock page in the newspaper?

SANDY: That was my husband's idea too, to buy the paper. I didn't know any-thing about it up to that time. And you make a lot of mistakes doing this and then you make some hits too. It's sort of like going out to the track; you don't talk about the losses. But the fact is, I'm certainly a lot better off than I was before.

I got into [investing] by accident with Merrill Lynch. I first put it into Merrill Lynch and then I got into a trust account at Southeastern Bank which I got out of that for a while. But you begin to get *The Wall Street Journal*. I remem-ber when my daughter was staying with me up in Indiana, that long ago, when I was starting the investments up there, I said, "You know, if I didn't work, I could read this paper and I'd make more money than I can working." She was very young at the time and she was amazed. It really was a continu-ation of the way I already thought from when I was married because we talked about investing. We bought some GTE stock—it was preferred stock—and he had some friends at the bank. He took all this stuff down to the bank and asked somebody that he knew whether we should invest in this. This was a long time ago, probably the late 1970s. And the man said, "Oh yeah, it seems good to me." Anyway, that was the first thing we did and after that I did it 'cause I read the paper.

I got a stockbroker up there in Indiana and I talked to him and he—oh this made me so mad too—he didn't want to talk to me. He wanted to talk to my husband and I was the one that was doing it, not him. (Sandy)

GIGI: I really feel for the people that are losing money in the market. But my tax plan will help everybody. People don't realize it's over ten years. So I may end up with a couple thousand to play with again. When I was work-ing I was able to put a little bit away a month. I have maybe a thousand dollars in my savings account now. And I have two stocks I'm going to buy. I'm going to buy GE and I may get Oracle again, I don't know. Bank of America is a 4.3 percent return. They were at fifty-two; I don't know what they closed at yesterday. That's a good one too.

CHERYL: If you're after dividends, look at something like Crescent Realty which is ticker symbol CEI—they pay between 8 and 10 percent—depends on where their share price is.

GIGI: I'm so afraid of real estate now. I've seen this happen, where it plateaus and suddenly sinks a little bit and then it takes so long to get up to a profit margin again. And they are saying that the new home sales was only up like a tenth of a percent or something. They were kind of concerned about that adding to a recession too. I'm going to buy two stocks with that little bit of money, start over again, that's how I've always done it and just let it sit. My timing has just been horrendously bad. But I love it. I'm not sitting here crying over it. It's like when I lost everything up in Michigan, I took $140,000 in savings and bought property and the rest I mortgaged. Then when I lost it all, I said, "Oh well."

CHERYL: And have you let [the broker] make all the decisions about what to buy and when to sell?

JACKIE: Yeah, he checks with me and he explains stuff but I just realized that it's out of my ballpark. As long as things have gone well, I just allow him to do that. I let my money sit for many years in a tax-sheltered annuity that collected very low interest, because I felt guilty participating in a system that perpetuated the corporate practices that keep poverty alive. And since I got hooked into joining the system, my guilt has continued. Allowing my broker to make the decisions seems to enable me to remain somewhat in denial of the reality of the impact of those decisions on other people.

You know people say, two reasons to save money is for security in your old age and also to have an inheritance for your children. Those are the two big reasons. There are other reasons, however. I like to do this. I talk to this friend of mine, Bob, and I tell him things. I see missed opportunities here. And you've got to have money to do it of course. I sold some stuff that wasn't doing anything. And I told him this story. Back at a mission I went to in church, from the pulpit, this was about five years ago. The priest ran down Time Warner because they were into that rap group that was X-rated. It was selling some odd records that were wrong and Time Warner was in the doghouse. And I knew this was the time to buy Time Warner. I told him the other day, now is the time to buy Philip Morris because of all that's going on. "Oh," he said, "they're going to go out of business." I said, "No, they're not; they're not going out of business." They'll do something else, but the stock is down. I know when to buy. I just know when to buy it. I have a very serious fault though. I don't know when to sell it. You've got to be good at both ends of it. Back in 1992 I told Jim, "It's time to buy IBM." And he said, "No, no, blah, blah." So I didn't say any more, I just bought. I put everything I had into it. And then I sold it. I made a lot of money on it, but I'd be a millionaire today if I hadn't 'cause they've split a couple of times. I'll give you an example. When I sold it, even though I made quite a bit, I kept four shares just to be on the books. And these four shares are now nineteen shares; that's how much they've split. It just makes me ill. (Sandy)

Gigi had a tax business and knows quite a bit about the market. Mary Lou subscribes to various services that fax and e-mail her daily. Barbara sells stock options to make her monthly income, regularly attending a technical analysis club in which she is one of only two women. Judy has taken responsibility for investing a trust fund and for her and her partner's investments decisions. Several women use Internet brokerage services.

Not everyone has invested or is still invested in the stock market. Edie bought an annuity in 1987 and promptly saw most of it disappear, so she no longer is interested in the stock market. Gloria, too, got into the market via mutual funds and then out. Jackie was disappointed that socially responsible funds often didn't earn as much

money as did other funds. Sappho said her whole family has a history
of buying stocks and losing.

In 1998 to 2000, when most of these interviews were conducted,
many of the women were receiving dividends or investing in stocks
for their appreciation, anticipating milking their portfolios for luxuri-
ous living in the next decade. Those were the heady days of the
NASDAQ, when one saw quarterly gains in mutual funds and individual stocks that rivaled paychecks. In the next chapter, I will explore what the crash of 2001 to 2002 is doing to these women who
had invested and were deriving monthly income from the stock market.

She and I both bought annuities and that was the year—I think it was
1986-1987—that there was the stock market crash and I lost like $350 which
was a good percentage of what I had put in there. And so it kind of made me
say, "Oh, I don't think I'm going to do that anymore." I think part of it is a decision that it's part of the world that I don't want to belong to. I don't like capitalism, even though I realize that I live in the middle of it and I have to kind of like
deal with capitalism 'cause that's really what happens. (Edie)

Money in Relationships

And we started to notice [on the checks that came in] that some of them
had joint checking accounts and we'd say, those two are [a couple]. (1960-
1968, Mary Lou)

Various options exist for managing money in relationships, and all
of them are present among this group of women. For some women,
joint finances signal love and commitment. For others this melding is
unnecessary.

Her name is on my house and my name is on her house. We have done
all of that. We are in the process of putting names on CDs and mutual funds
and we've opened up a joint checking account. Because this is basically a
new relationship in the sense that we're living together now. So there's still
some things that we have to do, but we're going to do all of that. (Dorothy)

For some, taking care of a lover, supporting her, is a point of pride.
For most of these women, their attitudes and interpretations of the
meanings of melding and separating finances have changed over time
and with experience. Early in life it was more common to support a
lover, or to merge everything. Late in life a greater tendency occurs to

have separate savings and checking accounts while jointly owning assets such as houses and investment properties. In Chapter 6 I will explore how partners have provided for each other. I have separated responses into early situations and later situations.

And she moved in with me and it was 1,000 percent disaster. She interfered with my business. I totally kept her. There's nothing more I could have ever done for her and it was never enough. And after two years I had to ask her to leave. Meanwhile, I'd put her name on my home to make her feel more secure, bought her a new car, bought her a big grand piano, everything. She had a $10,000 bank account, an IRA, never lifted a finger. Didn't even cook, I had cleaning people come in, and she wouldn't sign off my home. And every year she wanted more money to sign off. She didn't have one penny invested in it, nor did she have any sweat equity in it. Then I met somebody else and I had another partner and a partner in business and I had investments going.

So Kay moves in and then I started the investment company and gave her full control 'cause I'm running my other businesses. I also had a marketing company. And she's not working so naturally it would work out really nice. And then about a year and a half later I'm finding out, I'm getting calls, the gas bill on this building isn't being paid, the electric bill isn't being paid, people are moving out. I didn't know about it. She's not trying to re-rent the stores. It turned out to be a real mess and she's living right in my home. And I said, "Kay, what the heck is going on?" "Oh, I'm taking care of it." Then I started looking at the books. The rents aren't even going into the business account. Because her last name was {} and it was the {} Company, she opened up another checking account and put all the checks that were coming in from the rents into that. So she did a real show on me also.

So I'm stuck with all the bills. There was no way I could keep it up. I had to move to Florida to help take care of my mom. The other woman would not sign off. She was up to $40,000 to get her name off my house. Kay had wiped me out with cash. So I just told everybody good-bye; I closed the door and walked away from it all. (Gigi)

CAROLYN: Lucy made the payments. To buy the house her parents paid half the cost, Marge the other half.

CHERYL: So the house was going to be hers?

CAROLYN: No, the house was in both names, but she made all the payments. I was not at all happy with Lucy. She turned out to be much more possessive and protective than I wanted in my life. For example, she said, "You don't need to set up a charge account at such and such a store. Use my card." She was generosity itself. "You don't need a separate bank account. I'll put you on mine." Well, I felt like I had no independence.

CHERYL: Did you ever put any property in the name of you and a partner—a sexual partner?

NAN: Yes, I did.

CHERYL: So there have been times when you've fused your economic resources?

NAN: I did because I was conned into it. I just got talked into it. My guard wasn't up and I got sued for palimony also. I was lucky to get my home back. We settled out of court. I had some goods on this woman. We went in front of a mediator and I passed on to my lawyer to pass on to the mediator to go to her lawyer with what I had. She was suing me for $40,000 and she came back with $4,000 and I said, "Write it up as fast you can. I'll be happy to give her a check for $4,000 and get out of this and have my home back." Those were uncomfortable years.

CHERYL: What year was that?

NAN: 1988-1989.

CHERYL: So most of your relationship with people living in your home have not gotten as far as meshing financially?

NAN: No.

CHERYL: You kept that separate.

NAN: Right. If other people have owned properties, we kept that separate. However, with running a household, we put our monies together to join with each other. And if I was to buy a property with somebody I sure would have to have something written up by a lawyer first.

CHERYL: Were you ever supporting any of these women you were living with?

NANCY: Yes, for a brief period. Vollie went back to school and I did a lot of the supporting during those couple of years.

CHERYL: Were you paying the tuition for her?

NANCY: No. I had to write a lot of her papers.

CHERYL: Did you ever end a relationship because of money?

NANCY: No. It's never been a big issue with me, period. It's nice to have it, but it's not been anything that I took so seriously that if everything else was going right, that I would have broken up with someone over it.

She was in financial trouble when I met her. She was one of these people, if they sent her an application for a credit card, she filled it out and sent it back. So when I stepped into Alice's life, I paid off her house and made her tear up every credit card she had and got her financially back in shape. (Ellen)

CHERYL: Did you have both you and your partner's names on deeds and on mortgages?

DIANE: Yes. I'll never do that again.

There is no "I" in our finances. Yeah, we had savings accounts. We put our money together the minute we met practically. We said that once we got

$1,000, we'd feel like we had something. This was back in New York. And it didn't take us long to get the $1,000. Joyce handles our finances. (Addy)

Joanna had a ten-year relationship in which everything was separate except for a joint account for house expenses. Amelia has let her partner take care of all of their finances. As a consequence she was shocked to learn that she needed to file for bankruptcy several years ago. Kate says she used money to impress her dates, insisting on paying for everything.

But with aging often comes fiscal maturity. Several Whistling Women have changed their tune about finances in relationships. Now Kate and her partner have bought homes together and pool all of their incoming money, but have several separate checking accounts for their respective children. Barbara, who had a budget as a wife, now pools money with her partner. Jackie says that her partner has really helped her learn to manage her money.

CHERYL: I assume that you and June had joint accounts.

SHERI: We did and when that was settled out, there was a great deal of animosity, but that's all over.

CHERYL: And have you done the same kind of financial arrangement with Dot?

SHERI: No, Dot owns everything. In fact the last duplex that she bought, she put it in both our names and I said, No, let's not. I didn't want my name on it. I know that I'm inheriting, but in the meantime it's less confusing legally if everything is in her name.

CHERYL: So you have your own separate checking account and your separate savings account?

SHERI: Yes.

CHERYL: I would assume that when you were married that you had joint checking accounts and things like that. Is that a sort of model, do you think that if you were to set up house with another woman that you would want to do things like joint checking accounts and joint property ownership?

DAWN: I don't think I would. I've heard of too many problems with joint things, unless a couple has been together for years and years and they've got this all settled. And even at that, some people run into a lot of problems. I've heard of some pretty bitter breakups and problems with that. I haven't run into that situation yet and I don't know what I'd do.

It had always been that way, finances were kept separate. It didn't come up, I mean, no one ever asked me, "Couldn't we put our finances together?" So the first time I had done that has been with Martha. We have everything totally entwined. I never expect to have this one end. Martha has more money. Her father had made quite a bit of money. He died when she was two, but he left her and her mother pretty well off. She was working. She was working as a music manager in New York—music management company—booking artists into concert series and concert halls. I suppose I had a little more trust in Martha. Well, you learn a lot by the time you're fifty. I listened to the way she talked and I saw how she behaved with her mother and I got a sense of what she was about and I never worried. First of all, she had more money than I did. The other people were either at the same level or less. I thought she had been managing her own money for some time and she knows how to do it. (Nancy)

[Dotty and I held everything jointly but in this relationship things are separate.] When we bought this house, I did not have exactly half—maybe I was about $28,000 or $30,000 less. But she wanted to go ahead and get the house. So I agreed. I pay all the utilities and she's keeping a record once a month. So I'm catching up by doing that. That's the only way I wanted it. (Kay M)

In my past experiences in a lesbian relationship, I had always done a fifty-fifty split until we began to look at other ways to deal with money as a whole. That was in our lesbian ethics group. We looked at other ways to deal with inequities in women's lives. There is a great imbalance of power in lesbian relationships when one woman makes a lot more money than the other one does, or when one owns a house and the other one pays the owner rent. We examined questions such as: Should she, if they are no longer in a relationship, have part of that house or part of whatever they have purchased together? We began to explore the different kinds of ideas about how to manage money. So, for my last two relationships, we have changed that dynamic. Before my partnership with Jackie, I was working and making 70 percent percent more than my partner so we did expenses on a 70 percent to 30 percent split. Now, Jackie has a lot more income than I do. We pay expenses on that ratio of what percent her income is to mine. When I had a relationship with Doreen, it took all of my salary to put in my 50 percent. She put in her 50 percent of what it cost us to live together and she had money left over at the end of each month. She had a good retirement income. The ratio model works so much better—we both have money left over at the end of the month, so that I have discretionary money and she has discretionary money. She has a lot more than I do but I feel like I have at least $100 a month left over that I can play with. (Edie)

There are lessons here for all of us who have not retired. One of the most important might be that one doesn't get rich quickly and that fortunes level out over time; they are fragile. These women by and large reflect the Protestant ethic—which is clearly just as much a Catholic and a Jewish ethic as Protestant—that is, go to school, work regularly, save and invest, and reap. They also show us that the world of finance is not simply a man's world.

SUMMARY

The history of women in the workforce in the twentieth century was rocky before 1970. How did lesbian women of the 1940s, 1950s, and 1960s learn to support themselves without husbands and educate themselves about finances to the point that they live comfortable lives today? My conclusion is the same one offered in Chapter 4: It isn't husbands, but jobs with pensions, that make it possible to live a middle-class or higher existence in this country.

The narrators actually show more variety in their careers and degrees than the surveys of the 1940s to 1960s would suggest. Older narrators earned degrees or certificates in history, English, math, social work, education, nursing, and journalism. Among the younger narrators were degrees in education, art, music, engineering, business/economics, drama, and medical field degrees. Nursing credentials were earned by five women.

Six of fifteen women in the older cohort (40 percent) got master's degrees as did sixteen of twenty-nine of the younger women (55 percent). Two of the older women (13 percent) and four of the younger women (14 percent) completed PhDs. For the younger women, going back to school was spread out over three decades, while all the older women obtained advanced schooling in the 1950s, fairly quickly on the heels of their undergraduate degrees.

Fifteen women consider themselves to have maintained the same class standing they were born into as working adults. Typically this is the sentiment of women who were born into upper middle class families. Twenty-one women assess their socioeconomic class status to have been higher when they were working than when they were children, while five women say they dropped in class standing as working adults.

Financial education for these women came in many forms—successful parents and/or financial support from parents, childhood lessons about money and saving, house ownership, loans, friends and spouses who understood or wanted to understand the stock market, jobs with retirement clinics, handling accounts, and sometimes dumb luck, sometimes bad luck. Most of the wealthiest women in this project made their money in real estate, buying, improving or building, and selling houses. There are many cases of two women buying property jointly since 1946. Profits from the sale of these houses or from inheritance were often put into the stock market.

In the next chapter, the finances, activities, and communities of the Whistling Women are explored.

Chapter 6

Life After Sixty

On scale of one to ten, life now is a twelve. (Kate)

Retirement has been wonderful—the best years of my life. (Roberta)

What's to complain about? I recommend retirement to everybody. (Sappho)

I loved being in charge of myself. I think that was the main thing. The first morning I woke up and realized I can go where I want to, when I want to, was just an incredible feeling of exhilaration. And now being in this relationship and being with someone that is as much fun and interesting to be with has just been better. (Jackie)

It was this incredible freeing experience. I just love it. I get up in the morning and I say, well, what do I think I'll do today. Well, maybe I'll put in a fence, maybe I'll plant, maybe I'll go to a show, go to a movie. (Edie)

I'm glad to be rid of the personnel problems. Retirement is like being on vacation all the time. I've never been sorry I retired. (Kay M)

Retirement is an exploring experience in time management—you are afraid of things passing you by. (Marilyn)

I still have anxiety dreams about retiring. (Carolyn)

Retirement has been a disappointment. (Amelia)

I can't really say I'm retired. How can a person ever retire? I don't know. What would you do if you retired? (Dawn)

This chapter is divided into six parts: the decision to retire, financing, communities, activities, health, and future plans. When and why these narrators retired, what planning went into the decision and timing to retire, how they are financing retirement, and what they are doing in this phase of their lives are the subjects of this chapter. Academic questions are probed, such as why women retire from the labor force, and how successful they are financing retirement, given historically lower wages and shorter work lives, as well as examples and advice to be offered about financing these years and activities. Furthermore, in the course of these interviews I have learned about several amazing lesbian communities and the activities and life that have been created by these so-called "retirees." I will explore the sense of community these women have built in various places and the commonalties that they have found.

THE DECISION TO RETIRE

In this study, I, the interviewer, carried the notion that retirement meant the end of one job by choice and the collecting of money earned/owed from a pension or Social Security for previous work. This definition was in keeping with my assumption that most lesbians had not been married and all lesbians worked for a living. Considering my own work history and thoughts of retiring, I had assumed that lesbians would retire for all the same reasons that working men retire: they get tired of working, tired of that job, want to match schedules with a spouse, or company incentives made retirement logical.

I was surprised on four fronts. One surprise was that some of the women in the sample had never worked and thus can't retire. Another surprise was that some of the women never plan to retire. They enjoy their work or they must work. The third surprise was that some women retire two and three times. The final surprise was to read that "We have little idea of why women retire" (Gratton and Haug 1983, quoted in Dailey 1998, p. 26), a state that persisted in 1998.

> Inherent in feminist analyses is the assumption that women have dissimilar work and retirement experiences from men. Even if women have comparable levels of education or income, their social and family role commitments will make their retirement experience different. (Dailey 1998, p. 26)

It follows then that by paying attention to sexuality, particularly to those women (and men) who did not bear or raise children, it will be possible to shed light on what aspects of the retirement decision are related to family and social responsibility and what aspects of the retirement decision are related to gender. Do lesbians retire for different reasons than do men and straight women?

Why Retire?

The earliest retirements were in 1977, one from each age cohort. Looking at the older age cohort, two women retired in the 1970s, ten in the 1980s, and three in the 1990s. All fifteen women in this group worked and subsequently retired. From the younger cohort, one retirement occurred in 1977, six in the 1980s, thirteen in the 1990s, two in the year 2000, and five women are still working. Three women (younger cohort) never worked at paid jobs or never for retirement benefits and thus are not included in the following discussion (Table 6.1).

The average age at retirement for the older women was 60.93 while for the younger women it is earlier, 57.45 years, but if I add in the ages today of the women who have not yet retired, the average retirement age would be the same—sixty-one years. Early retirement, here defined as retiring before age sixty-five, occurred among 60 percent of the older women and among 86 percent of the younger women. This is clearly a significant difference between the two age cohorts and may be reflecting the better pension/retirement packets available in the 1970s and 1980s. It may also be reflecting money growth and the supplemental "pensions" of the "new" financial instruments such as mutual funds, IRAs, and annuities, which became available to many employees in the 1980s (offered to federal employees in 1981, says Carolyn), when several of the older women were already retired or close to retirement.

Sixteen (36 percent) of these narrators retired in the 1980s. Displaced workers—"persons with tenure of 3 or more years who lost or left a job between January 1981 and January 1986 because of plant closing, moves, slack work, or the abolishment of their positions or shifts" (U.S. Bureau of the Census 1988, cited in Calasanti and Bonanno 1992, p. 136)—comprised nearly 10 percent of the labor force in 1988. Perhaps reflecting the high number of lesbians working in public education or nursing in this sample, rather than in manufacturing, only three narrators attributed their retirement decision to displacement fears or realities. Two of these women worked for the federal government. One retired in 1982, the other in 1985.

TABLE 6.1. Retirement Statistics for the Whistling Women

Name	Retirement Year	Age	Working Now	Class Now	SS	Pension	Market	Rent
Older Cohort								
Claire	1990	65	no	um	x	x	x	x
Kay M	1978	54	yes	um	x	x	x	0
Carolyn	1985	65	no	m	0	x	x	0
Joanna	1990	66	no	lm	x	x	0	0
Bing	1989	65	yes	lm	x	0	x	0
Amelia	1985	56	no	l	x	0	0	0
Gloria	1980	56	no	m	x	0	x	0
Kay	1990	61	no	um	x	x	x	x
Cam	1989	68	no	m	x	x	x	0
Roberta	1983	63	no	m	x	0	x	0
Addy	1977	49	no	u	x	0	x	0
Vera	1985	62	no	m	x	x	0	0
Sheri	1982	55	no	lm	x	x	x	0
Mary2	1982	63	no	m	x	x	x	x
Diane	1983	66	no	m	x	x	x	0
Total			13%		93%	66%	80%	20%
Younger Cohort								
Mary Lou	1985	56	no	um	x	x	x	x
Nan	—	—	no	um	xh	0	x	0
Pat N	1982	52	no	m	0	x	?	0
Dawn	—	—	yes	um	0	0	x	x
Marilyn	1995	53	no	um	x	x	x	0
Sappho	1993	56	no	m	x	x	x	0
Edie	1997	60	no	m	xh	0	0	0
Sandy	1994	61	yes	m	x	0	x	0
Nancy	semi	—	yes	um	x	0	x	0
Pat M	2000	65	yes	l	xh	0	0	0
Dorothy	1995	65	no	m	x	0	x	0
Jackie	1990	59	no	m	x	x	x	0

Name	Retirement Year	Age	Working Now	Class Now	Income Sources SS	Pension	Market	Rent
Mary1	1999	61	no	l	d	0	0	w
Chris	1993	63	no	l	x	x	0	w
Ruth	1995	57	no	um	ny	x	x	0
Judy	1993	58	no	um	ny	x	x	0
Mitch	1989	57	no	mm	x	x	x	0
Jean	1984	53	no	u	x	x	0	m
Joyce	1977	43	no	u	x	x	x	0
Barbara	semi	—	yes	m	0	0	x	0
Kate	hasn't	—	yes	u	x	x	x	x
Ellen	—	—	no	um	x	alimony	x	0
Pauline	2000	66	yes	m	x	x	0	0
Jan	1998	53	no	m	d	x	0	0
Janet	1993	57	no	m	x	x	0	0
Bobbie	1995	59	no	lm	x	x	x	0
Liz	hasn't	—	yes	m	x	0	x	0
Rose	1980	50	yes	lm	x	0	x	x
Gigi	1993	58	no	lm	x	0	0	x
Total			31%		83%	55%	66%	21%

*working now: yes if regular schedule of 10+ hours/week or living off of wages.
ny = not yet eligible but will be
d = for disability payments, rather than Social Security
m = receives mortgage payments
w = receives welfare checks, and/or food stamps
xh = receives social security through ex-husband

All but one of the women in this sample provided information on their retirement decision. Among this group of narrators, ten reasons for retiring were given:

1. tired of working (seven)
2. uncertain future of job due to changes underway (four)
3. didn't want to be the "old fart" in the office (one)
4. spouse retired (four)
5. to ensure she had a retirement era (two)

6. company incentive (three)
7. sold business (one)
8. moved on, other things to do (seven)
9. disability, health problems (five)
10. could not remain in a repressive bureaucracy and serve clients with dignity (one)

I worked until 1983, retired from the diaper service. I got a lump sum. I was sick and tired of working. And I never would have worked a day in my life if I'd had money. I'd have traveled. I thought that I could manage with the money without working. I had money in the market. I sold my old house—put the money in mutual funds. Retirement has been wonderful. It's been the best years of my life. I was a person that never wanted a lot of responsibility and I gave up a lot of good jobs because of that. And I also never wanted to wear a lot of clothes. (Roberta)

I had planned to retire at fifty-five, but I found that I was hopelessly involved with Juana and I knew that I couldn't do that. She would have been so resentful of me being retired. Well, I worked till I was sixty and I was really getting antsy. And a lot of changes were happening to our jobs. People coming in were more and more incompetent—I didn't have a lot of patience with that and finally at the age of sixty-two, I decided, hell, I don't have to do this anymore. For a year I had trained my employees so that they knew how to do all the projects that fell in our domain. I had my desk thoroughly clean. I went on my annual vacation—I shocked the hell out of them—I never went back. (Vera)

I really was in the best situation I had ever been in my entire career. But I woke up one morning in February saying, I don't feel like getting up anymore. By the time I was able to go to make my retirement appointments, we were already getting into May. As long as it was May, I waited until June because then they have what you call double dipping where I got my salary for July and August and my pension for July and August. In 1993 I retired, July 1.

At the end I was teaching English as a second language and I was doing a lot of work not teaching. I had had it with kids. I was teaching adults, teaching teachers at times, doing workshops for teachers and things. But as the years went on, the less I worked, the less I wanted to work. The supervisor got a job in another district as a principal. Toward the end she also was able to pull teachers out of the classroom so she didn't need to budget for people like me as much, so I was getting less work which was fine. Last year I worked for another supervisor testing children for the gifted program and I hated it. I said, "I don't want to work at all." I was fifty-six.

I could have retired a year earlier, but I didn't. I was having a great time. I was out of the classroom; I was doing this night school job. Why retire? That last year it was just a matter of progression, having to get up in the morning, get dressed and be there. And the whole working in the school, I didn't mind working at the district office as much as I minded working in the schools and seeing and hearing and being part of that, it would bring back a lot of negative memories. (Sappho)

I was approaching sixty and I didn't want to work anymore. I really was going to stop working when I was sixty-two, but in the end I couldn't [stop at sixty] because I got cancer. And you can't get insurance, see, and then I would have lost my insurance after eighteen months. So I was working and then they were going to make me pay for the premiums and I thought, Why am I working? So I quit. I gave my notice, worked the next month. (Sandy)

I retired July (1999), went back to work in September because the woman they hired didn't work out, and I just finally stopped working last week. I really think I will enjoy retirement as long as I can find something to do to keep me out of mischief. I'm not really sure about retirement yet. I retired because I'm tired of working. I said if I lived long enough, I would retire at sixty-five. I turned sixty-five last April. (Pat M)

I left my job when the job situation was changing. One of the employees left and there were two of us and I was getting bored with the repetitiveness of it and there wasn't a future. And I'd worked long enough to be vested. (Marilyn)

I retired in 1984 at age fifty-two. I didn't have time to go to a job and when [the company] split up I got out. I was into remodeling and I was into running this bar. . . . Retired from the bar in 1986. I moved to Florida. (Cynthia)

When I retired, it was March 1985. Virginia had her Easter vacation coming up and we came to Florida. And of course our house was there. The relatives who had been renting it had left and we stayed there for about ten days till she had to fly back. And by agreement we left me there for Virginia to come down after school. I had some second thoughts [about retiring]. I could have stayed on longer. At that time, it was the middle Reagan years, and things were shaking up pretty badly in the federal government and I could see the handwriting on the wall. A lot of the jobs in my branch were going to be abolished when the incumbents retired. And a number of the incumbents were ready to retire and I didn't know what I was going to be left with as branch chief. So I thought I'd better get out while the getting was good. I worked in Social Security. (Carolyn)

At fifty-five I said good-bye to teaching/counseling. I thought it was handled better by the younger people coming in. I had a lot of interns. And I got to thinking, I don't want to be the old fogy, the old fart around here. I think it's time to let the youth take over. I'll move on. That's how I felt. (Mary Lou)

We planned—both of us were college professors—so we had retirement benefits. We had agreed, because we are about five years different in age, that she would retire at sixty and I would retire at fifty-five. (Ruth)

Dottie wanted to retire seventeen to eighteen years after we got together. She was sixty-two and I was fifty-four when she retired and she talked about wanting to go to Florida. I said, "I can't yet; it's too soon." But in January we had a heavy snow and I'd shoveled the driveway out twice in one day and I said to her when I got home that night, "The more I think about it, the more I think it might be a good idea to go to Florida." So I got a sabbatical and we took my sister's RV and started down the west coast of Florida. I didn't care much for it and I didn't know much about Florida. When we drove up the east coast, and got to Daytona, we drove out on the sand, I said, "This is where I want to live." So we bought a house right then. I had to go back and turn in my resignation. It took nine months for them to get a replacement. I had liked teaching but I was the library director and I hated administration—always trying to be tactful. (Kay M)

I only had about sixteen years in and I should have had twenty so they rationed my pension. But we were not happy, Addy's legs were bothering her. She's had a knee replacement and in the house in New York there were two flights of stairs. We just stopped working. A friend at the age of forty resigned from his job and started making a living on the stock market. And I said to him once, "I'm still teaching and I hate it because the kids were already getting a little too rambunctious." I said, "How do you do it? How can you live and support your family?" And we sat down one day and he showed me how. (Joyce)

I retired in 1980. I've never worried about money. It's always been there. I planned to retire early and I didn't plan financially, I planned in terms of the job and what I wanted to do. I planned to retire early because so many people that I knew died shortly after they retired. I said, "That's not going to happen, I'm going to retire as early as I possibly can and have fun." I always said that at fifty-five I was leaving. I left teaching nursing in a college. I've kept up my nursing license but I could never go back though because things have changed so drastically. (Gloria)

My university came up with a retirement package that occurred before I was sixty. They offered three years of retirement but no salary when I was fifty-eight and they gave six months' salary for sick days unused. I decided I couldn't afford to work anymore. (Judy)

I finagled some deal there where I could retire ahead of time and receive the credit for being there for another two years and my pension would be based on that also. (Mitch)

The reason I retired from each job: I either moved or went on to other fields. I like to be busy!!!! (Bing)

My son asked me to come to New York and home school his son. So I did that and never really went back to nursing. Then I met my partner and she was retired. (Edie)

I was working until a year and two months ago. But I retired on disability. I really didn't think about retiring—it was forced on me. (Mary1)

I retired because I got sick, physically sick. And the reason I bought the van was because I retired to travel and I can't drive very far without falling asleep and so I made it comfortable for myself. But I have recovered. And there was a time I couldn't walk from here to the car. I was very sick. I have this cardiologist that straightened me out and got me back together. I retired at sixty-two, I retired three years ago. (Jan)

Well, because I'd been wanting to for a long time. I was starting to have health problems. I have poor lungs from having smoked for many years and all of a sudden I started getting one cold after another, bronchitis, terrible things. And then one year I ended up with pneumonia by May, by the end of the school year. I said, "I can't go through this any longer" and sure enough the next year it started right up with another cold. (Bobbie)

We now have some idea of why women retire (à la Gratton and Haug 1983 and Dailey 1998). It appears that no woman retired because of social or family obligations, although the four women who retired to fit their spouses' lifestyle should probably be included in this categorization. In fact, four of the five women who have yet to retire are at least sixty-nine years old and have adult children; several have grandchildren. Clearly family and social responsibilities are not weighing on them.

I see nothing in the list of ten reasons for retiring that I would attribute to the narrators' being women, being mothers, or being homosexual. I see nothing in the list of ten reasons for retiring that would not appear in a group of forty-four men aged sixty or more. Later in this chapter I will present the activities that these women are engaged in now, which are in some cases different from what heterosexual women would be doing but different only in that the social groups are primarily homosexual women. I have no doubts that the type of employers, the prevalence of retirement packages, and the types of retirement packages offered by employers may, in a huge sample of retirees, differ between men and women, regardless of their sexuality, but it does not follow that the retirement reasons or experiences of women will be different from those of men. I cannot, with this data, support the statement found in Dailey 1998 that "Even if women have comparable levels of education or income, their social and family role commitments will make their retirement experience different" (Dailey 1998, p. 26).

I imagine, although I have not mustered the data, that far greater differences in retirement experiences occur between coupled and single people than between men and women.

The Choice Not to Retire

In 1996, 17 percent of women sixty-five to sixty-nine were still working, and 8.8 percent of women seventy to seventy-four were still working (Yutema 1997). Fourteen percent of people said that they did not plan to retire.

Among the Whistling Women, four women declared themselves semi-retired or not yet retired or said they never will retire. Barbara has a private practice in counseling with twenty to twenty-five clients, Dawn earns money as a city council member and through antique sales, Nancy continues to give private music lessons at a local college, and Kate does a variety of money-earning activities.

In addition, seven retired women are currently earning wages at some sort of self-directed work, two from the older cohort (13 percent). Sandy spends four hours a day, three times a week tending to an older woman, Bing works full time at a university residence hall, Liz works on a will-call basis, Pauline is doing freelance writing and part-time teaching, Rose sells items at craft shows, and Kay M drives people to the airport when they call. Pat M has gone back to the job she retired from to fill in a vacancy. Joyce was a travel agent working for commissions earlier in retirement. Only Pat M, Sandy, Bing, Kay M, and Pauline could be said to be working for the extra income. The others either continue to do what they have been doing for years, or happened to get paid for something they particularly enjoy doing.

Calasanti and Bonanno, in an article published in 1992, stated that 34 percent of all retirees work either for pay or for free and that 20 percent of younger retirees are employed full-time. In fact, figures from the late 1980s show that 23.4 percent of all retirees reversed their decision to cease working (Ruhm 1990 cited in Calasanti and Bonanno 1992). Fewer than 20 percent of workers move from full-time work to no work at all. For those who continue to work for money, low income is the strongest predictor of work (Calasanti and Bonanno 1992). One-third of the jobs for the working elderly come from the service sector, and the majority of elderly workers are female (Howe 1986 cited in Calasanti and Bonanno 1992).

The benefits of this extra income are enjoyed for a relatively short time (Calasanti and Bonanno 1992). Eighty percent of people in a partial retirement situation terminate their work before eight years have passed (as did Jackie; see the following) while the average length of time for partial retirement is less than six years (Calasanti and Bonanno 1992). The motivations for reentering the workforce, or for working in unpaid situations, are to survive economically, to maintain status, and to help others maintain or survive.

Whistling Women who came out of retirement to reenter the work force full time have done so out of boredom with retirement. Bing has retired three times and reentered the workforce four times. "I thought each time I retired would be the last and then I got bored. . . . Back to work I went, mainly for the need of companionship not so much money but it always helps" (Bing). Her reason for working is a rather obvious one, but not one of those specified by Calasanti and Bonanno—to avoid boredom or loneliness—and no doubt is a prime motivator for many older people who return to work after retirement. Boredom was also the motivating factor behind Kate's return to the work force, as well as Marilyn's. Kate has continued working for over ten years since retiring.

I moved into semi-retired supposedly when we sold the house in New York. But it didn't happen exactly the way we planned it because I was getting very bored when I came back down to Florida, and I was too young to retire. So I went and got myself a job in the field that I knew best which was substance abuse. I just had to do something. Then as I continued to work, I wanted a better job. So I went ahead and got a job as clinical director and I stayed there for several years. and then I decided that it was just too much and I wanted to go into private practice and I was getting my doctorate at that point. I've never had a pension from any of those jobs.

At the moment I have no plans for full retirement—I'm having too much fun. There's no reason to. I have every reason to have clients. (Kate)

Jackie retired early from a public school system in 1990 but continued to work another seven years.

And then I continued to work, I had a private psychotherapy practice a couple of nights a week actually because I enjoyed being a social worker/psychotherapist. Once I was retired, I had the freedom to choose my assignments. I had a sense of autonomy and creativity that my work in the bureaucracy of a large urban school district had not provided. In addition it increased my expendable income. I did a lot of freelancing and consultation... . I didn't actually have my last client contact until July 1997. I met Edie and I knew that I wanted to come down [to Florida to live with her]. I had been gradually phasing out the practice. I was really fed up with the New Jersey winters and was getting myself psychologically ready to come to Florida. (Jackie)

Marilyn has been fully retired since 1997. She first retired in 1985 from a state library in Ohio. Three years later, she and her partner moved to Florida and Marilyn "was ready to do anything." She went to work at "the newspaper" for nine years. That second job netted her a pension amounting to an extra $52/month.

Calasanti and Bonanno also included work by elders that was not remunerated in the statistics about work after retirement. Volunteer work and family work are engaged in by many narrators and for the reasons mentioned by Calasanti and Bonanno—to improve or maintain the status of others and communities. Here, volunteering is considered in the section on activities.

Why Florida?

Forty of the Whistling Women spend at least five months a year in Florida, and many of them are at least the second generation in their natal families to do so, and some are third generation to retire there. People at least fifty-five years old are less likely to move than their children are, but their moves are more likely to take them out of state. In the eastern United States, Florida is the most popular retirement destination, with a 10.2 percent growth in the retiree group from 1995 through 2000. Florida's population of fifty-five to sixty-four-year-olds increased 21.6 percent during this time, declined 5.1 percent for ages sixty-five to seventy-four, increased 14.1 percent in seniors seventy-five to eighty-four, and 26.6 percent in those over eighty-four (Yutema 1997).

Why move to Florida? For the same reasons their parents chose this state (multiple reasons included in tally):

To be near parent, sibling, or child	16
For the weather	11
Because lover was there/wanted to be there	10
Tax benefit	4
Already living there	3
Owned real estate/timeshare there	2
For the sea	2

The overwhelming reason for these women to choose Florida as a retirement location was to be near a relative or a lover. The tax benefits of making Florida one's permanent residence are becoming less as several states have moved to eliminate state income taxes on retirement monies earned in that state. Both New York and North Carolina exempt retirement monies earned in those states from annual taxation now. However, the options for places to move after retirement from New York or North Carolina are narrowing to just Florida, if one wants to keep the tax benefits of a home state.

Only five women knew gay women already living in Florida, but three of them said that the presence of a gay community in west Florida was an important factor in their choice of Florida as a residence. This gay community will be explored later in this chapter.

FINANCING RETIREMENT

If I was talking to someone I'd say, "Be careful. Save your money," really. (Chris)

Planning for Retirement

According to Yutema (1997), a large proportion of the near-retirement population has made no plans for retirement, including 28 percent of those aged sixty-one or more, beyond saying that they will not work once retired (31 percent), or work no more than four hours per week (20 percent). Fourteen percent said they will never retire. The majority of people have a hard time imagining retirement, which contributes to their lack of planning. However, the number of Whistling Women who planned retirement exceeds the number who did not.

CHERYL: So thinking all along that you were going to retire at sixty-five, what did you do to plan for it?
PAT M: Not a damn thing.

I didn't ever worry about retirement. When I moved from Texas to Ohio, I got the retirement money out in cash and deposited it and I didn't ever get transfer credit for that. But the state of Ohio has a good retirement system.
I've saved in order to ensure a decent retirement. I have bought some stock even. With my husband, we moved to different cities, so I've never

been on a steady track that I've been thinking, *Oh, I can't wait till I retire from this situation.* (Marilyn)

JOANNA: Well, I bought stocks and I always sold them and used the money for something else. So, no, I didn't have any particular plans in my head for retirement.

CHERYL: What did you imagine that you would do in retirement, money wise? What did you imagine your life would be like?

JOANNA: I thought I'd be with this woman I was with, but that didn't work out. But I hadn't really thought much about it. I didn't plan ahead.

NANCY: I just figured I'd work forever. Retirement wasn't a concept that I... it was not like I thought, *Now shall I retire or shall I not?* It just never occurred. I never even considered the possibility.

CHERYL: In the 1960s, are you thinking about retirement?

NANCY: Are you kidding? My mother probably never thought that and nobody ever told me that I should do that, so I didn't. I never thought about it and, as I said, I thought I'd be working until the end. It was not something that I thought about in terms of not having full health. It just didn't cross my mind that maybe I'm going to be weak and infirm and what's going to happen to me then without children to come to the rescue like they do, like I did with my mother.

I have a government retirement, a very good one, very good health insurance. Virginia and I did a great deal to prepare for retirement for both of us. IRAs, optional retirement. Of course, I kept track of what my retirement would be and we both bought stocks. In 1981 we bought our lot in Florida and in 1982 we put our home on it and started renting it out. It was paid for by the time we retired and moved down there in 1988. (Carolyn)

Well, I put some money away. And my God, if you have a chance to do that, do it. 'Cause if you get on a fixed income like I'm on, you can't afford to live on it. (Bobbie)

CHERYL: Did you plan for retirement?

DIANE: No, not until the last ten years when I got a job with a pension. Before that whenever I had a job with a pension, I'd take the money and go on a fling.

CHERYL: The annuity, at some point you've decided to put extra money into an annuity?

DIANE: Yes, two of them. One pays into the bank every month which I like a lot, the other one once a year.

CHERYL: That's some planning. When did you start doing that?

DIANE: When I got the money from the sale of the house, I began to use a financial advisor and tried to invest it to make it grow. Oh, it didn't. I don't think I have as much now as I had then.

I planned retirement. I put money into a tax shelter through my job for about twenty years. (Jackie)

I planned to retire at sixty-two—last year. I had figured out how I would save money, work extra, pay off the mortgage. Plus I had a little bed-and-breakfast that I advertised in *Lesbian Connection*. (Edie)

I substituted for twelve years which was a mistake, because I paid my own health insurance. So I picked up a full-time contract. I retired when I was sixty-five with eight and one-half years with the county. The plan five years before I retired really went into effect and that's when it paid off. I knew I didn't want to work beyond sixty-five and I knew at age sixty that I'd have to start thinking about how I was going to do that. I have a small villa. I had to start and replace all the appliances because I knew I couldn't do that after I retired. I wanted a new car. I wanted to be able to pay my bills; I knew what they were. I knew what my SS [Social Security] was going to be, I knew I couldn't make it on SS. I needed an additional probably $200 to $300 a month of interest income. So I got into the stock market. I thought, if I can use my head and just read the business page, I can do all right. I started while I still had a job—after I retired I wouldn't be able to keep money there. So when I retired in 1995, I got out of the stock market, put that money in CDs and I now I have the additional interest to pay the bills.

I also created a slush fund for one-time expenses. I had the county take some of my paycheck and buy savings bonds with the money—that's the slush fund. (Dorothy)

Two women planned early retirements and then health problems—cancer and aneurysm—kept them working until age sixty-five to maintain their health insurance until they were eligible for Medicare.

Predictably, there were retirement planners and nonplanners among the narrators. Among the nonplanners are those who assumed that their investments in properties, the stock market, and bonds would carry them indefinitely, a type of planning. Also among the nonplanners are those who knew they were earning a pension from their years of service to a school district or company. They are nonplanners in that they did nothing extra. For planners I include those who said they planned, those who contributed extra money to a fund that they could not draw from until age fifty-nine or later, and those who actually mapped out the last three to five years of their working lives with an eye toward retirement. Financial planners would have us all plan the way Dorothy and Edie did—before retirement, methodically adding up the expenses, replacing appliances and cars, paying off loans, debts and mortgages, and creating money accounts that will grow or at least generate semi-annual payments.

Piecing Together Retirement Financing

The sources of money for these narrators are the (1) federal government in the form of Social Security, disability, welfare, and food stamps, (2) employer money given in the form of a pension or retirement plan or current wages, (3) monies generated by investments—either stocks, bonds or rents or mortgages, and (4) money gifts from family or ex-husbands (alimony payments). A fifth source of money is the sharing of expenses with a partner or live-in relative. Table 6.1 presents some financial information for each narrator.

Social Security (SS) is available to most working U.S. citizens such that 93 percent of retired Americans receive monthly Social Security checks. A woman must either pay into SS quarterly and earn forty quarters to receive payment or have had a husband who paid in and a marriage that lasted at least twelve years, even if they are divorced. Women have the choice of receiving their husband's SS or their own, whichever is the larger amount. Edie had not paid enough quarters to qualify for SS when she turned sixty, but her twenty years of marriage and the death of her ex-husband earned her the money. Nan and Pat M have the same situation.

I never had to go back to work because I have Social Security. When I reached sixty, my ex-husband died and I collect his Social Security as a widow even though we were divorced. I was married to him for twenty years so I was eligible to collect his benefits when I reached age sixty. I heard somebody talking about that once and I said, "You're shitting me?" And she said, "No, you really can collect his SSI." And I called up Social Security and they said, "Sure." And I was overjoyed. I couldn't believe it: Here I was, I was only sixty and I was retired! It was like, this man gave me more in death than he could give me in life. (Edie)

CHERYL: Is your monthly income higher now than it was when you last worked?

JANET: Well, it varies because a lot of it is in the market. And I don't really go by the monthly income. When I need something, I withdraw.

CHERYL: Or sell?

JANET: I sell a mutual fund, withdraw from mutual funds. Soon after I retired, I was making more than I made when I worked. Money makes money. Once you get over the hill, the money makes the money. There were a few very good years. I'm astounded with what I have.

Bing has recently felt anxious about money and about being alone. She has just started working with a budget and although she isn't saving she is trying to spend frugally. Her VA hospital benefits are becoming more important.

Yutema (1997) found that among people sixty-five to seventy-four years old, our younger age cohort, 91 percent of them had checking accounts, 24 percent had CDs, 17 percent had savings bonds, 5 percent had other bonds, 18 percent had stocks, 14 percent had mutual funds, 35 percent had a retirement package or pension, and 37 percent had life insurance. Seventy-nine percent owned homes, 82 percent owned cars, and 26.5 percent had other real estate investments. For people older than seventy-four, our older cohort, 93 percent had checking accounts, followed by life insurance (35 percent), CDs (34 percent), stocks (21 percent), and then retirement packages (16.5 percent). Seventy-two percent owned cars, 73 percent owned homes, and 16.6 percent had other real estate investments. When someone owned stocks, stocks made up 34.3 percent of the assets of the younger group and 39.5 percent of the older group. Federal employees do not earn SS benefits—Carolyn and Pat N fall into this category—but the federal employee retirement packet is considered to be extremely good by those earning it.

Table 6.2 combines Table 6.1 for this sample of gay women with the national statistics for the general population presented in Yutema (1997) for a clearer picture of how lesbians over the age of sixty-five compare to the larger heterosexual population.

Yutema's statistics, although stated to be for the general population, are in fact female dominated since women outlive men in the United States. Given that we are comparing primarily populations of women, heterosexual versus homosexual, in Table 6.2, particularly in the older age group, there are some interesting differences here that haven't shown up elsewhere in this study, and some interesting similarities.

Among the differences is the significantly greater proportion of lesbians with pensions than is the case in the general population. The greater proportion of mothers in the general population, which often delays work or prevents them from qualifying for pensions, probably explains this difference. The significant use of stocks by lesbians for generating wealth is also interesting and probably reflects their status as sole or primary wage earners. Stocks are thought to be the baili-

TABLE 6.2. Economic Resources of Whistling Women and General U.S. Population (%)

| Resource | Older | | Younger | | 55+ |
	Whistling W	U.S.	Whistling W	U.S.	U.S.
Social Security	93		83		93.0
Pensions	66	17	55	35	32.0
Stocks	80	40	66		34.0
Rental/trusts	20	17	21	26.5	10.5
Still working	7	9	31	17	13.5
Home owners	86	73	90	79	
Veterans	20		03		3.7
Disability	0		07		0.7
Public assistance	0		07		0.3

Source: Yutema (1997)

wick of men, so that women in heterosexual couples may take less interest in purchasing stocks or in maintaining stock portfolios once their husbands die. On the other hand, the greater frequency of pensions among lesbians may mean that either their own retirement monies are invested in the stock market or that their employers offered stock market/investing classes that unemployed women or service sector employees don't have access to.

Older lesbians are also more frequently homeowners than are those in the general population, a statistic I can't explain, unless heterosexual women are more likely to be living with children or other relatives and thus don't need to maintain their own homes. Lesbians often have a history of independent living, and home ownership may be a significant symbol of that independence.

A larger proportion of lesbians sixty-five to seventy-four work later in life than do people in the general population, and this longer work life may explain the greater incidence of disability among lesbians of this age group. Conversely, it may be the type of work that lesbians engage in versus the women in Yutema's study that leads to their disabilities, although the two women in this study on disability don't appear to suffer from injuries related to work.

Many people have the stereotype that lesbian women are attracted to the military. That stereotype is upheld in the veteran statistics in Table 6.2 only for the oldest women. That statistic, however, is largely comparing heterosexual women to the homosexual women in this study and thus is strong support for the lesbian in the military in the 1930s and 1940s stereotype. Once we get to the sixty-five to seventy-five-year-old age comparisons—the post–World War II era—lesbians were in the military in the same proportion as the general population.

There is no significant difference in the reliance on Social Security or on rental/trust/royalty income between lesbians and the general population. Lesbians were just as successful in getting jobs that withheld Social Security and in working enough quarters to earn back their deductions as were men and heterosexual women. I am at a loss to explain why a greater proportion of lesbians would now be receiving public assistance. Historical analyses have long depicted women in general as being financially less savvy, less successful, and less rewarded for their efforts. Although these depictions don't hold for most of the women in this sample, they certainly seem to apply to two women, and three others who are held above the poverty level by the incomes of their partners.

Economic Status as Retirees

The average Social Security check for people sixty-five-plus is $7,972/year. Twenty-eight percent of American households headed by individuals over seventy-five years old have an annual income under $10,000. Women older than seventy-five and living alone had an average annual income in 1995 of $10,619 and were 47 percent of the households in their age group (Yutema 1997). Women who live alone have the smallest incomes of all older age cohorts. Because the majority of individuals older than sixty-five are women, women have, on average, lower annual incomes in retirement or past age 65 than do households sixty-five with retired male earners (Table 6.3).

Annual income can be estimated for thirteen of these older women based on their monthly income figures (Table 6.4). One of the other two women (fifteen total in cohort I) maintains two houses, so she is in the upper half of the distribution in Table 6.4. The lowest income

TABLE 6.3. Percent of Women-Headed Households with Income Ranges in 1995

	Age 65-74		75+	
Income	Multiple	Alone	Multiple	Alone
under 10,000	38	39	46	47
10,000-19,999	38	38	39	39
20,000-29,999	12	11	8	8
30,000-39,999	6	6	4	4
40,000-49,999	3	3	1	1
50,000-59,999	1	1	1	1
60,000-69,999	1	1	.4	.4
70,000-79,999	.2	.2	.2	.1
80,000-89,999	.1	.1	.1	.1
90,000-99,999	.3	.3	.1	0
over 100,000	.4	.4	.5	.4

Source: Yutema 1997, p.102

TABLE 6.4. Regular Annual Incomes for Individual Whistling Women

Income per Year	Older Cohort	Younger Cohort
54,000	1	1
> 48,000		3
45,000	1	
> 36,000	3	3
36,000		1
33,600	1	
25,000-36,000	3	3
24,000		1
18,000	1	
17,580	1	
16,800		1
15,000		2
12,000-24,000		4
12,000	1	2
< 12,000		1
5400	1	
3555		1
?	2	6

woman receives government assistance and shares expenses with a partner. The annual incomes of the twenty-nine younger women can also be estimated (Table 6.4). The poorest woman in this group lives alone.

In all, 5 percent of the narrators receive less than $10,000 per year and 23 percent receive $15,000 or less. The national average for women over fifty-five living in poverty (income less than $8,590 in 2001) is 13 percent. The highest regular annual income any individual woman has is $54,000.

Certainly living with someone, pooling financial resources and splitting living costs raises a woman's standard of living. Living arrangement, then, is relevant not only to happiness and longevity but also to financial health and security.

Six percent of women eighty-five-plus live alone in the United States, as is the case with one woman who is eighty-five in this project. Currently living with a lover are ten of the fifteen women (66 percent) in the oldest age cohort. Seven live in houses that they own or co-own, and most of them have lovers who are younger than they are (two exceptions). Of the five women living alone, one has just recently moved into an assisted care situation which she enjoys, one lives in a lesbian RV park in her own home, one moves biyearly between Boone and Florida, one is a sorority house mom so she lives on a college campus surrounded by considerably younger women, and one lives off and on with her son, moving almost yearly.

Of the twenty-nine women in the younger cohort, seventeen or 59 percent were coupled in 2000. Twelve were single. One of those has had four affairs since 1997. One couple rents, as does one single woman, but the rest live in homes they own. One single woman shares a house with her gay brother and has a lesbian renter. (Lesbians sixty-plus may have a much lower incidence of other family members living with them than the heterosexual population.)

When the incomes of women who live together are pooled or joined, we get the distribution seen in Table 6.5. There is little overlap in the distributions of the two categories. Single Whistling Women

TABLE 6.5. Single and Joint Household Incomes of Whistling Women

Income Bracket	Joint	Single
< 10,000		1
10,000-19,999		4
20,000-29,999		5
30,000-39,999	1	2
40,000-49,999	2	2
50,000-59,999	2	
60,000-69,999		
70,000-79,999	1	
80,000-89,999		
90,000-99,999	1	
over 100,000	1	
?	8	3

TABLE 6.6. Socioeconomic Class Now

Class	Older Cohort		Younger Cohort	
Upper/upper middle	4	27%	11	38%
Middle	7	47%	12	41%
Lower middle	3	20%	3	10%
Lower	1	7%	3	10%
Don't know	0	0%	2	1%

manage with regular annual incomes from $50,000 to less than $10,000, most of them receiving less than $30,000, while women in couples in this project have household incomes starting at $30,000 to over $100,000. Yutema (1997) reported that 4 percent of households headed by someone aged sixty-four to seventy-four had incomes over $100,000 and that the average net worth for someone in this age range was $104,100. In this case, in which the incomes of twenty-two households are known, the percentage of households earning more than $100,000 is 4.5 percent. At least three women mentioned in their interviews that their partner's income was their economic salvation.

Socioeconomic Class in Retirement

As was the case for other periods in their lives, I asked each narrator to label her socioeconomic class now (Table 6.6). Half of these women believe that they have maintained their status, be it upper, middle, or lower class, in the transition to retirement. Thirty percent, however, feel that their socioeconomic class has fallen with retirement, most often from middle class to lower-class status (n = 7) but also from upper class to middle class (n = 3). Surprisingly, 15 percent say their class status has improved in retirement, from middle class to upper class (n = 4) and from lower to middle class (n = 3). This impression is certainly helped by moving out of Chicago or New York City to Florida where real estate prices are lower, and by not having to pay state income tax any longer in New York.

So I'm okay. As a matter of fact, down here in Gulfport, I'm rich. (Sappho)

Retirement has been a lot better than I imagined. Well, financially I'm a lot more set than I ever dreamed I would be—better off now than I was when I was working—I made a lot of money selling property. (Cynthia)

I didn't feel like I had enough money for retirement until I got with Edie who is an incredible money manager. She made me a rich woman—with the same amount of money. (Jackie)

GIGI: I'm not in an emergency state. I took a part-time job when I was able to, earning $6 an hour. I'm used to earning $40-$50 an hour. Earning $6 an hour to pay for my medication and then I got really sick, that's when I ended up in the hospital.

CHERYL: So how long did you do that airport job?

GIGI: Four months, and then I got sick a year and a half ago.

CHERYL: You don't have any kind of wage labor now?

GIGI: No. I went back to work in September or October, after I got out of the hospital. I went back to work and worked for three months. I got bronchitis again in January and I had to quit. That's where I am right now. No, I have no job.

CHERYL: What socioeconomic class would you put yourself in now?

GIGI: I don't know. I owe money, I don't own the house outright. I don't own my car. I owe on everything. I'm not destitute and I've got lots of things I could sell if I had to. That's another thing that kept me going, I've been doing a lot of sewing too. I was a collector most of my life; I managed to keep some good things, art objects and stuff.

I get $711/month and $51 food stamps. The biggest disappointment with retirement is not having enough money to really do what we'd like to do. I had money in retirement which is almost all gone now. So I really don't know what we're going to do. (Mary1)

And trying to figure, you know, well, if I had the money, would I really get out of Florida or what? And if I had some money on the side, something I could count on, I don't have any real bank accounts. My mother left me money but I threw that out the window. My brother is very good to me. At Christmas and at my birthday and things like that, he comes down and he spends time with me and he brings a couple of hundred with him, which is good. And that's only started the past couple of years. But you can't depend on anything because, I mean, he's eighty already. This isn't going to go on forever. You get spoiled. (Chris)

While retirement may appear to be a era of self-determination, it isn't. Retirement is a world of uncertainty, particularly financial uncertainty. One doesn't know what health problems will occur and thus what costs will be entailed, the longevity of the partner or a supporting family member, the longevity of oneself, or even the financial health of the retirement fund or company in which one has invested.

Stock Market Activity Since Summer 2000

The 2002 collapse of Enron threatened the pension investments of several states and companies. The collapse of the NASDAQ stock market in summer 2000-2002 and the Dow Jones Industrials in 2002, and the steep decline in interest rates from 2000 through 2002, diminished interest and dividends earned and caused some companies to eliminate dividends.

It is clear that money invested in the stock market is supposed to grow as share prices increase and is supposed to generate quarterly if not monthly dividends. A large percentage of women in this project have invested in these financial instruments and were feeling quite successful with them when these interviews took place from 1997 to 2001. The NASDAQ market—primarily with technology and biotechnology stocks—began what is so far a two-year downturn in late summer of 2000. Its value was above 5,000 "points" or dollars using a formula for the share price of 100 companies, and, in October of 2002, its value was 1,300 points, a decline of over 75 percent! It should be clear from the information given in Chapter 5 and this chapter that the stock market investments by the narrators are significant.

The expected impacts of the fall in stock market values are smaller dividend checks, smaller interest payments, and the dissolution of real value of money in mutual funds and individual stocks. Of course the losses in real money from the devaluation of individual stocks and funds are realized only if the woman sells, but this money was supposed to be essentially "saved" by investing and growing, so that it could be pulled out at any time—no doubt many women have had to sell at losses in order to make some payments. I have recorded a few reactions to the market downturn in March 2001 from Gigi and Janet and a few comments in October 2002 from Jan, Sappho, and Claire.

JOYCE: We work with the stockbroker that we've been with for fifteen or sixteen years who I trust implicitly. . . . She's a vice president; they're all vice presidents, I think, at Smith Barney. We're very conservatively invested. We let them hold all proceeds and all we do is write checks on a Smith Barney money market. Anything that comes into the account goes into the money market and we write checks on it.

CHERYL: Have you always used the dividends?

JOYCE: We never see them, I just see them on a statement and then I write checks against them. . . . And so far we have not been hurt. [July 2000]

CHERYL: How has the market activity since August 2000 impacted your retirement?

GIGI: I lost $90,000 so far. [March 2001]

CHERYL: Does it mean that you have less money coming in monthly?

GIGI: It means I have no way of bringing in money. Before, if I needed a couple hundred for the doctor or if my car needed a repair or something, I could sell a stock. I can't do that now. I have nothing that's worth anything.

CHERYL: So you're not getting any dividends, any interest?

GIGI: I lost that. My IRA is down to half of what it was and that was nothing to begin with really.

CHERYL: What has the downturn in the market since August 2000 done to you?

JANET: I was shocked. [March 2001]

CHERYL: Are you having to refigure the next five years?

JANET: No, I've still done well.

I've lost 45 percent of my mutual fund . . . money stolen by rich white guys. They have more money than they or their families could ever spend and should be made to return the money. (Jan, October 26, 2002)

[My pension is invested in the market so that] in 1993 it was $2,800, it went up to $3,800/mn [in 1999], and now it is $3,000-3,100/mn so I'm okay. (Sappho, October 26, 2002)

Fortunately I invested in real estate as well as the market, with two rentals, so, no, we are not hurting. (Claire, October 26, 2002)

LESBIAN COMMUNITIES

Does being old and homosexual offer an additional communality on which to build a community consciousness? . . . My research suggests that, at least among the present sample of homosexual males over fifty, being homosexual offers little more commonalty than being old. (Lee 1987, p. 47)

We recruit women to come here through *Lesbian Connection*. (Edie)

I'm telling you, the brains down here, brains alone, first rate and then besides brains, compassion, capacity for really giving a damn. I've never encountered anything quite like it in all my wanderings, very impressive. (Diane)

While John Lee, in the study quoted previously, couldn't find any community base among older gay men, gay women have formed several vibrant communities around their common sexuality in Arizona,

Florida, Alabama, and North Carolina. More and more lesbian women are coming to Florida because of their knowledge of lesbian communities that are politically and socially active.

Gay community appears over and over again in this project to be the result of one or two women initiating opportunities for others to get together. A woman known to me only as "Lily" in Washington, DC, opened her small home to dozens of women once a week for several years and created a community there in the early 1970s. A narrator who went to those meeting then started OWLS in DC, a group that still organizes social gatherings for older lesbians. One woman in Provincetown, Christine Burton, started Golden Threads, a networking opportunity for lesbians, and from that convention which has met annually for over fifteen years has now sprung the annual Silver Threads convention in Gulfport, Florida (St. Pete Beach area), organized by one of the narrators in 2001 and 2002.

Two women started RVing Women, and then two lesbian RV parks in Apache Junction, Arizona. Their example led two other women from Cincinnati, Gina Razete and Cathy Groene, to start the Carefree residential community in Fort Myers, Florida and the Carefree Cove residential community outside of Boone, North Carolina.

Kay M was the conduit into a gay community around Bradenton, Florida, for several of the narrators who credit her with introducing them to activities and groups of women for the first time in their lives. She is also the one who sent me the letter that connected me with the Florida population in the Boone area. But Kay M was living with very little gay community in Pennsylvania and then on the east coast of Florida until her friends Amelia and Jan enticed her to move to the Sarasota area after her partner of twenty-eight years died.

Edie, an ex-lover, two other women, and Mary1 and Pat M opened a feminist bookstore in Madeira Beach in 1982 specifically to create a lesbian community. Out of this bookstore community grew Salon and the Women's Energy Bank (WEB) that offer so much to the St. Petersburg area. Individuals cause communities.

St. Petersburg/Gulfport/Tampa/Sarasota

Hundreds of lesbians, over and under age sixty, live in this area of west Florida. They have created and now sustain dozens of regular businesses, activities, and funds for women's needs.

WEB, founded in the early 1980s and centered in St. Petersburg, is a major creator of and magnet for lesbian and feminist activities. *Womyn's Words,* its monthly newsletter, is one of the main organs for announcing activities in the west-central Florida area. It is assembled by a group of volunteers and has been in publication since 1983, supported by paid advertising by women/gay-friendly businesses and services. A 2,000-volume feminist library was maintained from 1984 until 2001. The accessibility project matches women with needs with helpful women, a breast cancer fund assists women with costs of prevention, detection, and treatment of breast cancer, a women for women fund for limit emergency monies, and a female to feline fund for vet bills. WEB also distributes cell phones for calling 911, has a speakers' bureau, puts on cultural productions and films, has a Web site, offers free notary services, and organizes a monthly dinner. Monthly Salon gatherings in St. Petersburg feature special topics/discussions, along with newsletter production work.

In the area one can find meetings of a group called LOAF (lesbians over fifty and their friends), a women's chorus, Crescendo, and a gay men's chorus, and several awareness or support groups and shelters for HIV women and battered women. There is a women's bookstore in the area, Brigit's Books, monthly women's dances and potlucks, a bay fishing group, an S&M bar—Master Quest—with a women-only night, and the Clio Foundation in Gulfport, devoted to the history of women in Florida. There are groups for reading, ethics, education, and support and socializing (LIFT, 45+).

A hotline and education network, a lesbian law firm, a Dignity group (gay Catholics), a gay Christian magazine, five MCC congregations, a gay Unitarian group, a gay Jewish group, gay youth groups, a tennis league, and a chamber of commerce are also present. Chapters of PFLAG, AA, Women Outdoors, and NOW have formed as well. Until recently there were chapters of two other national organizations SOL (Slightly Older Lesbians) and OLOC.

Less-frequent lesbian/gay events include the gay pride parade in June every year, which began in 1983 with fifty people, a Take Back the Night march, and an annual lesbian convention—Silver Threads in January.

When my lover and I came here twenty years ago, there was no community. So we started the Salon. We opened a bookstore first of all so we could meet women. We knew the bookstore wouldn't last because there was no women's community here. It was called the Well of Happiness. We knew that women would know what that name meant. We sold feminist books and it was very radical to be doing that here in St. Petersburg nineteen years ago. And then we started the Salon, a place where women could meet each other. So to me, yes, community is important as a place. We don't need a building in that way, in that sense of place, but we do need to have a place where we can see each other and where we can gather. In the larger feminist community, I think that certainly Michigan Womyn's Music Festival and the National Women's Music Festival in Bloomington, and NOW meetings are community places. (Edie)

The women that opened that bookstore later closed it, but they were organizers and they organized the WEB, which is the Women's Energy Bank. Now we're talking about early 1980s. Now in 1997 we have a publication monthly, *Womyn's Words,* with a calendar of every activity. WEB is now a foundation . . . and then there's the SOL group. All your Saturdays are taken. The SOL group meets, that's slightly older lesbians, meets the first Saturday. Then OLOC, which is the old lesbians, meets the second Saturday. Of course everybody goes to everything, you understand. (Claire)

St. Petersburg has a neat gay bar here that's had its ups and downs but they have a big open area so you aren't in the smoke. (Marilyn)

Right, there's plenty to do down there. The lesbian and gay community as a whole has grown and grown; it's wonderful. They have all kinds of social events. They had a big thing over at Tampa stadium last year that had 7,000 entertainers from all over the world. I have three or four areas very close by where I am and I know lesbians in all these different cities. (Nan)

And, of course, Gulfport is just being totally taken over. It's an old-turn-of-the century town with brick streets. I bought a duplex there in February. . . . But the old casino there has one of the best dance floors—old wood dance floors—and so we have dances there. Hundreds of women there, all ages. . . . of course, there's so many gay and lesbian galleries in Gulfport. (Claire)

SAPPHO: But that's when I really discovered Gulfport and I saw all these lesbians moving around. So I came the following January of 1995.

CHERYL: How important has the lesbian community in this area been in your decision to buy and move down here?

SAPPHO: Oh, very important. I didn't want to live in a segregated community. I liked the fact that there was a large lesbian population, gay population down here, but it was in the real world.

The lesbian community, I would say they're all very supportive, close knit, I would say there's the core of the active ones that keep it going. (Dawn)

Several of the narrators live or own business property in this sleepy little town of old bungalows, doves, and sandy yards east of St. Pete

Beach, called Gulfport. In much of Gulfport the streets are lined with cars or houses with rainbow flags and window stickers. There is a lesbian bar. The Clio Foundation is located there and is where many of the interviews for this book were conducted. Monthly women's dances are held at the casino, and women's picnics in the bay front park. Over 400 women have been known to attend the Valentine's Day dance and dances at other times of year.

> Two of the women next door went up there [Maine] and did a civil ceremony. That's a really gay community over there. I love it. Next door, Glen Oaks Manor (Sarasota). (Diane)

> The social life in Sarasota was wild. There must have been 150 gay women there that we could have called at any time. (Mary Lou)

> Most of our social life is visiting our gay friends in Sarasota and Venice and having them visit us, going places together. (Carolyn)

Fort Myers

> I am putting up a two-bedroom and two-bath house in Carefree with a 12' x 21' enclosed porch. We love to spend time there; the entertainment there and the social activities there are terrific!!! (Claire)

Carefree gated community near Fort Myers is primarily a lesbian residential community on fifty acres with two lakes, begun in 1996. The developers set out 278 RV and manufactured home sites on streets named after beloved women, and added an elaborate clubhouse. This clubhouse offers rooms for billiards, parties, dances, spa, crafts, and TV and fronts on a large swimming pool. Tennis, putting green, bocci court, nature trails, and fishing are some of the outdoor activities. The owners' association brings in lesbian entertainers and sponsors interest groups, breakfasts, dinners, and other activities.

Boone, North Carolina

The community in Boone/Blowing Rock/Banner Elk tends to be as seasonal as the Floridians. Most of the Florida women (about fifty) come in the months of July and August and know each other from their lives in Florida. Several come as early as April and stay into October or early November. Monthly brunches are scheduled on either the third or fourth Sunday starting in June and continuing through September. The local university employs thirty to forty lesbian staff and faculty who attend the summer brunches in small numbers as do other gay women living in town, and who have various gatherings throughout the year in smaller groups of friends. A gay film festival is held in October at the university and an MCC congregation meets at the Unitarian house. No gay bar or particular public gathering place is located in the area.

Carefree Cove, eighteen miles out of Boone, is the second Carefree gated community to be developed. It is planned as a log cabin retreat with ninety home sites on 100 acres and sixty-five undeveloped acres and a clubhouse.

Apache Junction

Zoe Swannigan and Laverne King founded RVing Women and imagined an all-women RV park. Sometime before 1995, they purchased two existing parks across the street from each other in Apache Junction, Arizona, and moved into one of the parks. (They no longer live in Apache Junction.) There are 225 lots on eleven acres with 400 women resident in the winter and about sixty in the summer heat. The lots are 60 × 35 feet and cost between $15,000 and $20,000 with a monthly membership fee of $100 to keep up the grounds and pay the five employees. Streets in the park are named after appreciated women. The park features a clubhouse, library, pool, spa, and recycling center. A neighborhood council handles disputes between residents (Schmidt 1999). Vera lives in the other park and gave a short history of the two parks during her interview. She moved there in 1995 from Los Angeles.

The parks are today occupied by lesbians, primarily from the northwestern states although from other regions as well, and most have a history as RVers. Word of mouth is the advertising mechanism, but currently all lots are owned and developed. Vera says that within six months of the purchase of the parks, there was a waiting list to buy in. There is an elected board of directors, a clubhouse, and a park coordinator, Julie, who introduced bocci ball. When an owner decides to sell, the park board is given first opportunity to buy the lot. In the past, on Sunday nights, there was a program, Her Story, "where anybody could volunteer their story. One Sunday we did it here and one Sunday we did it there. We had pretty good rapport" (Vera).

Many of them since they got here have elected to buy park models. Some of them have done what we call "adding on." You use as much of your space as possible, as long as you leave a space to put your car. And you would be amazed what they can do with that space. It usually consists of a living room, a bedroom, another bathroom and a utility room. (Vera)

Alapine

Located on a sizable piece of land in Alabama, Alapine began selling parcels and planning an older lesbian care facility several years ago. The project has been largely the effort of several women who were associated with The Pagoda, a women's retreat in St. Augustine, Florida, that began in the 1970s. Narrator Rose has begun building a house there and will eventually leave Florida.

Electronic Communities:
Newsletter, Magazine, and Online Resources
for Lesbians Sixty-Plus

Golden Threads is a "global networking service . . . created to end isolation and loneliness among midlife and old lesbians." It was started by Christine Burton, who was the subject of a POV documentary. It has a newsletter and an annual "convergence" in Provincetown, Massachusetts, in the summer.

Old Lesbians Organizing for Change (OLOC): See details in section "retirement activities" below.

GLARP, or Gay and Lesbian Association of Retiring Persons, is modeled after AARP and is a national organization. It has a Web address, travel discounts, and is gathering information on housing and care options for older homosexuals.

Pride Senior Network: There is an online newsletter, *The Networker,* which has short informational pieces for senior lesbians (www.pridesenior.org).

ClassicDykes On Line, a Web site (www.classicdykes.com), was started in 1998 by Kristine Abroy for midlife and beyond lesbians.

Butch-Femme.com has a subgroup, Fine Wine, "for mature butches and femmes 47+." This site is for those who actively identify as butch or femme.

Coalition of Older Lesbians can be found online at <www. dykesandtheirdogs.com/CoalitionofOlderLesbian.htm>.

DragonflyCottage.com has women's stories. The founder was married for 25 years and has two children, so there is information particularly aimed at other ex-married women.

LGAIN or Lesbian and Gay Aging Issues Network is a subgroup of the American Society on Aging. The newsletter *Outword* presents professionals addressing concerns of older gays and lesbians.

SAGE, Senior Action in a Gay Environment, is a social service organization uses volunteers and staff to work in all 5 burroughs of New York City. It also maintains a drop-in center in the West Village, phone: (212) 741-2247. It is "the oldest and largest community based inter-generational social service agency dedicated to lesbian and gay community senior members. It has a task force to access the availability and quality of long term care options for lesbian and gay seniors" (www. sageusa.org).

Reddotgirls.org is a Seattle based group for lesbians 40+.

RETIREMENT ACTIVITIES

I asked each participant what she did with her time currently. The responses were varied but somewhat predictable as activities engaged in by many retirees. The most frequently specified activity was reading (n = 17). Several women belong to one or two gay book clubs, or church book clubs. Two women specifically mentioned the luxury with retirement of being able to read the newspaper in its entirety. Other women mentioned reading particular genres of literature such as mysteries or history or gay literature. One woman can't read at night because she is on oxygen.

Equally common in specification was visiting, entertaining, and socializing (n = 17). I am certain that even more women would list this as a major activity if asked. I have included those women who attend regular bridge groups, game groups, dinner groups, coffee groups, as well as those who mentioned entertaining visitors and relatives. Two women specifically mentioned biweekly visitations by children.

Exercising (n = 14) involves sessions at a club, swimming, walking, and golf.

Traveling was specified by thirteen women. Traveling in a van, camping, buying an RV or motor home, going west, going south, and going to see children were some of the motivations for travel.

Artistic activities were noted by twelve narrators. The artistic endeavors most popular are writing, stained-glass making, and painting. One woman is on her community Arts Council.

Getting on the Internet or e-mail, going to church (see discussion of religion below), and volunteering are equally popular (n = 9). Working with strays is the most popular volunteer activity (n = 4) but one person mentioned Habitat for Humanity and local museums, and two women drive carts in the local airport. Edie doesn't believe that people should volunteer free labor for businesses that make money, but she does a lot of organizing and maintenance work for grassroots groups. Sappho also stated that she doesn't want to volunteer because the agencies usually want a fixed schedule. "I would like to volunteer as the mood hit me."

Eating out was mentioned by fewer women than would acknowledge this activity if asked (n = 9). Several women eat out every midday and then eat a light dinner at home. Sappho revealed that as a working woman in New York, she envied those women who could "do" lunch. Now that she is retired, "doing" lunch is one of her pleasures.

Attending meetings of gay or women's groups occupies a lot of time. OLOC meetings were mentioned by seven women, 45+ was mentioned by seven women, five women mentioned WEB/Salon attendance, and five talked about lesbian activities in Gulfport. One or two women each mentioned several other groups. A description of OLOC, 45+, will follow shortly.

Old Lesbians Organizing for Change and the Old Lesbians Organizing Committee started in 1987.

There was a woman [Barbara MacDonald] who wrote a book called *Look Me in the Eye* with her partner whose name was Cynthia Rich. She's the sister to Adrienne Rich. And when that woman wrote her book, that started the movement of old lesbians in a sense; it was a door opener. And in 1987 they had what they called a celebration of old lesbians and it was in southern California on the campus of [California State University at] Domingus Hills. (Vera)

OLOC is a national organization for lesbians sixty years and older with a steering committee of eight women. Its purposes are to confront ageism, explore and name the oppression, share individual stories, educate, and become a force in the women's movement and the lesbian community (www. oloc.org). In addition to its Web site, there is a newsletter, the *OLOC Reporter*, with editorials on various topics and a column on health issues.

Barbara, in many ways, objected to young women doing their thesis or their PhDs or whatever and interviewing old women and the old women never, ever saw these theses. They never knew what the final product was. And she was really adamant about that. OLOC embraced that and adhered to it over the years. Barbara died earlier this year and I have been doing everything I can to change that attitude. Because my attitude is, if we don't share with the young women that are coming behind us, they don't have a history. (Vera)

[OLOC] meets in St. Petersburg. I don't go anymore. I was one of the first ones that started it. It first started in Florida, on the east coast one year and then the west coast the next year. They could see right away that the women were older and they didn't want to travel all the way across the state. So they finally decided that they would have two groups. I went here for the first couple of years and then I just got bored with it. They weren't having any kind of programs that I enjoyed. In St. Petersburg, a couple of the members were younger and somebody decided that they couldn't come anymore, if you were under the age of sixty. I really was very much disturbed about that. So a group of the under sixty started something, [LIFT] but I've never been. (Kay M)

As a lesbian my age, sixty-six, who came out later and came out with these younger dykes, women, Michigan, and music and all that, that's a whole different head set than women my age that toughed it out in the 1950s. And they didn't want to have anything political. The point of OLOC is: I'm proud I'm old; I don't need your help; I don't want sociologists defining who I am. It's run by a core group in Houston and Arizona, some really strong outstanding women; some are from Michigan. And they do a newsletter and they have national conferences. But although we took that name of OLOC, the group never really wanted to be out there that much. (Marilyn)

We haven't had an OLOC chapter here for at least three years—the women didn't want to be political; they changed their name to LIFT (Lesbians in Friendship Together) and they do a lot of social activities. (Jackie)

I was in charge of [45+] for several years. It's a group that meets once a month, the second Saturday of the month. It's getting more and more difficult to keep the younger people. They don't want to take the responsibility of getting the programs, putting up the tables and chairs and cleaning up when we have· a dance twice a year. So I've been involved with that ever since I've been here. (Kay M)

Attending theater or museums and being volunteer ushers is a favorite pastime of at least seven women. One woman was president of her city's symphony board for several years.

CHERYL: What did you imagine retirement would be like?

CAM: Different. I've had an awful hard time managing my time.

CHERYL: You mean, like it's one o'clock before you realize it and the day's half gone?

CAM: Yes. I paint and I'm good at crafts. I could use my time more wisely.

CHERYL: So you imagined that you would be painting a lot in your retirement?

CAM: Yes. And I thought I would take care of my home, and we have someone come in who doesn't do the job that I could do. And yet, I don't want to do it. And do you know what, I feel guilty about all these things. But, by damn, I've been there, done that. I just feel that in this stage in my life, I'm due to just lay back. But I'm disappointed in myself. And too, I don't have the energy that I had when I was thinking about retirement.

I'm so busy. It's a good thing I'm not working 'cause I couldn't squeeze it in. The OLOC group that we're with is very social. We're having a New Year's Eve dance, I'm involved in decorating that tonight. I'll buy the decorations and all this kind of stuff, plus one of the gals is a New Year's Eve baby and we're having dinner for her at my house, a birthday dinner before we go down. Of course this is the holidays, so it's probably a little worse. But there's something going on every weekend and if there isn't, then Nancy and I make something. Nancy is who I'm with now. And we just make something. And I've got a whole list of things to do and sometimes we'll just end up going to the movies and going out for dinner. We travel a lot. We spent two weeks in Albuquerque, New Mexico, for the balloon festival in October. We spent a week in upper Michigan; we spent a week in Canada last summer. We spent a week in London—or a week and a half, it was. There was a cruise to Mexico. (Dorothy)

CHERYL: How many of these women have two communities, like you come up here for part of the year? How many of these women actually do that?

CLAIRE: Not too many. In the first place, many of these women are still working or they take a vacation here. Although one of the women in the group has a place on Cape Cod she goes to. The Tampa Bay area gets a lot of easterners as opposed to Sarasota which gets more midwestern. Iowa moves to Sarasota. A lot of people from Maine move to the Tampa Bay area. The Tampa Bay area is really quite large. It includes so many communities. It's two counties, Hillsborough and Pinellas. For some reason, we get a lot of people from New England, Pennsylvania, New Jersey, New York, Newfoundland, Nova Scotia, Labrador. It always interested me that people who live on an island, vacation on an island. You'd think they'd go to the mountains or something. . . .

CHERYL: Do you sort of lump these two organizations together, the National Gay and Lesbian Task Force and the Human Rights Campaign? I don't yet understand their differences but I know they are very different.

CLAIRE: I'll tell you, I don't spend enough time on it to know because I concentrate my time and energies on those things I think have a chance to work. And OLOC (Old Lesbians Organized for Change), the march on Washington, OLOC led the parade. They were in lavender and white with banners.

CHERYL: Is this a national organization?

CLAIRE: Oh yes. We have the largest chapter in the country in St. Petersburg. But all of our activities are publicized in *Womyn's Words*. In other words, the Women's Energy Bank is sort of the overarching organization and there is a board. It is sort of the sorting house, clearing house, anyone can go and be involved.

Religion

I pray for a Catholic lover but God keeps sending me health insurance. (Dorothy)

Most of the United States would probably characterize lesbians as steeped in sin and thus areligious and even irreligious. Albro and Tully (1979) found that the majority of the gay women in their report disavowed any religious affiliation, but these women were on average much younger than the Whistling Women. Instead, for older lesbians, usually raised as children in a state-recognized faith, religion is important to them and an activity of theirs in retirement.

The Metropolitan Community Church (MCC) is the most popular religious organization attended by these narrators, probably because of the presence of two congregations in the west Florida area. The MCC was founded in 1968 in Los Angeles by Reverend Troy Perry, who had been defrocked by the Pentecostal Church for his homosexuality. Vera and Mary1 were both members of that congregation, although several decades apart, and both women know him personally.

Currently, more than 300 MCCs are found throughout the world. Over the past thirty years, more than 200 MCC congregations have been targets of arson and firebombing, and many more congregations have been victims of vandalism and desecration. Thirty-two parishioners were killed in a 1973 New Orleans fire (Fedukovich 2002). There are five congregations in the Tampa Bay area, in St. Petersburg,

Tampa, Sarasota, and Venice, with a woman pastor. The Boone MCC
began in 1993 and was founded by its current pastor, Cindy Long.
The congregation meets Sunday evenings in the Unitarian House. The
only narrator to have attended the Boone congregation is Roberta. In
2002, this congregation broke from the MCC.

MARY1: Yeah. Well the first time we went to the MCC here, the pastor was absolutely wonderful. As a matter of fact, he's retired in California and
Tijuana now and we're still in constant contact with him. I've always considered him my pastor. He was wonderful. And everyone that's come after
him has not been churchy. I don't know how to explain it, but they're just
out for the money.

CHERYL: No respect for the ritual?

MARY1: No. I belonged to MCC in Los Angeles when it first started and I was
a member of the church that burned down in Los Angeles. I even had a
Holy Union in that church. So I was MCC in the very beginning and loved
Troy Perry, the founder. So usually when he comes down to one of the
churches, we go to see him.

So taking communion at MCC is like, well, that's good just in case. That's
how your parents taught you to do, just a touching-all-bases kind of thing.
(Marilyn)

GIGI: Methodist by upbringing. And now I'm MCC. Religion has always been
important.

CHERYL: Do you go weekly?

GIGI: Yes, because it's kind of like a mainframe for me right now. . . . It's important because it's a good support system for me, emotionally and physically and socially.

CHERYL: How did you find the MCC?

GIGI: I was very active in it up in Detroit. And that was twenty-some years
ago. That's how I found MCC with my gay community in the Detroit area.

CHRIS: I haven't been [to MCC] in months. But when I go there, I get my shirt
and tie on and jacket, dress up, I'm comfortable. Around gay boys, I'm
comfortable if I'm dressed as a man.

CHERYL: And you mentioned mass, do you also go to mass sometimes?

CHRIS: I used to go to mass all the time. Now I sit home and watch it on television.

CHERYL: Were you going to MCC and mass at the same time?

CHRIS: Yeah, I'd go to mass on Saturday night and I would go to MCC on
Sunday morning.

CHERYL: Now why don't you go to MCC?

CHRIS: Well, for a while there, even with the luncheons, I was trying to avoid
this person I knew. You can't get rid of her and I just didn't want to get en-

tangled. Even down here I'd go to church, she'd happen to be in the neighborhood or something. But we're in the same group so what can I say? You know, you're going to meet her. . . . I stopped the luncheons, then I stopped the services, but I kept up the dances.

And I started going to Metropolitan Community Church which was founded by Troy Perry. And I met Troy and his mom and several others and they were just so warm and so welcoming and so kind to me. So I'd get invited to picnics and dances and I got to meet a lot of people. . . . I started going there in 1971 or 1972. They had two choirs. And I just loved to go and hear them sing. They used to do concerts a couple of times a year and wherever they did it, I would always go. I love the music, but I can't manage to get a grip on the rest of it. . . . When I got my first lesbian partner in 1975, we had a Holy Union at MCC. What I got was that they tried to pick a little bit of every possible denomination and incorporate it into their services. And of course most of it went right over my head. (Vera)

I do go down to the MCC in Venice probably once every three weeks. We have one just a mile away, an MCC church, but I like Sherry, the minister, a lot, so I go down to her church in Venice. (Kay M)

Patricia and Gigi go to MCC every Sunday. Sandy was "heavy into MCC" but has now gone back to the Catholic Church. Mary2 is not comfortable at the MCC church because there is hand holding and embracing when they go to communion. Mary Lou thinks the MCC is too evangelical, as do Ruth and Judy. Roberta enjoyed attending the Boone MCC but finds it hard to get out now.

The MCC church has offered the gay or lesbian person not only a friendly environment within which to explore and express religious thoughts but also a catalyst in gay community formation and in activism. It is the setting for dozens of gay marriages that many of these women have attended, as well as the other social events mentioned by Chris.

Then I went to the Metropolitan Community Church one day and I met Kay. She knew all these people here. So then it was like, my God, is there anyone around here who is *not* gay for God's sake? (Gloria)

The MCC church in St. Petersburg is huge. It's larger, I think, than the Catholic cathedral—the building itself. It was a theater. They have concerts there. We have been to the coffee house which is on Saturday night for women; it's women only. It's widely attended. (Claire)

Well let me tell you what I did. When I got involved with MCC, I became an immediate lesbian activist. I joined everything that was out there. (Vera)

Pat M started out in an MCC church but she and small group of others grew disillusioned with that particular congregation and left to found a new church, in which she became ordained.

Catholicism was named as the religion of choice now by five women. Jan, a lifelong Catholic, is one of the few narrators who said she goes to church every Sunday.

CHERYL: Have you stayed in the [Catholic] church?

JAN: I have. I think people question that in me, but I only answer to me and my thoughts about that.

CHERYL: Have you sought out any particularly gay congregation?

JAN: I have a couple of times. I've gone to Dignity a number of times and didn't find any comfort from the group at all. I find more comfort by myself in my own church.

CHERYL: And would you say that your sexuality is known in the congregation?

JAN: I don't believe it is and I would think that they would probably reject me if they knew. I feel pretty certain of that.

CHERYL: How often do you go to church now?

JAN: I go to church every Sunday, holidays, holy days.

Past lives and reincarnation and well as psychics were referred to by several women (n = 4). Barbara believes her sons were brothers in another time, and has several stories demonstrating reincarnation. Kay M has several past lives Web sites bookmarked. Dawn has done a past life regression. A psychic has brought Amelia back to God.

I am religious now. I went to the MCC every Sunday but about two years ago I had a problem with God and stopped going. Of course it wasn't God; it was me. Then recently a friend gave me book by Sylvia Browne. She's a psychic. It's called *Life on the Other Side.* I have a whole new feeling about God now. I'm not afraid of death. In fact, I want to die so that I can go see this place. She better not be lying about this. Now I go to MCC about every other week, to see my friends, not to [worship their way].

I believe in reincarnation now. The Council decides. And there is all this research and learning to do—maybe I'll choose to come back or maybe I'll just stay there and learn. I want to see how I've done with this life. (Amelia)

KAY M: Many years ago I read a book about Edgar Cayce and it just struck me as being correct. I suppose that was what initiated my interest in medium/occult and the psychic and UFOs. I believe strongly in UFOs, that there is something there. I believe in ghosts. There was a woman, a friend of mine in Pennsylvania who had a ghost in her house. I stayed a couple of weekends hoping to see it myself but I never did. She knew who this woman ghost was who had drowned in a pond on the property. She did some research and found that out. [All of these research tools have] developed within, say, thirty years. Elizabeth Hoffman has written several books on the psychic and we were good friends. Knowing her was really what started me believing about that sort of thing. I met this Unity minister many years ago. I went to church because I liked her. But I found that the Unity message was very helpful. It's a very upbeat message that can make you believe you can do anything.

CHERYL: Have you ever been to a drumming circle or to a coven?

KAY M: No. I'm not into Wicca or that sort of thing. I have nothing against it, but it doesn't interest me at all.

And I've done past life regression. So I know that I've been a male in other lives. And I've been a woman in other lives. (Dawn)

Other groups mentioned were Louise Hay and the Science of Mind beliefs (n = 2), and the Unity Church (n = 4). Gloria is quite involved in the Unity Church and Pat M is a minister in this church. Liz reads scripture daily but then said she could do without religion.

I know there're a couple of gay synagogues, two of them on the west coast of Florida. I went to one and people were really strange. And the other one I haven't been to because I just haven't felt like going. I was curious. I started a Jewish group once of homosexuals. The gays and the lesbians, there were ten of us and we had ten different answers as to what Judaism was, what our Jewishness meant to us. So when you're with a Jewish group, there's no steady answer. (Nan)

Several women said they were spiritual, but didn't care for mainstream religions. Diane went to the MCC, but it and others do nothing for her. She says she is "profoundly religious but in an offbeat way." Janet also said her personal religious beliefs were very important to her and that she attended the Catholic Church with her lover. Two women called themselves witches or referred to coven meetings. Marilyn has been a member of a coven and circles and is a user of astrology but goes to MCC "just in case." One woman each said she was Methodist, Presbyterian, and into Eastern religion.

A few other women had things to say about religion in their lives.

Now my grandfather, the minister, was very supportive of me. He knew my lifestyle for some reason and he said, "Just don't hurt other people. Live a good life." (Gigi)

I was brought up believing in Jesus. While I was in college, I taught Bible school in the summer. I believe in God, you know. But I believe a good Christian person is a person that's good, honest, moral. . . . I've never had that problem [with religious beliefs and being lesbian]. I believe God loves me whether I'm gay or straight. I firmly believe that, because it isn't a choice that you have. (Jan)

And for a long time I believed the Bible literally, that this was an abomination, you're going to hell. I don't know that I ever thought that much about it, other than the fact that, you know, I was okay with it. Of course, now you come down to the Catholic background and is it a sin? Is it a sin you must confess? And all I ever said was I don't think it's wrong and I don't think if it's not wrong, it ain't a sin. Of course, maybe that's why I'm a Protestant minister today. (Pat M)

CHERYL: So there wasn't a biblical problem with the relationship?

CAM: No, not from me. I don't know if Susan ever felt that or not because she was the finest Christian I have known.

CHERYL: We haven't talked about religion. Is religion important to either one of you?

RUTH: Not in the sense of organized religion. Neither one of us are active in religious organizations.

CHERYL: Have you tried MCC?

RUTH: No. We've not gone to the church. We've gone to some activities that have been sponsored by the church.

JUDY: MCC, I think it would be a problem for me because of the fact that I think it's more evangelical in nature.

RUTH: I don't think either one of us could stand that. If we went to a church, we'd be more likely to go to the Unitarian church as being at an intellectual level that we would find refreshing.

CHERYL: Are you all into goddesses?

RUTH: No.

CHERYL: Prior lives?

RUTH: No.

Out of respect for friends, I attend weddings and various other services at gay churches and synagogues as well as mainstream houses of worship, but organized religion turns me off! (Jackie)

I've been to all kinds of religions. I've been to Unitarian, I've done the Pentecostal thing; I've done Jehovah's Witnesses for years; I've done Presbyterian. I really don't know where I stand right now, I don't go to church. I do pray. (Dawn)

DIANE: But I'm deeply, profoundly religious in an offbeat way. I don't like church. I like church for the music; I go to every church in town because of the music. And if the music isn't good, I don't go back.

CHERYL: So religion is very important to you today?

DIANE: Yeah.

CHERYL: But not a church, not in a building?

DIANE: Not in the traditional way. I've also been looking a little bit, peeking into American Buddhism. It's like the story, the blind man and the elephant. You know that story. We ain't got a hold of the whole elephant, none of the religions here have got it, but there's a glimmering. I hope there won't be any survival of the ego after death.

In fact, in a nationwide survey of people fifty-five and older, Yutema (1997) found that 42 percent of people sixty-plus attend religious services at least weekly. Three percent said they don't believe in God, contrasted with 60 percent who said they prayed daily (Yutema 1997). Among the narrators, eighteen women said that religion has no place in their lives, one said she was agnostic, and one said she was an atheist. It appears that older lesbians are a little less religious than the general population, given that 46 percent do not have any interest in religion and 4.5 percent don't believe in God, but they also are more religious than the other studies of lesbians found and probably more religious than most churchgoers would assume.

Computers/Internet

I asked most of the narrators if they had a computer. WebTV often satisfied their computer needs, rendering an actual computer unnecessary. Thirty-four women have e-mail accounts and seem to use them daily. Those accounts greatly aided this research project. Three women said that they had been working with computers at work prior to retirement, and three other women sent their first e-mail in the three years since they were interviewed (two of them in the older age cohort). Several women have more than one computer. Mary Lou got her first computer in 1988 to research the stock market. Jackie said she's addicted to the Internet. Janet says her life is on it. Barbara has three computers at home and one at another house. Joanna has two laptops and WebTV.

GIGI: I do everything on the computer. The computer kept me sane.

CHERYL: How long have you been computer savvy?

GIGI: Well, my labs were all computerized. I was one of the first. Fifteen years I would say.

CHERYL: What kinds of places are bookmarked or are your favorites on your computer?

GIGI: Well, I must have 300.

CHERYL: They fall into what kind of categories?

GIGI: Financial. I have things for retail, the weather. I have what are called My Sites which are beautiful both sound and visually. I collect angels.

CHERYL: Are you on eBay then?

GIGI: No, not yet I haven't been. I'm thinking of putting a couple things on eBay to sell. I have many, many interests. I have a thirteen meg hard drive there which is nothing but Favorites. Everything from mountain climbing to butterflies. I have so many varied interests; I just love it.

I love my computer. (Pauline)

More informants used the computer to e-mail than to search the Internet. One woman met a lover online, and others search for medical information, browse Amazon.com and Borders Books, send greeting cards, play games, visit museums, and look at art. Several women research stocks and do online trading, investigate vacation rentals, pass family photos and news through a family Web page, look for lost friends, visit cooking sites, get news on WNBA, baseball, and ice skating, and look into NPR or CNN programming information.

Eight women have no computer or WebTV and have no desire to get into this technology. Three of these women are in the oldest age group (20 percent) and five are younger (17 percent). Complaints aired about the computer and Internet among those who do use them were eyestrain, inefficient searches, viruses, arthritic hands, and the time the computer demands or sucks out of a day.

I hate machines. I call the broker. I will use a friend's Internet but I'm not going to sit there playing with it myself. I'm a people person. (Mitch)

I still can't get used to a dishwasher. (Cynthia)

I made it a point to get a computer but it's hard. But I want to keep up with it as long as I can. (Marilyn)

HEALTH

Assessing health among the general population of women, Yutema reported that in 1995, for women age sixty-five to sixty-nine, 64.2 percent have no limitations, 35.8 percent have limitations, and 26.8 percent have major limitations. For women seventy-plus, our older age cohort, 59.5 percent had no limitations, 40.5 percent had some limits, and 2.9 percent had major limits. There is not a substantial population of invalids until eighty-five-plus, when 35 percent have difficulties (Yutema 1997). The oldest woman in this project, aged eighty-five, is wheelchair bound and tethered to oxygen.

Forty percent of the narrators in the oldest age cohort reported no medical problems. Among the other women, one has knee problems and lupus, one has high cholesterol, rheumatoid arthritis, and glaucoma, one has had a heart attack and has emphysema, one an aneurysm, one has arthritis, two have knee problems, and one has had breast cancer.

Fifty-five percent of the younger women reported no medical problems, but the medical problems in this group are more severe than those of the older women. Lung problems were reported by three women, two of whom were on oxygen during the interview period, three reported back problems, and three have hearing problems. Two women each have had polio, breast cancer, knee problems, and arthritis. One woman each mentioned high blood pressure, multiple heart attacks, heart problems, angioplasty, diabetes, and multiple sclerosis (MS).

Truly bad health is being experienced by the oldest woman in the older group—she is wheelchair bound—and three women in the younger group, or 6.6 percent and 10 percent respectively. Thus, the number of lesbians with poor health seems to be in line with the health problems and needs of the general population of older women.

These health problems have consequences beyond pain and medication costs. Hearing problems led one to seek out smaller groups in order to follow the conversation and participate in it. The arthritis takes its toll on sexual activity and makes computer use uncomfortable or impossible. Polio limits vacation plans and the duration of shopping trips. Oxygen delivery through a mask prevents reading in bed and, because of cost, severely curtails airplane travel.

DIANE: Well, I can't believe what a wreck I am because it just isn't my vision of myself. But I've got a whole alphabet of disorders, would you like to hear them? COPD, IVD, HCVD, GDA, I guess that's it. All systems are down, except my urinary system seems to be okay.

CHERYL: Would you say your health is poor?

DIANE: I guess I would be classified as poor, but I don't feel real poor yet. A little more of this and I'll begin to whimper and snivel a little, but not quite yet.

CHERYL: You've gotten a lot more mobility in your hands since I came.

DIANE: Yeah. I can do this now. When you came, I could hardly do this. Torn rotator cuffs are a bitch; it's the biggest pain I've ever had in my life, more than having babies, definitely, and more than pleurisy. It's big time. My friend drove me home the other night from the opera. I'm shrugging out of my glorious satin brocade opera cloak and I tear the damn thing again. I screamed, I couldn't believe my own voice, it was the worst scream I've ever heard in my life. My friend is about to faint and I can't stop screaming, poor lady. I thought, geez, I'm going to have to call 911 for her. This has just been a bad couple of weeks. But I've had a bad shoulder forever. . . . Now my head and neck and shoulders are out of commission. And the bottom half—as you can see—doesn't work well. And the obesity adds to it.

GIGI: Then I got sick for four years. They diagnosed me with MS. So I wasn't able to work for four years. I lost everything. I didn't know that you can apply for Social Security and that you can apply for food stamps 'cause my family never did that. I never knew anybody that did that. And Cynthia was working and I had enough money put away and the building was paying for itself. But I did, I lost everything, every penny I had. It's a good thing I had the apartment building we were living in or I wouldn't have had any housing.

CHERYL: Did you lose it or did you spend it?

GIGI: I paid doctor bills with it.

CHERYL: What about health insurance?

GIGI: Well I even lost that after a year. I had a tiny, tiny IRA which I couldn't touch. I had no income coming in whatsoever. And the cash I had had, I bought the business with. I ended up supporting the business, so I'm void of cash again. So my mother's still alive and I had a little cash reserve but that was it. But then when my doctor's bills started—I'm horrendous up into doctor bills again because I can't pay them. The disability hadn't kicked in yet. Then I filed for disability and that was six months. And then it's another six months before I got Medicare. I didn't have any health insurance. I didn't have anything. I couldn't buy medicine and I couldn't get the proper care because I just didn't have the money. So I had to wait until the disability came in. Then I was getting Social Security.

CHERYL: How were you able to care for your mother and be disabled?

GIGI: I wasn't entirely disabled then. I was also taking care of two other women, going for a day or two to help them out. I hurt my back. I thought that's how I did it. I was in a wheelchair part of the time. I used a walker. I use a cane. My mother never saw me do that. I never allowed her to see that. I'd take the wheelchair up to her room at the hospital and then walk in. I didn't take care of her physically—I couldn't. I had help here. We had a nurse every other day. My mother was taking care of me.

My lungs are gone. I was very, very ill. Everything went. I had a total shutdown. My lungs, I had a heart attack while I was in a coma, I woke up with diabetes. When I woke up, I was paralyzed. I was in the hospital and nursing home for two months. I lost my memory. I was having an affair. I had just broken off one affair and the other nurse came down.

I used to golf three times a week. I used to bowl two and three nights a week. I can't even swing a golf club now the pain is so bad. I can't walk around the pool without being out of breath. It is poor, [my health]. I take sixteen pills a day.

PLANS FOR SELF, PARTNERS, AND FAMILIES

Family members provide the bulk of care to elderly members. Fortunately, 40 percent of lesbian women over age sixty have children found the study by the National Gay and Lesbian Task Force (Outing Age 2000) and 45 percent of women sixty-five and older have at least three children reported Yutema (1997). Sixteen percent of those women in Yutema's study were childless. Forty-five percent of the Whistling Women have children. But even having children doesn't assure one of care by familiar persons or for free in even a short-term health crisis. Sometimes the children have rejected the mother because of her homosexuality, they live too far away to be of assistance, they aren't inclined to offer help, or they are financially worse off than Mom is.

See, since my children have this negative feeling, I don't know how much help I would get from them. I suspect not very much. I've already seen how it's been in the past. I had a mastectomy too and some other things since I've been here and they have not helped me. I had to have a dressing changed on my back and here I have two nurses [meaning children] and it's all I could do to get them to do it. It had to be done every other day before I went back to the doctor and I really had to talk them into it. One did it one time and one did it another time. (Sandy)

I don't depend on [my two sons]. I'm sure they would be available, but I prepare so I don't have to depend upon them. (Barbara)

In 1995 the average cost of nursing home care was $126 day or $46,000 per year. Medicare covers some short stays for the first 100 days after a surgery, but allows nothing for long-term nursing home care. Medicaid is used for long-term care but has a high copayment rate and has strict income and asset rules that must be met before it will pay anything. One of the frequently mentioned differences between married couples and gay couples is that Medicaid will allow a spouse to keep a home when the incapacitated spouse enters a nursing home, but gay couples have to choose between their home or health care for the sick partner (see Sheri's testimonial in following text) (www.pridesenior.org/Networker/Winter _2002/3Ms.asp).

Eight women have purchased long-term care insurance policies (four in each age cohort), and one from the oldest group has nursing home insurance. At least two women, both from the oldest age group, mentioned that they pay for optional health insurance.

In-home health care is an increasingly popular option for women whose health is fading. Women are 72.5 percent of the caregivers and most of them are age thirty-five to forty-nine (39.4 percent), fifty to sixty-four (26 percent), and over 64 (12.4 percent) (Yutema 1997). Several of the narrators have been involved in this industry either formally with home health care companies or informally by personally hiring on to help an elderly neighbor or distant relative. For women in couples, the other woman is usually considered to be the one who will provide home health care. One couple in this project has purchased adjacent condos and a long-term care policy that will pay someone not living with you to come into your home and care for you. In this manner the couple will be able to care for the sick partner and financially reimburse the caring partner. We hear from the oldest women first:

It's a regular insurance policy. You pay a premium, but it has advantages. I mean, in other words, if there are several bodily functions that I am not able to perform, then by this policy, I can hire someone to come in and perform them for me. I do not have to go to some care organization. This would be an individual. In-home care. [The premiums] depend upon your age. It increases with age. I paid more than my partner did because I'm older. But it's not cheap.

This is our first year [paying the premium]. We just met Debra. She and one of her associates came and gave a presentation at an OLOC meeting. This is where networking is so essential. . . . She sold us a policy, we introduced her to friends, and she came and made a presentation. And because we do not live together, I can hire [my partner] to take care of me and vice versa. But you can hire a woman from our community. And who would know about this kind of a policy except an insurance person with our orientation? (Claire)

CHERYL: Your health insurance?

DIANE: Inadequate.

CHERYL: Is it Medicare?

DIANE: Yeah. I have a supplementary thing from the New York State Retirees System which is very stingy.

CHERYL: They pay for it?

DIANE: Yes. The good thing about it, it has a pharmacy thing. But they say no to virtually everything else. They won't even pay for my oxygen.

CHERYL: Extended care or long-term care policy?

DIANE: No. The nest egg will go for that. Poor children aren't going to get a dime. It's going to be all used up because I think I'm going to live to be ninety. I think I will. My father did; maybe I will. And so far, it's doable [She's eighty-five].

GLORIA: I don't plan to be incapacitated. I don't foresee anything like that happening. I still believe that what you see is what you get. And I don't see that in the future. I see myself to be able to take care of myself always.

CHERYL: So are you saying that you would commit suicide?

GLORIA: Oh no, I'm not saying that. I really do not expect to get any catastrophic illness. I hate to even put that suggestion out there though is what I'm saying. The universe hears everything you say and if you say it, you're likely to get it. So I'd really rather not talk about that. . . . I don't know [if I] would want to live in the house alone. So it might be a smaller facility, retirement type place where there would be activities around.

They don't let anybody starve out in the street. If I didn't have a nickel and I had to go to a nursing home, I could go to one. I'd be taken care of. A lot of women said, "Oh, my children will take care of me." I see so much of that in Florida. The husband dies and the women move closer to their children so they can be taken care of. I don't have anybody that's going to take care of me, so I have a policy—a nursing home policy—in case I need it. And I want to be cremated. (Kay M)

The only thing that I've ever said to anybody is that when the times comes for the nursing home or whatever, long before that my name will be off my money. Somebody else's name will be on it and qualify me for Medicaid right away. And save whatever I've got to spend on me. A country as rich as this that can't afford to take care of its elderly people, there's something wrong somewhere. Other than that, I really haven't thought about it. I just assume that when it comes, you do what you have to do. I could get in and out of my house in a wheelchair 'cause there's no stairs. There's no up and down inside the house. (Dorothy)

Well, I certainly wouldn't want to be a burden on Jan. So I don't know. You can only hope that you only know for a few days and it goes quick. (Mary2)

In the present, [my partner] would be my biggest resource because I trust her implicitly and because she's a nurse and because she and I really have spent a tremendous amount of time communicating with each other about what's important to us, what we want and what we need. She's totally respectful of my nontraditional use of health care and I know what she wants. So I couldn't ask for anybody better at this point. What will happen a little bit down the road, I don't know. You might be interested to know that two years ago we organized an "Exit Group." It consists of seven women: two lesbian couples, one single lesbian, and two single heterosexual women all over sixty who meet regularly to discuss end of life issues, such as living wills, durable power of attorney, suicide, etc. The focus is on having women who know our wishes so that we and our caregivers (partners, children, friends, whoever) will have support for the kind of dying process that we want. (Jackie)

Yeah, there would be [a place for suicide] if I was terminally ill and suffering. I think it's a viable alternative to suffering. The people who were good to my parents, I'd give them extra money on the side. It's pathetic in a nursing home and a retirement home. It's terrible. I'm a homing pigeon; I like houses. I love to keep them nice. (Mary Lou)

I guess if I got sick now, it would be in-home [care]. I haven't given it much thought. I know that insurance-wise I'm taken care of. And then when those other choices happen, I'll make those choices as they happen. I wish there were more facilities for lesbians. It would be really neat to have like kind with you. That's an interesting question. (Nan)

All narrators have Medicare, Medicaid, or a company insurance plan. In the U.S. population at large, 1 percent of people over sixty-four are without insurance, 97 percent of elderly are covered by Medicare, and 31 percent have some group health plan (Yutema 1997). Some of the Whistling Women have purchased long-term care insurance, but very few have cancer insurance or an optional additional health insurance. One woman mentioned that the health insurance from her retirement package was far better than Medicare but that it had been superseded by Medicare when she turned sixty-five. Two women with health problems indicated that they had tried to purchase long-term health care insurance but were rejected. Three narrators have veterans' benefits and VA hospital privileges. Most of the couples have done the paperwork required to give their partners power of attorney for health decisions, have wills, and have trusts. A small proportion of single women have taken these steps.

In several situations, lesbians have networked to care for a sick member of the community. It is often this type of arrangement that the helping women imagine for themselves, but in order for it to be a reality, the community has to stay together and have several long-lived members.

The one girl I was seeing came down as soon as she found out I was in ICU. They had a whole group set up on the computer. I used to be with a lot of groups. My sister knew a lot of my friends, so they set up a thing. They could get in touch every day. And so Vicky came down and also my friend from New Jersey and they were here for a couple of weeks. (Gigi)

SHERI: Dot wanted everything that was right to protect me, I know she did. Because when she signed off as trustee of her estate, she was well on the way and the lawyer said it would be good if you could get her to sign off because then there's no question. Sometimes if a person becomes incompetent, then it has to go through a court and they appoint a guardian. The lawyer said, "You want to avoid that, you don't want that to happen. If you can get Dot to sign off, then you're the trustee and you don't have to worry about that anymore." 'Cause she knows I'm a worrier. It took me days and days and days of explaining to Dot, because she has a nephew who might contest if he knew what was going on. He'd be right down there to get control. If he knew that she was incompetent, he'd be right there to grab control. The lawyer knew this. So it took me several days of explaining to Dot, if you will sign off, sign this paper and make me your trustee, then Gary cannot come in here and claim anything and he cannot take charge. I said, "Do you want me to be in charge or do you want Gary to be in charge?" "Well, I want you to be in charge." I said, "Well, then please sign this." So one day she said, "Yes, I will sign anything." She was having a good day and she seemed to understand. So I called the attorney's office and we went down and she signed it. Since she's been in the assisted living place, I've had to remortgage the house to get the money to pay for her keep. The duplexes maintain just about, but there are always things that come up that take more money than you expect.

CHERYL: So in dealing with Dot's illness, you've always had the piece of paper that said, This is why I can be in the room?

SHERI: Oh, absolutely. And everybody seems to understand that too. Of course I always had the paperwork. But I do that for another person, too, who's in assisted living. And she's no particular friend, except that I guess I'm the only friend she's really got when it comes right down to it. She had a stroke in October 1995 and she called. Of course Dot was home, and Dot and I went right down there and took her to the hospital. As soon as she said her hand was numb, I knew she'd had a stroke. So we took her to the hospital and she was there about five days. And then everybody pitched in, bringing food and checking on her every day and this and that, but little by little they all drifted away. And the only ones that were left were Dot and me.

CHERYL: So you have a legal arrangement with her now?

SHERI: I have a legal arrangement. I found out that she could afford to buy into assisted living on a lifetime contract. And I took her up there and showed her around the place and talked with the people and she agreed and she bought into one of the efficiency places where you just have one room and a little kitchenette and a Murphy bed that comes down and up.

CHERYL: Can she lower the bed?

SHERI: Well, she could at that time. She'd just push a button. And she lived there until just last year, the spring of 2000. She began falling a lot and I said to them, "I think she's got to be moved to assisted living." And they moved her that very day. But in the meantime, as soon as she had her stroke and got settled, she went to her attorney. I took her but she went in and she made out a new will and she did the power of attorney and a health surrogate and all that stuff. She had to go and have a cancerous uterus removed a couple of years ago. I just carried a folder with all that stuff in it and said to the doctor, "Look, this is it." And they don't give me any trouble. She's been moved twice more since then. She's in a situation now, she's got Alzheimer's or dementia or whatever you want to call it. Her mind is going.

DOROTHY: Last summer we had to sell her villa, her condo. Her partner had died the April before of lung cancer and she had been diagnosed with Alzheimer's. So we put her in a nursing home; it's an assisted living center. And she's really very happy and very comfortable because now she doesn't have to remember anything and there's no responsibilities. So my friend takes care of her during the winter and I take care of her during the summer. We take her out and take her places and go over and do stuff. But everybody cares for each other.

CHERYL: How many women, would you say?

DOROTHY: In terms of really being close, people you can call in the middle of the night, I'd say that there's twenty-five [in my Detroit community].

JACKIE: I feel that there are a number of women in our community to whom I've already become close and I would be there for them and I think they would be there for me.

CHERYL: Have you seen anything like what you're imagining in action?

JACKIE: What I've seen really is what Edie was involved with when she went down and was a part of that whole group that nursed Blue Lunden. That's quite a story. You may have seen the documentary on her that did all the LGBT film festivals about 2000. She was a major activist whose last years and death took place at Sugar Loaf in Key West. Women from all over the country became part of her caregiving team during her long, painful death from cancer. And that's what we're hoping, that that kind of thing can be created without having to go to Woman's Land in order to have it happen. Have you heard about this Crone's Nest [Alapine] that's being developed?

MARILYN: Terese Edell is the icon [in Cincinnati community] . . . There's community for you. She is being supported; women do come in regularly to help her, move her.

CHERYL: She's immobile?

MARILYN: Yeah. I went to Muncie this past June to the National Women's Music Festival in Indiana and she was in her wheelchair. But her being there just gave her her strength back.

CHERYL: Can she sing still?

MARILYN: No. But she is composing music—classical music—with the aid of a computer.

CHERYL: So she's still earning money?

MARILYN: Possibly, I'm not sure.

CHERYL: But it would be your impression that it would be community money that's caring for her?

MARILYN: I don't know about the money. But instead of impersonal nurse's aides, and she probably has that too, but women from the community come in to help her.

A few plans are in the works for assisted living, nursing homes, and progressive care for lesbians in the United States. Women's Land is one of those possibilities and is closer to reality than anything else in the United States. It alone promises to offer facilities exclusively for lesbians. Planning is underway for gay and lesbian senior housing in San Francisco, Rainbow Adult Community Housing, with one-third of the units subsidized for incomes under $40,000 and a progressive care unit (Kerman 2002).

Meanwhile, a few towns have opened day care centers and activity centers. Fort Lauderdale is to open the first day care center for gays and lesbians in the state of Florida in the summer of 2003 at the MCC Sunshine cathedral. They estimate that there are 15,000 homosexual seniors in Broward County alone. (Thor-Dahlburg 2003). Los Angeles and New York City also have gay senior centers with computer classes, exercise classes, therapy groups, bridge and lessons, a calling group, trips, dinners, dances, and, in Brooklyn at the YWCA, there is the Griot Circle for elderly black lesbians.

Euthanasia was not a subject about which I questioned the narrators, but four of the narrators specifically mentioned that they favored assisted suicide, two from each cohort. Yutema found that among people sixty to sixty-nine years old, sixty-three percent said that euthanasia is an option, but as people age, apparently they change their minds. Of those seventy and older, only 53 percent said it was an option (Yutema 1997).

The looming crisis in care for childless baby boomers or those who have only one or two children, who began retiring in 2001, has already existed for large numbers of lesbian and gay elderly. Might our ways of coping and supporting be instructive for the larger retiring population of the next fifteen years?

SUMMARY

Retirements began for this group of women in 1977. The average age for retiring among the oldest cohort was 60.7 years and for the younger cohort 57.45 years. Ten reasons for retiring were given. Nothing in the list of ten reasons for retiring would I attribute to the narrators' being women, being mothers, or being homosexual, and I must conclude that lesbians retire for the same reasons as men do. Those reasons may be different for married women.

Most of the narrators planned retirement, at least as far as putting away money in optional investment accounts. A minority of narrators planned more actively. A significantly greater proportion of lesbians have pensions than is the case in the general population, and they use stocks for wealth generation to a greater extent. They are homeowners to a greater extent, and a higher (though small) proportion of them are receiving disability checks and public assistance.

Five percent of the narrators receive less than $10,000 per year, and 23 percent receive $15,000 or less. Twenty-seven narrators (61 percent) were coupled in 2000. Single Whistling Women manage with regular annual incomes from $50,000 to less than $10,000, most of them receiving less than $30,000, while women in couples have household incomes starting at $30,000 to over $100,000. Half of these women believe that they have maintained their economic status in the transition to retirement, 30 percent say it has fallen, and 15 percent say it has improved.

Gay women have formed several vibrant communities around their common sexuality in Arizona, Florida, Alabama, and North Carolina. The most common activity in retirement is reading, followed by entertaining and socializing. Thirty-four women have e-mail accounts and seem to use them daily. The Metropolitan Community Church (MCC) is the most popular religious organization attended by these narrators, but being spiritual apart from any formal religion is even more common. Twenty women said that religion has no place in their lives. It appears that older lesbians are a little less religious than the general population, but they also are more religious that the other studies of lesbians have found and probably more religious than most congregations would assume.

Forty percent of the narrators in the oldest age cohort reported no medical problems. Fifty-five percent of the younger women reported no medical problems, but the medical problems of those in this group are more severe than those of the older women. Most of the couples have done the paperwork required to give their partners power of attorney for health decisions, have wills, and have trusts. A small proportion of single women have taken these steps. Lesbians are depending on long-term care policies, on their children, or their spouses, on the lesbian community, and on good luck.

You start to be concerned that you'll have enough money to last you. . . . You start thinking about your health care and whatever disease might come your way, how debilitating they are going to be and how are you going to be cared for. You start thinking about housing, if you don't own a place, where are you going to go where you won't have to move every year or so. . . . Most likely you are through with menopause and you don't want to talk about it anymore. You've been there, done that. That's how we came to sixty and over. (Vera)

Chapter 7

Words and Us

I once perused a large and extensively illustrated book on sexual activity by and for homosexual men. It was astounding to me for one thing in particular, namely, that its pages constituted a huge lexicon of words; words for acts and activities, their sub-acts, preludes and denouements, their stylistic variation, their sequences. Gay male sex, I realized then, is articulate. It is articulate to a degree that, in my world, lesbian "sex" does not remotely approach. Lesbian "sex" as I have known it, most of the time I have known it, is utterly inarticulate. (Marilyn Frye 1990, pp. 310-311)

BEING WORDLESS

Throughout this project, I have been struck by the number of narrators who said that they knew no words, had no words, used no words, gave no words to their loving of women, to their lovers, to their friends and family, to themselves. The words of Adrienne Rich beg to be repeated:

Whatever is unnamed, undepicted in images, whatever is omitted from biography, censored in collections of letters, whatever is misnamed as something else, made difficult-to-come-by, whatever is buried in the memory by the collapse of meaning under an inadequate or lying language—this will become, not merely unspoken, but unspeakable. (Rich 1979, p. 199)

Adrienne Rich, a writing teacher, and Marilyn Frye, a philosopher, are decrying lesbian silences, lesbian, and in fact women's, speechlessness. Both women have struggled to identify this phenomenon of speechlessness and to put it into words. So have many of the narrators, but many of them seem to have been able to cope with the lack of words for decades.

[She] and I didn't know we were lesbians. We lived together thirteen years! (Cam)

JOYCE: We both didn't know what to call it.
CHERYL: So you had no words for it?
JOYCE : No words for it, except that it must be something bad, abnormal.
CHERYL: 'Cause you didn't know of anybody else doing it?
JOYCE: Absolutely not.

CHERYL: Did you have words for what you were doing?
GIGI: Other than loving her? No.

One time when I came back to Virginia from DC to visit her, she said, "Will you touch me? It's been so long since I've been touched." I believe it was after that, she said, "Do other women feel about each other the way we have felt?" And I said, "Oh my, yes." It almost makes me cry right now. Because her best friend—I know she was gay, but she wouldn't do anything. She said, "I don't understand why Peggy doesn't touch me, why she doesn't hug me." They were very good friends, very close friends. (Cam)

When we moved in together, I don't think she could help but think that. But we did not talk about it. (Cam)

CHERYL: Did you know anybody else besides her? Did you have a community?
CHRIS: No. And in those days, that was back in 1951, we don't talk like that. Everything was hush-hush.

CHERYL: What words did you have for yourselves?
CAROLYN: I'm not sure that we had any. I don't think we had any name. I don't think I knew the word "lesbian" then even. In my work, part of which was transcribing psychotherapy sessions, I learned some vocabularies that I had never known before. But I don't think that was included.
CHERYL: What about terms for body parts and sexuality?
CAROLYN: No, I don't think there were any.
CHERYL: So it would be touching without talking about what was going on?
CAROLYN: Mostly.

CHRIS: No. I had the mental set that it would be unspecified catastrophe if it were known.
CHERYL: But you don't know of any [disasters]?
CHRIS: No, I do not. Well, my god, if they happened nobody would talk about it.

People would say, "Come back to our room. We're going to have drinks and we're just going to visit with each other." And I'd be aware when I walked into the room that there was an energy here that was different from any place I had ever been and nobody talked. Years later, I'm still friendly with that woman. We've had a friendship now for forty-six years and she was just down visiting us, as a matter of fact. But about five years ago I said to her, "I wish I had asked you a whole lot of questions when we first got together. It would have made my life a lot less painful." And she said, "I wouldn't have answered." She said nobody talked about it then. And so there was no communicating. We hung out together, we did things together, we went places together, but nobody ever described who they were. Nobody asked me any questions; nobody offered any mentoring of any kind. . . . And I [had] no one that I [could] talk to. It was dangerous. I mean, I didn't know it was dangerous. My gut told me it was dangerous to risk discussing it with other people that I was close to. So I just played the game. (Jackie)

CHERYL: Did you talk about it?

JACKIE: Not really, no. And she was extremely conflicted. . . . And it also impacted on our relationship then in a very painful way for me because there was no talking, there was no commitment, there was no validating the relationship. So she would come home and tell me about this professor. By then we were both on the faculty of the graduate school of social work at Rutgers. And she was very interested in this one particular [male] professor and would come and discuss that with me in the same way that you do with a friend, not intending to be hurtful. Just assuming that that's what one does . . . and I would go out to be with some other friends or go to a meeting and would come home and would find that they were up in the bedroom. And it never occurred to me that I had any reason to object. I thought, well, that's what she wants and it's clear that that's what important to her. It didn't feel good. As I say, the relationship was never specified and it was never validated. So probably from her point of view, it was like that we were roommates and so that behavior was totally appropriate for roommates.

But then I finally told her what I'd been doing all these years, because I didn't have any sisters to talk to. I never told anybody all those twenty years about [my gay husband]. (Marilyn)

ELLEN: I always had these children and I always thought I'd try to protect them. I never had any gay literature or a gay magazine even. I don't even remember reading at that point in my life, I was so mentally screwed up. I was raised a good Catholic and good Catholics get married and procreate and live happily ever after.

CHERYL: How did your husband and your son take [your announcement that you were gay]?

ELLEN: Well, my husband knew from the beginning but he didn't really believe me when I told him early on. So he never said anything about it.

Yeah, I pray about a week over it and then I say, "We have to talk." So we went up to this lot there behind a supermarket and I told her what's happening to me. The first thing she says, "I've got to tell you something. You can't talk like this to people. You can't tell people these things." 'Cause she had been like this all of her life and she knew all that stuff. I said, "Well, I'm telling you. You are, aren't you?" She said, "Yes, I am." She said, "But you can't talk like this; you can't do this." (Sandy)

I didn't know where to go with my emotions. I had no friends that were gay. I didn't know about the bars. I didn't know about all the various places that I could go to meet people. And so I got married and that was it. I had two children which I love dearly. (Joanna)

In Adrienne Rich's words, these women were living in "a culture of manipulated passivity" (1979, p. 14). Life and love without words, acknowledgment. A woman doesn't know that there are lesbians in the world because her parents, her siblings, her doctors, her teachers, and book publishers don't want her to know. She doesn't come out to herself because she has no words. She doesn't come out to her parents because her parents don't want to know. She doesn't come out to her children because the slighted spouse doesn't want them to know. She finds the words to tell her husband and he doesn't believe her. She gets married because she has no words. She stays quiet because she has no words, because she thinks she's crazy, because she thinks she's bad, because she thinks something is wrong with her.

Marilyn Frye is angry when she recounts her reading of the gay male sex book and pleading when she writes about it. Adrienne Rich is angry and pleading when she writes the essays in *On Lies, Secrets, and Silence*. Men are so much more articulate about their bodies, about their acts, about their feelings, about what they want, what they like, what they don't like, even who they are, than are lesbians in both women authors' experience. Several narrators said they preferred no words, no labels, naming their sexuality wasn't important to them. I believe this is so and will explore this further later in this chapter. I believe some men feel the same way. But I am suspicious of why these women reject words. We have learned to make our way, to communicate through looks and places and proximity to one another and touch. Could it be they reject words now because our language has so utterly failed us for forty, fifty, sixty, seventy years? "The vocabulary will arise among us, of course, only if we talk with each other about what we're doing and why, and what it feels like. Language is social. So is 'doing it'" (Marilyn Frye 1990, p. 314).

LEARNING WORDS

The words to name her sexuality eventually did come to each of these women. These were words that in some cases saddled, in some cases freed, in some cases directed, but they were perhaps, most importantly, words with which they could communicate something of importance to another woman or a husband, or a child. The guessing could end, the unspeakable could be uttered, a group or community could be found, could be joined. "When women can stop being haunted . . . by internalized fears of being and saying themselves, then it is an extraordinary moment" (Rich 1979, p. 38).

As a matter of fact, the way that I came out to my mother was we went to this meeting and my friend came up to me and she had a shirt on that said "Mother Nature is a Lesbian." And my mom saw that shirt and so the words were out then. And then later on, I told you that my mother probably would have been a lesbian. Well she said to me later on, "I knew what was going on. I just wished you hadn't used the words. " We said, "Mom, if we hadn't used the words, we couldn't have taken you any of the places that we did." She used to love to go with us to different places. She used to come to Salon and she was very much at home with women. But she didn't like the words. And I think that's because of her own internalized homophobia. (Edie)

It was archaeology—my profession, which thinks sexuality is irrelevant to anything it does—which gave us the word "Lesbian" from texts found on tablets, poems written by Sappho, words lost and then found, recovered in excavations on the isle of Lesbos.

Nan Boyd (1997) makes several interesting and important distinction in words used for and by homosexuals. From concerns about gender and gender issues come the terms "queer" and "queen." From medical pathology literature come the terms "invert," "deviant," "homosexual," and "lesbian." From civil rights and liberation movements come the terms "homophile" and "gay."

Gertrude Stein used the word "gay" to mean living "in the life" in 1922 (Faderman 1991, p. 67). Letters and newspaper articles in the early part of the twentieth century reveal that "homosexual" and "lesbian" were the most common terms used by the San Francisco press in the 1930s, 1940s, and 1950s. Tennessee Williams used words in letters written in the 1930s such as "queer," "fairies," "fag," and "butch," and the word "jam" to mean straight society (Chauncey 1997; Boyd 1997). "Gay" began to appear in the San Francisco newspapers in the 1940s, but outside of the San Francisco area, "gay" was still cryptic to outsiders into the 1950s (Boyd 1997). The term first appeared in *The New York Times* in 1963, in a book review (Katz 1983).

Other in-group ways of referring to lesbians in the 1930s were phrases such as "a dash of lavender," "lavender," "dyke," "bulldyke," "bull dagger," "drag," "sil," "trapeze artist," "jockey," "mantee," "daddy," "poppa," "husband," "top sergeant," and "spook" (Faderman 1991). More general terms for homosexuals were "pansy," "belle" (from the 1930s), going to "the club," "the life," "in the life," (1930s), "boy" and "girl" to mean homosexuals and "man" and "woman" to refer to straights (Chauncey 1997).

Within lesbian circles words arose like "butch" and "fem," most probably borrowed from men's usage. Words probably originating in women's circles in the first half of the twentieth century and used by the women in this project were "dykes," "diesel dyke," "stone butch," "soft butch," "daddy-butch," "kiki," "bull dagger," and even "old granddad."

CLAIRE: I used to use the word "old granddad," too, because I knew a number of women who for all the world were like old granddads.

CHERYL: That was something you made up?

CLAIRE: Yeah. But they were kind of heavy, gone to fat, and ponderous, you know, weighty in their conversations—old patriarchs.

From among the women in this study came a number of different opinions about the words used to identify their sexuality. Twenty Whistling Women preferred the term "gay," and three were equally happy with "gay" or "lesbian." Eight women preferred "lesbian," including two women from the older cohort. Sixteen women expressed a strong dislike for the term "lesbian." Dorothy never felt that "lesbian" was a negative word. She used it for herself while she was married in the 1950s and 1960s. She said, "I happened to like it. Being lesbian separated me from the boys and I liked that." Nancy, in the sixty to seventy age group, prefers the term "lesbian" because she likes the classical tradition of Sappho. "Lesbian" is kind of classy, she thinks. Mitch looked up the word "lesbian" in the dictionary at age twelve and remembers reading that it was a phase that ended by age eighteen. Nan just started using the word "lesbian" in 1995 even though she's never liked its sound or its implied segregation. Amelia says it was years before she could say "lesbian" and not feel so awful about it.

I was standing in an elevator once and I wouldn't date any of the men in the business at all. And I was standing in an elevator one day and somebody said to me, "Are you a lesbian?" I said, "No, I'm American." I didn't hear another word from them. (Addy)

I was in school doing my thing and reading all about my own life. I never really liked to get involved with . . . first of all, I hate the word "lesbian." I think it's the worst word. I prefer the word "gay" and I never ever have used the word "lesbian" with regard to myself. It's a label. It's a jacket and I don't like that. (Barbara)

CHERYL: Does "lesbian" grate?

CAM: Yes, it does. I don't like the word. But I'm getting used to it. I think it's an ugly word. It's an ugly-sounding word. The sound of it bothers me.

Well, as I said, I chose "lesbian," not as a label, but as a choice of that's my identity. Not "gay," because I don't feel like I live a gay lifestyle. I live a lesbian lifestyle. That means a lot of different things. (Edie)

Five women denied any label, saying they hated labels. All but four women felt negatively toward the word "dyke."

Negotiating words for ourselves, even deciding to identify ourselves by a sexuality, is not a simple thing to do. Wanting to be part of all homosexuality, rather than separate, women from men, leads many women to prefer the word "gay," and they resist or resent giving this word over to men for their exclusive use. Mary's words reflect this frequently expressed sentiment well. "I don't like the term 'gay and lesbian.' I thought we were all one, and that phrase irritates me" (Mary1). Nevertheless, she uses the word "lesbian" when talking about other lesbians to lesbians and the word "gay" when talking to straight people she works with. Remarking on the separation of gay and lesbian, Addy and Jan correctly attributed the split in terminology to lesbian women's groups who saw women's concerns being forgotten by a media fixated on gay men's lives and gay men's concerns, and by gay men's groups who were forgetting that gay women had equally valid but different concerns.

CHERYL: Which word would you use now for yourself first?

JAN: "Lesbian." Oh definitely.

CHERYL: So you made the split in your own vocabulary about the same time everybody else did.

JAN: Probably. I learned a lot by going to Michigan [Womyn's Music Festival]. A lot of my friends didn't want to say that, they wanted to remain gay.

Women older than seventy-one in this sample seem more comfortable with the words "lesbian," "homosexual," "butch," "dyke," and "queer" than are the younger women, a result more of being active in the 1940s and 1950s than of age directly, I think. Lesbian culture of the 1970s and 1980s disparaged the perceived role-playing words "butch" and "dyke" and the marginalizing word "queer" in favor of "lesbian" or "gay." "Lesbian" was easier for a feminist to say than a nonfeminist (and few in this sample of women consider themselves to be feminists), but "gay" was easier for everyone to say and hear. By the end of the 1970s, however, gay liberation and gay rights movements were strong enough to have seduced most women into using the word "gay."

"Dyke" was the word that most frequently elicited a negative reaction. Many informants were quite turned off by this word and described mannish, truck driving, uneducated women who offended the senses.

Addy doesn't like "queer" because she doesn't feel queer. Bing and Carolyn think "queer" only appropriate for men. Roberta doesn't think "gay" is appropriate because "there's nothing gay about this life." Addy prefers "gay" but adds, "Although, I don't see a whole bunch of happy people." Chris rejects all these words, describing herself as "a gentleman" instead.

Perhaps the most poignant thing about language and words for women who are in this study is that words may be a gift, a luxury earned and granted. Words have often come only with retirement, with community membership, or with the death of parents or divorces. This point will become stronger as I turn to a consideration of "coming out," a very powerful moment when lying and secrets stop and words take center stage.

But the terms "gay" and "lesbian" has never been negative for me. Partly, I suppose, because by the time I got to the words and what they meant, I was an adult and there was no reason for it to hold any negativity. (Kay)

I just recently started using the word "lesbian" because it's used so much here [in Sarasota]. (Cam)

OTHER PEOPLE'S WORDS

Many of the women in this study have read *The Well of Loneliness,* written in 1928 by Radclyffe Hall. Many of them read the book as adolescents, including Sappho, Chris, and Roberta. Gigi's father gave it to her to read at age fourteen. Carolyn, at age fourteen, was given the book by a married librarian. Nancy read a borrowed copy in college, as did Claire. Mary2 read it in the 1950s. A male psychiatrist suggested the book to Nan in the 1970s; a male friend recommended it to Joanna. Ellen read the book while she was going through her divorce in 1976. Pat N read it in the 1970s. Sandy read it in the late 1990s.

KAY M: I read *The Ladder* and I read *The Well of Loneliness.*

CHERYL: Do you remember when?

KAY M: Oh yes, 1942. When I read that book, I knew. Six or eight months ago I got an e-mail from this guy who I know who's maybe fifty years old. And he said, "I've recently read a book called *The Well of Loneliness.* Have you ever heard of it?" I wrote him back and said, "I was probably reading that book on the day your mother gave birth to you." Yes, that was very impressive. And there was a little group of us in Tulsa that read it and talked about it and lived it.

CHERYL: So you read it again twenty years later?

KAY M: Oh, I've read it several times and I have the biography of Radclyffe Hall.

A girl at work gave that to me on my desk and said, "This book reminds me of you." This was before the service. I read it and you know what, everything she was doing in there, I had done it. Even where she went out and bought a pearl ring. And for the woman I was going with, I was working on Fifth Avenue, beautiful jewelry stores everywhere and I had a pearl ring made for her and this was before reading it. (Mitch)

I can remember when I was in college having a gal who lived across the hall I suspected. Then she became a graduate assistant and was living elsewhere. And she said, "I've got a book you might like to read." So I said, "Oh, all right." But she said, "You're going to have to read it in my room." So when I had a few spare moments I went over and I read *The Well of Loneliness.* So that's how I found out about her. (Claire)

I didn't get any real awareness that this had happened to anybody else ever until I stumbled across *The Well of Loneliness.* These two women were essentially extremely lonely, that they had no similar friends. And that by and large it was a rather sad plight. But I identified with both of them. (Carolyn)

And I picked up *The Well of Loneliness* and I wanted to be like this woman. (Chris)

We were the only two, till I read a couple of books. My father gave me *The Well of Loneliness* to read. (Gigi)

CHERYL: Did [*The Well of Loneliness*] scare you?

DOROTHY: It didn't scare me at all. I think it said, Hey, I'm not the only person in the whole world that feels this way. There's somebody else. Then you start to put two and two together and you think, Well, geez, maybe people can live together.

The quotes above summarize nicely exactly why parents and publishers were hiding these words/stories from young women. So widely read is *The Well of Loneliness* among older lesbians that the first lesbian bookstore in Florida chose for its name "The Well of Happiness," ensuring instant recognition of its subject matter to most lesbians of the area.

But *The Well of Loneliness* offered neither precise words nor a model of successful living for a female couple. The same can be said for *The Children's Hour* by Lillian Hellman, mentioned by two narrators. These books offered images of women struggling to make their place in an unsympathetic society, of destiny without courage. The personal stayed personal in these stories. The recently popular *Fried Green Tomatoes at the Whistlestop Cafe* (Fannie Flagg) continues this genre tradition—the love that shall not speak its name—offering courageous, yet still wordless, characters, but characters who do manage to live together.

Messages gleaned from *The Well of Loneliness* were articulated by some of the women. Nan remembers "how cloistered women had been and what a tough time that they had. I really felt that women made themselves separated instead of being part of." Carolyn recognized that "the two women were essentially extremely lonely, and that they had no similar friends. And that by and large it was a rather sad plight. But I identified with both of them." This book caused her to realize she wasn't the only girl with these feelings, and had the same effect on Dorothy. Chris wanted to be like the main character, Stephen, and Mitch felt she already was the main character.

A number of other books were mentioned during the interviews as being pivotal in a woman's coming out, in her sense of herself. Joanna mentioned *Lesbian/Woman*, Marilyn talked about *Liberating Masturbation*, Maryl spoke fondly of *Patience and Sarah*, and Gigi of *The Price of Salt*.

The Ladder, which was published from 1956 until 1972, was also mentioned by several informants—Mary1, Mary 2, Bing, Kay M. This publication, which was put out by the Daughters of Bilitis, began in 1955 and specifically decried the butch and fem "role playing," as they saw it, and the bar scene. Bing spoke specifically of the importance of DOB and *The Ladder* among her crowd. Mary1 tried to start a DOB chapter in early 1980s in Madeira Beach, Florida. Bing remembers that "someone was always coming to town bringing literature." She and her partner subscribed to *The Ladder,* wrote to the publication, and usually passed each issue around town.

Libraries and bookstores were filled with other people's words and are fond places for many narrators, providing much testimony for the protection of free speech. The WEB maintains a library, as do the clubhouses at Carefree and Apache Junction. Mitch snuck into the adult section of the public library to look up the word "lesbian" in the big dictionary. Other narrators had memories of the importance of bookstores and libraries.

There is a group in Tampa now, women that are meeting. They have a library over there of all gay literature. The Center for Human Rights or something. They have a regular library over there. (Sandy)

MARY1: I read all about [lesbianism] in the library.

CHERYL: So in Boston, you're kind of researching these feelings and your notion of who you are?

MARY1: Yeah. And it's funny because we used to go to the library to get books to read about it, you know, and they were always under cover at the desk. You couldn't take them out, they were reference books. And that same library, many years later in the 1980s, when I went back to Boston to take care of my mother, that very library was an MCC church now. The library that wouldn't tell me what lesbians were or what queer was, is now the MCC church! I thought that was very fitting.

We had a bookstore open in Phoenix. I used to go up there all the time and get books, on my breaks from the hospital. See, [my partner] didn't know I was there. I thought that was great. I couldn't believe it—a bookstore, wow.

But there was a bookstore that was a major focus of Cincinnati's gay community. It was founded and named Crazy Ladies Bookstore because if a woman questions authority, she's deemed crazy. And it was run by a collective for many years. (Marilyn)

Women's bookstores were also the source of women's music, an innovation of the 1970s and early 1980s. Two narrators spoke of the importance of these words in their lives.

Oh yeah. A store with all books and everything about lesbians and music. I discovered Olivia music, brought home Cris Williamson's *The Changer and the Changed.* Could not believe all those women were lesbians, singing on a record! That was wonderful. If we had had these things in the 1950s, how different life would be for a lot of people. But we had to pave the way. But I loved it. I was thrilled to go see her perform in October here. I love Meg Christian. I have all the albums. I have all the Olivia albums. (Mary1)

Through music is how we educated ourselves about lesbian community. Actually through Chris Williamson and Meg Christian and Margie Adams's music. Margie mostly, for me, because Margie spoke from her heart right to my heart. I took those words that she would say in the song and I would hear them over and over in my heart and I would realize that there was much more for me in my life than what I was experiencing. I must say that women's music, for me, is one of the most incredibly freeing and informative ways of learning about lesbian culture. (Edie)

Mainstream newspapers and magazines had their part in providing words and images to these women when they were young. Greenwich Village was made accessible to Mary1 and Cynthia by these venues.

CYNTHIA: I would try to find all the information that I could get and I would hide and read it. And then I started reading [about] my ambition—I started reading about Greenwich Village in New York [in magazines] and we'd hear stuff about it. And I wanted to go there so bad. And it seemed like such a faraway land to me. I was about fifteen to sixteen years old.

CHERYL: Did you cut these stories out and hide them?

CYNTHIA: Oh definitely. I think that's when I started thinking that's definitely what I was.

A long story in a local Washington, DC, news magazine facilitated the formation of a small lesbian community there in the 1970s, which was vitally important to Joanna.

JOANNA: There was a woman in northern Virginia who had an open house every Wednesday night. She had a little tiny house not much bigger than this room. She had an open house every Wednesday night and there'd be thirty to forty women there, all crowded into one little room.

CHERYL: How did they find out about [the Wednesday night gatherings]?

JOANNA: I found out about it because she was written up in the *Washingtonian* magazine and she had been on the *David Susskind Show,* which was a television show. She was from the New York area originally. So she was very active. . . . I don't know what it said exactly, but there was quite a long article. And then of course they had the *Gay Blade* newspaper, which is now called the *Washington Blade*. You could pick those up all over the city.

Since 1983 *Womyn's Words* has been published by Women's Energy Bank of St. Petersburg. *Womyn's Words* is the major source of information about activities in the Sarasota-Tampa-St. Petersburg area. In addition to announcements, it carries lesbian-friendly ads for services and for real estate, news, and poetry. Jan referred me to the publication, as did Jean. Kay and Sheri pick up free copies at the MCC church.

They had been down to visit and had made contact through *Womyn's Words* and they subscribed to *Womyn's Words* and so when I was getting ready to move down here, I subscribed to *Womyn's Words*. (Joanna)

MARILYN: We'd been to Tallahassee to see a friend, we were just kind of exploring around. We just sort of drove around here and then we started subscribing to *Womyn's Words* to get a feel for what the community was.
CHERYL: How did you find *Womyn's Words*?
MARILYN: Advertising in *Lesbian Connection*.

Yeah. I've got poetry in *Womyn's Words*. I write a lot of poems. (Dawn)

Faderman notes that within a year of the Stonewall Riots, hundreds of gay publications and organizations had sprung to life (1991). For those individuals who choose to speak, read, or write about their sexuality, the twentieth century ended with dozens of print outlets to help them do so. No longer is there a dearth of words. In the St. Petersburg-Sarasota area are women-focused magazines such as *Girlfriends, Lesbian Connection,* and *Womyn's Words*. *Ripe* is a magazine for older lesbians produced in Forest Hills, New York. There are correspondence and networking groups for lesbians such as Golden Threads, Silver Threads, and Wishing Well (also named with reference to *The Well of Loneliness*), and at one time there was *New Dawn*. Addressing the greater gay population of the Tampa Bay area are newsprint magazines such as *Watermark, Southern Voice,* and *Gayellow Pages*. But to be interested in the content of these papers requires that a woman identify by her sexuality, and see herself as part of a larger regional, really national subculture.

COMING OUT

The problem of speech, of language continues to be primary.
For if in our speaking we are breaking silences long established,
"liberating ourselves from our secrets," this is in itself a first
kind of action . . . the terrible negative power of the lie in relationships between women [can be broken]. (Adrienne Rich
1979, p. 185)

Madgey's still single and I don't think she's ever had another affair. They
[professional church women] just don't come out. (Cam)

CHERYL: So, do you teach this third woman the words, the acts?

JACKIE: The acts, to the extent that she was open to it. And she was comfortable, she was totally comfortable with being with me. But until the day she
died, which was several years ago (she died of a metastasis of melanoma
that reached her brain), she was still struggling with coming out, and
never came to terms with it.

Coming out was the most important political act a gay person
could do according to both gay liberationists in the early 1970s and
gay rights advocates in the late 1970s and 1980s. Calls to come out
have continued with each decade, with each Gay Pride march, with
each celebrity revelation, and even in the second Silver Threads conference keynote address (2001). I can remember an eleventh grade
Sunday School teacher instructing us: do the thing that you fear and
the death of the fear is certain. I thought of coming out then and there.
To come out is arguably good for the individual, good for her family,
and undeniably good for the cause of both gay liberation and gay civil
rights.

Thirty-five women in this sample consider themselves to be out,
nine do not. For only one of them was coming out expressed as a conscious political act, a statement to the world that she was joining the
ranks of a national gay movement.

To me, the personal is political. If I ever had a motto, it would be that the
way I live my life is a political statement. That's the reason why I'm out. (Edie)

Instead, coming out was far more often a discovery, a process, a
change in social status, even a retrospective awareness. Private, quiet
acts, most of these women experienced, with ripples only in their im-

mediate families; mothers became single parents, mothers lost children, married women became divorcees, stay-at-home wives became working women, addresses changed.

> There was no great decision point, I would say. I sort of oozed in. I knew from when I was very, very young that I was different and I knew what my desires were, but I never . . . I sort of moved gradually into participating outwardly. (Claire)

> CHERYL: Do you have a coming-out story?
> GLORIA: No, it was a gradual thing. When I moved here to Florida, there was nobody around that I knew who was lesbian.

Eve Sedgwick says "coming out is a matter of crystallizing intuitions or convictions that had been in the air for a while already and had already established their own power-circuits of silent contempt, silent blackmail, silent glamorization, silent complicity" (1992, p. 53).

> We went to Puerto Rico together. And at that time I was really coming out. I had to talk to someone, so I did speak to her. I said, "I feel that I am going to have a relationship with this woman. She said, "How would you know?" I said, "I don't know, I just know. I met her once. I just know that I'm going to end up having a relationship with her and I believe she's gay." She said, "How do you know that?" I said, "I don't know how I know, I just know." And I did know. (Barbara)

> Never come out to a straight woman. (Diane)

> But they all knew. It wasn't like I was revealing anything. I thought maybe I was, but I wasn't. (Ellen)

The alternative to being out is cast as a condition known as "being in the closet," a generally disapproving label applied by "out" people somewhat disparagingly. It means that the closeted person is frightened, even homophobic, and immature. "Why would one do this [stay in the closet]?" is the oft-asked question by people who consider themselves to be out. A widely read academic article that offers a close inspection of why people choose "to closet" themselves, stay in the closet (when they could come out), is *Epistemology of the Closet* authored by Eve Sedgwick (1992). In a comparison of Esther's (biblical) decision to come out as a Jew to a husband/king who is permitting the killing of Jews and a gay person's decision to come out, Sedgwick makes the following distinctions for the gay person:

1. A sexual identity is open to debate—by parents and friends—and the individual may not feel up to fielding all the questions and challenges to this "confession."
2. There is uncertainty about who knows what so there is uncertainty about what to tell whom.
3. There is the potential for serious injury to both the hearer and the speaker.
4. The sexuality of the hearer is likely to be implicated and cause discomfort for the hearer.
5. Telling may disconnect the speaker from friends and family while not aligning her with another coherent group/family/culture.
6. To come out is to bring into chaos understandings of gender.

The comments by narrators give ample evidence of these potent reasons why a woman would not "come out."

When I was in school and I was a teacher—you did not—you were not out. If you were, you were unemployed and not admitted in polite society. The only people I saw who were out were so flagrantly different and appeared to be gender distortions. I didn't want to be like that. (Claire)

That was just about it. We knew of a group in lower Westchester. We went a couple of times. Doreen was hesitant and would say, "What if somebody sees me there? They might out me." And I told her, "If they see you there, they're in the same predicament. If everybody's in the closet, they're not going to tell because they don't want to be outed either." That was the only way I could get her to come along and find out what more was out there. (Edie)

BOBBIE: Well, in general, probably I'm still hanging on to the closet, having survived ridicule and finger pointing all my life, I'm not anxious to take it on.

CHERYL: Was the source of the ridicule and finger pointing your sexuality?

BOBBIE: Yes. But I managed to escape most of it. Some of my friends didn't.

CHERYL: People get fired?

BOBBIE: Oh, people did subtle things like just silently and steadily withdrawing their children from their class, stuff like that. And the two friends I've had for years who were PE teachers had the jeering of the neighbors and the ridicule and stuff like that. But my partner and I managed to escape most of that. We kept our house and the yard nice. We went to Europe every summer and got the hell out of [Seattle].

But see, in the 1950s there was this McCarthyism and I worked for the U.S. government and you know, you just didn't say anything or you didn't get caught in any activities or you'd get fired. (Joanna)

I think that a lot of people did it privately, like ourselves. But I think that when you marry and you have children, you have a lot to lose by coming out. Because at that particular time or any particular time, it was not accepted. (Kate)

CHERYL: [Did] you have a gay community?

MARY1: No. She was not out, didn't want to be out, didn't want anyone to know she was gay. She worked for Los Angeles county in the court system and you're very much afraid of losing your job.

CHERYL: Did you share those fears or would you have been living differently if you were with somebody else?

MARY1: I don't know. I was always afraid of losing my job.

And I said, "Yes [I'm gay]." I've thought so many times since then that I should have lied to her, but I didn't. I didn't lie to her. I told her, "Yes, Roberta and I are a couple" and the whole thing. Well you know, she turned against me. You hear about parents not accepting their children. You never hear anything about children not accepting their parents. (Sandy)

ROBERTA: Well, mostly we were trying to stay very deep in the closet as far as the public was concerned because things were so very bad in those days. They were terrible. I had been writing her some letters while I was in the service because she came home first. And the landlady found the letters and threw us out in the middle of the night and was going to call the police. It was very, very bad. And then, of course, I lived through the days of Anita Bryant too. I was in Miami at the time and it was dreadful. The bars were raided and we had a mayor . . . whose daughter was gay and he went on a vendetta about gays. He even had raids at the gay beach where he had both ends to that beach cordoned off and had the police cars come in there and the police were even running into the ocean to try to pick up mostly the fellows. It was terrible. And you wouldn't go to a gay bar without worrying to death that you were going to be raided. . . . 'Cause don't forget, we were all in the closet.

CHERYL: So everybody you knew was closeted. You didn't hang out with anybody that was out there?

ROBERTA: Nobody was out in those days.

So, no one was "out" in the 1940s, 1950s, and 1960s, for many reasons. Faderman (1991) documents in some detail the chain of events that led to the fears for homosexuals expressed by these women. A tolerant 1920s, when people were being told that to repress sexual energy was to lead to neuroses, bisexuality was thought to be a part of a healthy development, and women were envisioning careers, gave way to a panicked 1930s. With one quarter of the U.S. population in financial trouble, women were to leave their jobs to men, to go home.

At the beginning of the 1940s sentiment turned again—women were to move to the cities, do men's work, become comrades, patriots. With the war over, normalcy became an obsession, even a national duty to rout the threat of communism in the late 1940s and 1950s. Faderman makes the comment that the 1950s were probably the worst time in history to be a woman who loved women. Many professional schools no longer admitted women. A presidential executive order issued in April 1953 mandated that any government employee could be and all new job applicants must be screened for deviant sexuality. A 1955 report on Homosexuals and Citizenship in Florida specifically targeted teachers as state employees (Mitchell 1964). Even admission to state colleges put the would-be student through a battery of written questions about sexual tendencies. The military branches made a concerted effort to rout out homosexuals—new recruits were asked numerous questions, and told to inform on lesbians in the ranks—and succeeded to their satisfaction. They even placed "spies" on softball teams. Mass media presented homosexuality "as a chief cause of American ills."

By the 1960s, however, the communists had been held at bay for over a decade, and various minority groups were taking actions to change their own plight. The country was being sensitized to injustices; unhappy people were learning organizing strategies. But the literature and popular understanding still depicted the homosexual as sick, deviant, unproductive, and hideous. It would certainly be hard to envision why one would pronounce to a family, boss, co-workers, husband, and children a state of mind, a behavior that most did not understand and all popular media stated to be pathological. Faderman wrote that women concluded that the popular images of lesbians did not apply to them and if they kept quiet about their love for other women they would not have to own those images. Furthermore, a woman would have to be 100 percent sure another woman was a lesbian before talking about herself or making an advance, because to be wrong could be disastrous.

Researchers have documented that 60 percent of 203 gay women in a 1984 report did fear job discrimination if their sexuality was known (Levine and Leonard 1984). "Coming out" would require a social milieu that could absorb the estranged brave soul and give her a new family, a new sense of accomplishment and purpose. Above all, it would require words—other people's words, gifts of words. Such a milieu did not exist in rural or suburban areas of the United States before 1970, and existed only in bars in the largest cities prior to that decade. Places made notorious through magazine and newspaper articles were Greenwich Village and the Castro section of San Francisco. Even after 1970, it was books, magazines, bookstores, and newspaper articles that bought a budding gay culture to the attention of most of these women. Some of these women needed this new community, some of them did not.

That's easy, [I came out in] 1947. That's when I literally came out for myself, as myself. And then I continually went down to the Village to see all these people because now my world opened up. (Addy)

I'm not basically an open person. I get to know people slowly and I do not feel that sexual identity, persuasion, preference is something that should be common knowledge. Heterosexuals do not feel compelled to identify their sexual preferences and, indeed, I would prefer they not inform me of these things. So I respond accordingly. I have known people for many years and gotten along very pleasantly and they know very little about me and we have a nice time together and I know very little about them. People can't seem to deal with the present. And I think this is part of the reason that people don't listen. I mean when it becomes important to me, I'm out. My picture was in the *Gazette*. (Claire)

BOBBIE: Well, we grew apart. I wanted to be out more and more, be more and more social and she just needed to be in a closet.
CHERYL: Were you wanting to become more political?
BOBBIE: Yeah, a little.

JACKIE: Right. And then simultaneously, because I was out and meeting people, I found that there were some projects going on that I could get involved with through the lesbian/gay coalition of New Jersey. I got on this committee that was doing workshops for teachers and parents and anyone else that was interested, sensitizing them to the needs of lesbian/gay adolescents. And then my name started to be out all over the place and it was like wonderful.
CHERYL: Didn't lose your job?
JACKIE: No. And it just brought me a richness of experience and people.
CHERYL: I want to clarify here, what would you say now was what you were missing in the twenty-two-year relationship?
JACKIE: What I was missing was community.

When Ellen decided to pursue her attraction to women, she did so with words. She placed an ad in *Psychology Today* and in The *Wishing Well*, a correspondence club for lesbians she had seen advertised in the back of a mainstream women's magazine. The responses she received were supportive, introduced her to the subcultural language, and gave her a girlfriend. Those response letters also cost her custody of her three children and were retained as evidence by a Michigan court.

Numerous authors have spoken of, even documented, the benefits—social, physical, mental—of "coming out." Friend (1980) argued that the greater the number of interactive roles in which the homosexual person is out, the higher is his self-esteem. Archbold (1982) argued from his interviews of public older homosexuals that earlier rejection of "society's lies about homosexuals makes it easier to reject the myth that aging equals . . . unhappiness." Berger (1982) noted from two different theoretical positions that hiding one's homosexuality led to emotional problems.

The findings of several studies of work satisfaction for homosexuals are relevant to this study of retired lesbians. Kronenberger (1991), Williamson (1993), and a National Defense Research Institute study (1993) projected that being closeted can lead an employee to want to leave the organization or negatively impact work performance. Nancy Day and Patricia Schoenrade asked 900 gay people, both "closeted" and "out," questions about job satisfaction, trust in top management, role ambiguity, role conflict, conflict between work and home issues, and commitment to continuing in their job. They were surprised on several fronts. "Out" workers socialized with colleagues significantly less than did "closeted" workers. "Out" workers "showed higher affective commitment, higher job satisfaction, higher perceived top management support, lower role ambiguity, lower role conflict, and lower conflict between work and home." But being open or secretive about one's sexuality at work created no difference in job stress or commitment to continue with the current employer. Perhaps even more surprising was that "out" workers did not differ significantly in any category from heterosexual workers (Day and Schoenrade 1997).

I think of how I was never able to be honest with any of [my fellow teachers in nearly forty years of teaching]. I think of how I had to hide my life. I think of the conversations with other faculty about their private lives and how I was never able to share mine! When I was younger of the gay men who accompanied me to faculty "events" as my date. Of later when I was older, how I just never went, or was never asked about my life outside of school. (Bobbie)

After five years of retirement, Bobbie is angry about the teaching profession's censorship of gay teachers, the environment that censured her significant relationship, her being. She is angry about the silence.

Or does hiding one's homosexuality lead to emotional problems? The Day and Schoenrade study suggests that there may be some work-related issues that differ between out and secretive homosexual workers, but job stress did not differ between the two groups, nor did resolution to continue working. Cracks are beginning to appear in this mantra: "come out" and be content. For instance, Berger (1982) found no correlation between self-concealment and self-acceptance in his group of gay men. Lee was startled to find that

> the capacity of some of my respondents to be quite content in old age after a lifetime of undetected deception—of wife, children, fellow employees, and even in some cases professional helpers—was frankly astonishing. (Lee 1987, p. 57)

Lee concluded that "successfully staying in the closet is one way to avoid storms" and those in his sample of older gay men who had managed to avoid storms self-identified as happier and more content with their lives than did those men who had come out years earlier. "The disappointing conclusion that staying in the closet is more likely to lead to a happy old age for homosexual men than is going public appeared to be true for the forty-seven men in my study" (Lee 1987, p. 57).

Nine of the narrators do not think that they are out (although the definitions in use differ). Of those nine, six said they were happy or very happy when asked about their life satisfaction. The other three were not asked that question, and neither were most of the other women. But no one who was asked about her satisfaction with retirement or with life, answered "unhappy." The most negative comments heard were "I'm 70 percent happy," and "I'm not at all happy with my sex life."

With only one exception, these women were not activists during the first fifty years of their lives. Many of them have done little that gay rights activists have identified as doable. There are notable exceptions to this picture of passivity in this sample, but they are quite few. In the sense of campaigning for gay liberation or rights, very, very few of these women were "out." "As homosexuals have become organized, a generational consciousness has emerged, namely, that gay liberation is for the young. Older homosexuals have expressed a painful loneliness amidst their younger liberated brethren" (Lee 1987, p. 49).

And I'm so happy for young people now that can just be out and do what they want and not have to worry about that kind of stuff. I remember one of the last couple of years that I taught, standing there in my library at that time and looking at this publication that came out from the school district. It was an in-house publication. It came out once a week. It announced local meetings and stuff that was going on in the district. And here was a meeting for gay teachers. I thought, *In my lifetime, now who dares go to that meeting and be seen?* (Bobbie)

Young kids are better at being out. (Bing)

I just have many, many straight friends and I don't think it's necessary [to be out]. If they know, fine; if they assume, fine. But I have no need, probably a lot to do with age, you know. (Joyce)

No, they didn't like the word "dyke." Now "dyke" is used. But it doesn't have the same connotation that it used to have. It used to be used for very masculine women. Now, I see some very feminine women that wear heels and dresses call themselves "dykes." I was around young people so much that I pick up on and understand all this because I was constantly surrounded by young people. And they brought me up to date very quickly. But some of my friends even, people I've known for years, would be very insulted to be called a dyke, even by other gay people. (Cynthia)

I think it's [a national gay movement] wonderful. I think it's great. And I think if I was born at this time, I would be part of every group available and probably marching in parades and all kinds of different things. But at the time that I was born and when I came out, it was completely different. I'm sort of like structured already. I think that what you're brought up with at any given time is really what you carry on with you. (Kate)

Oh yes, we talked about it. And the consensus with our group anyway, and I think mine personally, is that I will probably never walk in a parade and carry a placard. However, I feel very special that I have gotten a lot of benefits because so many people have done that. I feel very grateful to them. I feel sort of bad that I can't do it myself. But we did talk about that, that is something that we weren't sure that we could do. But, hey, somewhere along the line it's going to benefit us. And it has, it really has. (Dorothy)

To what extent do older homosexuals see gay liberation activity (parades, protests, passage of pro-gay legislation) as contrary to their interest or believe that younger homosexuals act as a different class of people at places such as gay bars, women's picnics, or meetings of special-interest groups (Lee 1987)? Lee concluded from his study that older men—homo or hetero—are more similar than different, and that generational class conflict is the major problem facing all of our aged (Lee 1987). Many of the women of OLOC would agree that ageism in the lesbian and gay communities is a problem for them.

Lee even reported that "many older homosexual men still interpret the closet and the secret society not as furtive, but as adventuresome and special" (1987, p. 63). The same has been recorded for lesbians. Bullough and Bullough (1977) related that in the 1920s and 1930s, lesbians valued the secretiveness of their lifestyle and saw it as a symbolic part of being "in the life." Lee (1987) repeated the same comment for older homosexual men. This badge of secrecy is probably an overlooked component of "being in the closet," but none of the narrators mentioned this aspect of their sexuality.

Unaware of the secrecy badge, I was surprised, even shocked, after my first interview in this project, and then the second, and the third, to hear these women say they hadn't participated in any form of political activity related to homosexual liberation or rights. Many of them had never belonged to any gay organization or been to any gay events, didn't know of any gay entertainers, had never contributed to a gay candidate's campaign, never boycotted a product, had no stickers, flags, or jewelry that indicated they identified with a national gay liberation or gay rights movement. After twenty-five of the interviews when I had spoken with only two women who had been engaged in any political activity, I began an article on their lack of activism which I planned to present at a gay and lesbian studies conference. But I couldn't get beyond the first page, and I abandoned the project until I started this chapter.

Why was I expecting these women to be activists? Because I assumed that they had suffered knowingly, from homophobia, I expected them to be fighters. Because being closeted did them psychological harm, I expected them to be fighters. Because there were ways to be active, I expected them to participate. They seemed to me meek, closeted, cowardly. This interpretation was the result of my own coming out in 1971 and being an activist frequently throughout that decade and occasionally since.

As I continued to ponder these stories and my reaction to them, I began to ask myself a series of questions. Must these women have done something "activist," that I valued, in order for me to respect them? Had these women really done nothing to further gay rights? Were these women closeted by my definition, and if so, were they cowards, were they "unliberated"? Was being "out" a requirement of mine? Was making decisions out of self-interest bad?

The answer to all of these questions is "no," I would now say. I understand being out in a totally different way now. For starters, every one of these women, in loving another woman, in living with another woman, in rejecting the prescribed heterosexual role in favor of an alternative social role, made a statement that was not lost on the people around them. These women are not cowards, they have risked much, and suffered some, regardless of how vocal they have been. Their actions made it safer for another woman to follow the same course, be that leaving her husband, validating a close friendship with another woman, deciding not to marry, or taking up life with another woman. If they thought that being discreet was in their best interest, they did the same thing I did. I thought being "out" was in my best interest. It is impossible to know if more women risked being lesbian because of my activism in the 1970s, witnessed mostly by other gay people, than did because of the actions of one of these "inactive" women. As Katz has pointed out, "Some have argued that all homosexual emotions and acts constitute 'resistance' (even 'revolution') in a society organized to maintain heterosexuality as the dominant form of human relationships" (1983, p. 158).

And what would they have said before 1970? One social theory (social constructionism) teaches that self-identity forms within available social constructs. Homosexuality among women was a nascent, almost cultureless phenomenon prior to the 1960s. It was a quiet, wordless, social construct. I had assumed there were more brave souls prior to the 1970s than we post-1960s lesbians were aware of, yet it had never occurred to me that it takes a vocal culture to give identity to people, to give voice to people, to give cause. There certainly was something to be spoken about—an injustice, many injustices, human rights, love, topics filled with activities and examples when other subgroups were identified in U.S. culture.

But, in a quiet, wordless, nascent culture there is nothing to speak. I now think no greater number of brave people in 2004 exists, just greater emphasis on identifying a sexuality now than before 1970. It helps tremendously that homosexual rights have become a human rights issue, but the fact that it did not happen until the 1950s in this country and then was not expressed beyond several small groups until the 1970s is not the fault of any of these women.

The other realization I came to is that some of these women have refused to identify themselves by their sexuality, or even to take/wear a sexuality. David Halperin (1995) and Michel Foucault (1988) have argued that sexuality—hetero, homo, bi—did not exist as a concept before the 1880s. Sexuality was the invention of medical personnel, and psychology. Prior to that decade, the biblical examples of so-called homosexuality, famous in contemporary arguments, were aimed at all readers/hearers of scripture. Anyone was potentially seducible by errant sexual practices. Everyone had to be vigilant, prayerful, resistant. There was no concept that these temptations were stronger for some people than others. No one classified oneself by a set of sexual practices. But since the 1880s, such labels, categories, and sexualities have emerged, and individuals have been encouraged to identify by sexuality. In fact, having a sexuality is part of U.S. culture now.

What I've come to realize in the course of this project is that apparently all scholars, and thousands of professional services people, and I have assumed that now everyone learns to classify oneself by a sexual identity. I suspect that still plenty of people, particularly those whose sex lives began before 1969, have not conformed to expectations that they take, wear, and be a sexuality. Plenty of people still exist in that pre-1880s world in which one didn't have a sexuality, didn't reduce oneself to sexual activity for an identity. I see this in the women in this sample who said they didn't want to pick a word to label themselves, or who didn't care what word I used for them, or who said that their sex lives were their private business, not the world's business, or who omitted any sexuality descriptor when I asked them to pick ten or so descriptors for themselves (e.g., Catholic, New Yorker, mother, etc.). Foolishly, I have expected everyone not heterosexual to name, take, and wear a sexuality and then defend it. Because I have been eager and happy to identify myself by a sexuality and then to flaunt it, brandish it, I expected everyone else engaged in homosexual behaviors to do the same. (Heaven forbid that all the heterosexuals would politicize their sexuality!)

Words. For over thirty years now lesbians have been whispering, speaking, singing, writing, convening, hearing, reading. These are all political acts, personal actions with political implications. These narrators have paved the way for untold numbers of other women.

I have a lot of trouble with women who feel like you need to be out no matter what, that you need to be out wearing the sign "I am a lesbian." I have a lot of trouble with that because it's very individual and each individual needs to decide that for herself and what's safe and what isn't safe. (Rose)

Women have often felt insane when cleaving to the truth of our experience. Our future depends on the sanity of each of us, and we have a profound stake, beyond the personal, in the project of describing our reality as candidly and fully as we can to each other. (Adrienne Rich 1979, p. 190)

Chapter 8

Lesbian Spaces, Gay Faces

Many people, including many social scientists, consider community to be rooted spatially, in a place. For a gay community, the obvious places are bars. However, the bars, before 1970, were found in the larger metropolitan centers—much of the rest of the country was still dry into the 1970s. Kennedy and Davis say that for working class lesbians in the pre-Stonewall era, "bars for lesbians created the possibility of group consciousness and activity" (Kennedy and Davis 1997, p. 27). They go on to assert that "bars were the *only possible place* for working-class lesbians to congregate outside of private homes" (Kennedy and Davis 1997, p. 28), emphasis added. Whistling Women frequently mentioned bars in their narratives, and the memories were often vivid. Most striking in their narratives, however, are the glimpses of class differences in particular. Because of the association of bars with nonworking or working-class women, bars were not the usual places most of the narrators went.

Other place-based communities occurred at gay beaches, at hospitals in Indiana, at the Miami Diaper Service. Several significant communities in the stories in this study existed like super-amoebas—at a particular woman's home in Washington, DC, at a bowling alley in small-town Georgia, at a military base in Detroit, at colleges and universities in Chicago and New Orleans, at the roller derby rinks, at ballparks, at Buckeye Lake in Ohio. Beginning in the 1970s, women's bookstores offered shelter. Surely working-class lesbians found these places.

Greenwich Village existed as a mecca from 1935 to 1990, often only a distant imagined place where one was free to be oneself. For those living in New York City or New Jersey, Fire Island was yet another dreamland. In the mid-1990s St. Petersburg-Tampa and Carefree, in Florida, and Apache Junction, Arizona, assume importance of place for retiring women.

Fixed places to congregate were less common than one might assume, and at least one narrator said she thought bars were unimportant in lesbian history. Most lesbian socializing, as presented in these stories, had no place association beyond that of a town or county. Far more important were the lesbian spaces without places—social groups with revolving meeting places for weekend house parties, or ephemeral spaces like the lesbian correspondence group of Wishing Well Lesbian Connection, and Womyn's Words. In 2004, Olivia Cruises are floating spaces.

Although a few women disclaim any interest in gay community, far more women acknowledge the changes—the new freedoms, the leasening of fear over the course of their lives, the literature, the presence of others like themselves. They feel connected to a national sense of numbers, a national community with few actual places, and more spaces—the Gay Olympics, Gay Pride parades in hundreds of communities every June, lobbying efforts in Washington and many states, state referenda for rights, news coverage of efforts to secure rights, TV and movie stars "coming out," organizations with chapters in dozens of towns—like MCC, 45+, OLOC, and caucuses for gay practitioners of dozens of academic and professional occupations.

During the interviews for this project, it became clear that elements of a U.S. lesbian history were available and should be pulled out for posterity. In this chapter I want to record the information about lesbian places and spaces remembered by these narrators. In many cases the information is frustratingly sparse and overshadowed by lengthy treatments in other academic works, such as the histories of gay life in Philadelphia, New York City, Buffalo, San Francisco, and Boston. Nevertheless, these memories reveal lesbian participant perspectives, which are valuable in and of themselves.

I also want to explore the relationships of these women with gay men. The degree to which the narrators identify as feminist, as lesbian, as gay, as part of a larger gay rights movement is revealed by their comments on men. This chapter is divided into three sections, then: Greenwich Village, bar subculture, and gay men.

GREENWICH VILLAGE

It is probably because most of these women grew up north of the Ohio River that Greenwich Village loomed so large in the narrations.

Its reputation was based on the establishment of gay bars and restaurants there and in Harlem, in 1933 when Prohibition ended. Such establishments were virtually nonexistent elsewhere in the United States in the 1930s. The significance of Greenwich Village in many of these lives—as a symbolic and an actual place—will be apparent in the extrated quotes. It was the locus of safety, freedom, and other lesbians—it was part mythical, it was part real.

Greenwich Village was the symbol of community. So many of these women knew no lesbians other than their lovers for many decades of their lives. They learned about this gay place from family and friends, from magazines and newspapers. Cynthia read about Greenwich Village in magazines while a girl living in Ontario. She said she was desperate to go there. Some went there while young without recognizing an affinity; others went there as teenagers to feel affinity. Several women ran away to Greenwich Village, others stayed at the margins. Mitch's father didn't believe that gay people really existed. He insisted that cross-dressing men in the Village were there for tourists. She finally went to see for herself. Other narrators flocked there as well.

But I remember when I was sixteen or seventeen (1937), running to Greenwich Village to see the gay women because I was fascinated. I didn't really know what it was all about, but I felt like I belonged over there. (Roberta)

But when I had a date with a guy he took me down to Greenwich Village (1945) in New York to a club called the 181 Club which was a very famous, famous gay club in New York City in Greenwich Village. I think he did it as a joke or whatever it was, but we went to this club and this was where all of the girls wore tuxedos and the men were in drag for shows. And I was sitting there and I was all dressed up—believe me when I tell you I was dressed to the nines. And we were sitting there and he invited this one girl over to sit at our table, one in a tuxedo. And they came over and you know how at nightclubs they take pictures, and he said, "Let's take a picture." Well, I was so nervous with this girl sitting next to me that I moved all the way over to the fellow that I was sitting with, my date. And when the picture came out, my body was leaning all the way over toward her. That's when I literally came out for myself, as myself. And then I continually went down to the Village to see all these people because now my world opened up. (Addy)

And on this trip we ended up in Greenwich Village in New York City on a Saturday night. And we were in a bar and it was the first time I had ever seen gay people. They were gay. They were women that were dressed like men and I heard my father or one of the other guys that was in our group say,

"Well, there's a couple." And I didn't know what they were talking about. It struck me then, damn, this is odd, women dressed like men. I could understand that but I'd never seen it. (Gigi)

MARY1: We packed sandwiches and a suitcase and got on the train at North Station [Boston] and got off at Grand Central. At that time it cost . . . I think it was like $6 to go to New York City.

CHERYL: So why New York City?

MARY1: Greenwich Village.

CHERYL: So you were looking for a safe place to be yourselves?

MARY1: Right.

CHERYL: And how had you heard about Greenwich Village?

MARY1: We'd read about it in the paper.

And so I decided to go to New York one day and I just up and went. I had no connections, I knew nobody in New York. I knew it was a place gay people went and I went to a bar on Barrow Street and ran into a group of women that were obviously gay. And they all lived out in Queens in the Sunnyside area and told me two or three places that I could find out there that would be economical but still not a dive. (Pat M)

All the bars in New York that were for the girls began with an L. And she and I went out this one night and we didn't know anything. We were in the Village and we had made up our minds that we were going to find a bar. In those days you didn't ask the cops. Now you can ask the cops 'cause I did at one point. But years ago, in 1951, they'd probably throw you in jail. And there was talk about these women, women cops that would come around and strike up a conversation in these bars and if you went for it, you'd end up in jail. So I took a chance going to these bars. They were nice; they weren't bad. But this one night we found this place. We went down to the Village and we followed these girls, two girls, and I said, "Oh, look there. Let's follow them." I mean they could have been walking down to the park or down to see the water, who knows? But they were in and out of streets; they were down this street and we were about a block back. And they go down this side street and we stopped and watched them knock on the door. This guy comes to the door. All they say is, "Hi." And I thought, they got in with a "hi." So we go and knock on the door. He looks and says, "Hello, girls." The door opens. Well, I tell you, you'd think you had just walked into heaven. The smoke—the place was packed with women—the smoke, it was like a fog in England. Didn't know anything like that, I had never been in a place like that, never. We were like twenty-one or so (1951). This was in New York down in the Village. (Chris)

One time this group of friends and I went down to the Village. There were four of us that went looking. Jen and I had not started any kind of affair yet and the other two were straight—but one of them had heard there was a women's bar, a gay women's bar, so we went to look. We were all giggling and too scared to go downstairs. Finally, one of the straight ones said, "I'll go down and check it out." She went down and the rest of us were giggling at the top of the stairs. She came back up and she said, "Well, it's not open and I can't tell much about it because all the chairs are turned over on top of the tables." This was like late afternoon. I don't remember the name of the place. (Nancy)

So I went with my friend. One day we were at a singles party and it was bad. So I don't know how we decided we were going to go to a gay bar. We didn't know what the hell we were doing. We figured, well they say most prostitutes are lesbians and we knew where a lot of prostitutes were so we went there. And they thought we were crazy. We knew where this gay guy was going to be right now, a friend of ours, so I said, "Let's go there," and he was there. And we said, "What do we do?" And he told us the hotline number to call up and they gave us a whole series of bars to go to. When we finally walked into a bar . . . we walk into this bar. I said, "Oh my God, this is like a sorority rush party or something like that." And my friend said, "Well, what do we do now?" And I said, "I don't know." We went up to the bartender and said, "We're virgins. What do we do?" Well, she connected with somebody and had her experience and decided it wasn't for her. (Sappho)

CHERYL: Was Greenwich Village ever important?

BARBARA: Only because the bars were there and we would go together down there. And I showed [paintings] in the Village and I had friends that lived there. It wasn't the focus of my gay life.

CHERYL: Do you think that you would be where you are now if you hadn't been living so close to Greenwich Village or living in New York City?

BARBARA: That has nothing to do with it. I felt it had absolutely nothing to do with it. I would still find women attractive.

CHERYL: And be equally comfortable?

BARBARA: I don't know, I can't say 'cause I'm not there. I grew up in a time when gayness was not really very accepted.

CHERYL: But perhaps in the one place where it was accepted?

BARBARA: Well, not where I lived, it wasn't.

Most of the lesbian bars are closed [in 2000]. There are very few women's bars left. There's a couple but not like there used to be when I was running around with those from the group [in NYC]. (Sappho)

The importance of the Village, in the imaginations of lesbian youths in the 1930s and 1940s, as well as today, cannot be overstated. (Its gay male history is explored at length in Chauncey 1994). In this blessed spot on earth were other people like themselves—imaginary friends and family. It was a spot where one could risk being oneself all the time, not just in the dark.

THE SUBCULTURE OF LESBIAN/MIXED GAY BARS

It is true that most of the lesbian bars in the United States have closed by now, making a history of bars and bar life possible and necessary. Cynthia explained that she closed her women's bar in upstate New York in 1986 because of liability issues—moral and financial. The movie *Last Call at Maud's* explores some of the reasons why that twenty-five-year-old bar in San Francisco closed in 1989. The owner said that lesbians stopped drinking in 1989 and the tremendous expenses made it impossible to make a profit. More generally, neighborhood bars failed in large numbers. Lesbians, for instance, were choosing to go to dance clubs in San Francisco in the late 1980s.

Bar life in Greenwich Village and Harlem in the 1930s was soon augmented in the 1940s by gay/lesbian bars elsewhere in large cities where Prohibition Era laws were not in place. These new bars were supported by the growing urban gay population attracted by wartime industry and ports. Prohibition sentiment in state laws prevented bars in places such as Wichita for decades. (They became possible in Boone, North Carolina, only in 1985.)

Studies that I am familiar with make it clear that bars were invaluable for creating community and educating women about their sexual persuasion. It also seems that bar culture created the phenomenon of butch/fem (explored in Chapter 4), as recorded in studies such as *Boots of Leather, Slippers of Gold*. Socioeconomic class differences were most evident in the reactions of many of these narrators to the women they saw or met in bars, which I explore in Chapter 7. As Cynthia remarked, based on her years of bar-going and owning, "upper class women didn't come to bars."

Kennedy and Davis (1997) point out that there was very little class mixing in lesbians bars where mostly working-class women hung out, unlike male bars where there was a thorough mixing of classes. Their explanation is that lesbian culture never eroticized power differences. Career women were afraid of being seen and losing their jobs so they did not go in bars often, and rather than being attracted to working-class women, middle-class and upper-class women were repulsed (see comments following, and in Chapter 7).

Lesbian bars, and gay bars in general for that matter, were often located in the bad part of town and were described as dirty, dark, and smoky. They were often unrecognizable from the outside, except for the lack of windows and the difficult access. Many women's places had a separate room or floor for men, or were establishments frequented by straight men during the daylight hours. The bars usually had bouncers and prearranged signals indicating the presence of police.

Few gay/lesbian bars were raided or closed in Buffalo during the 1940s. Under Governor Rockefeller, however, Buffalo bars were harassed and closed relentlessly in the late 1950s and early 1960s. "From this point on into the 1970s no bars [in Buffalo] managed to stay open for more than several years" (Kennedy and Davis 1993, p. 145). In New York City, the presence of a single homosexual made a bar "disorderly," and hundreds of bars in the city were closed and staff and patrons arrested. Gay bars hired floormen to prevent touching and campy behavior (Beemyn 1997b).

Nor was it only a governor who cracked down. In 1942-1943 the Armed Forces Disciplinary Control Board initiated antivice crackdowns in many U.S. cities, particularly ports, to regulate the impact of so many service personnel. "In San Francisco between 1942 and 1943, these efforts resulted in the citation or suspension of almost 100 bars and night clubs, many of which served a gay clientele" (Boyd 1997, p. 86). The names of gay bars were listed in newspapers from the late 1940s into the 1950s.

Gay bars have been called crucibles of political awareness (Kennedy and Davis 1997). Only one political action was reported in the stories of these narrators, that by Jan in Pittsburgh, protesting a policy to exclude black clients. Black lesbians didn't shift into bars until after the 1940s and then "not completely," although some bars in Chicago and NYC had black clientele in the 1940s (Beemyn 1997). It seems that in large part the political potential was unrealized.

Bars were beloved by some clientele, looming as large as the college or high school experience. I wonder where young lesbians of the next decade will find each other? The Internet, already a significant place for lesbians to meet, is a very different experience from walking into a gay bar.

CHERYL: You didn't go to bars?
CLAIRE: No. I never have walked into a gay bar alone.
CHERYL: And why is that?

CLAIRE: I didn't know who might be there or how much that place would be watched. In those days, there were surveillance teams with various police departments. I had a friend who was the vice president of the Cleveland Trust Company in the personnel department. And she went to a women's softball game and saw a bunch of the girls sitting across and there among them, laughing and joking with them, was a man she knew to be with the police department. This is how they gathered, I don't know what information. I don't know what they were looking for. But there were raids and those places were not safe.

CHERYL: How about today?

CLAIRE: I haven't been to one that would interest me enough to go back to. They are smoky and loud and I don't find them pleasant. If there were one that was not loud, not smoky, and pleasant, I would certainly go.

There was a place in Chicago out near Skokie called the Midget and the back room upstairs was lesbian. And I can remember going there with some friends from Cleveland and that's what visitors would like to do, take us to a gay bar. They were afraid to go into a gay bar in their hometown but when they were out of town. . . . But the group that frequented it was not a group I would want to know.

CHERYL: Who were they?

CLAIRE: Well, I don't know. I'd say that they were probably heavy drinkers. They were, once again, women who were trying not to be female, denying themselves. And that was not pleasant.

CHERYL: Did you run into them a lot?

CLAIRE: Oh, there was a lot of that out there.

CHERYL: Was that part of the butch-fem or not?

CLAIRE: It was a totally different thing because there could be two of them together. It was a kind of—you have to consider it a mental aberration. You are denying yourself. I am not who I am.

It was in Chicago and I was still in college. God, it was scary. And a friend of mine, Sonny—I've always thought I ought to try to find her. One night we decided we'd go to a bar called Billy's. And we heard it was gay and I had been there a couple of times. So we went into the back room and we had no more than got in and sat down than I see these two hulks standing in the doorway. And before you knew it, we were all in the paddy wagon. Now there were people there, mixed, a guy and a gal, and they were probably gay but they were mixed. They told them to leave. But they put all the women in the paddy wagon, so we all ended up in the bullpen. And one by one taken in and questioned. And unfortunately it happened to be in my neighborhood. I thought to myself, Oh God, if my family wonders where in the hell I am, 'cause we had left from my house. It was getting late. And I thought if they call the police station, they're going to call where they'll find me. They'll say, "Oh yes, we've got her here." So I sweated that one out. But anyway, they took us one at a time and interrogated us and I said, "I don't know what you're talking about." I said, "We just decided we'd have a drink." And so they interrogated everybody and apparently a couple of times some of them. And somehow or another I ended up then being the last one and I find out my friend said, yes, she knew what it was. I could have killed her. But anyway they got me back in and finally they said, "You're the last one and you're hold-ing everybody up. As soon as you sign this, everybody can go." And I thought, Oh God. So finally I said, "I don't know what you're talking about but if I'm the one that's holding everybody here. . . ."

And then they let us all go. But when we got to court—we had to go to court. When we got to court, the balliff came up as we were being checked in and said, "That policewoman is really out to get you." But apparently Billy's had a good lawyer and we were all dismissed. What happened was in those days the people in the neighborhood probably complained or else they didn't pay up. It was all a payoff scheme. And so they either missed a payment or the neighborhood was putting pressure on them and so they had to set up a night. (Mary2)

Then I met this schoolteacher and she took me to a bar in Washington, DC, and she said, "You've got to come with me." And I walked in and there's a whole room full of queers. She said, "Everybody here is queer." I just could not believe that every female in that room was gay. And sure enough, the bar scene really was not for me—the loud music and some of the people that were there. Not that I'm a snob. They were changing partners all the time. (Amelia)

I had friends that I had met in the bars, some that I would not invite to my home, absolutely never. And I was right about that. I invited one person that I didn't want to invite and the next day she called and wanted to borrow money. So many people I wouldn't invite; I just knew them in the bars. I don't think I was a snob, but I just didn't trust a lot of those folks. And still today, you have to be cautious of people. I think so. (Jan)

In 1986 I was down here in Florida and I got a call that my friend Rod who had introduced me to the gay life had had a stroke and was in the hospital. So I got Scott to take care of the cat and I took off and went up there and I stayed with a person who was also a friend of Rod's. She was about four years younger than I and Rod kind of thought maybe we could get some-thing going. But anyway, I stayed at her house and that was the first time that I was ever in a gay bar or a gay establishment where you could dance and have a drink and have dinner and that sort of thing—1986. I was all eyes and ears. I thought that was a whole lot of fun, yeah. You could dance and you could hold hands and that sort of thing.

And I said then, I've been cloistered for thirty years. Because June and I—I used to tease her, beg her, please, take me somewhere. I said, "Let's go to Buffalo, someplace." No, no, no, they are just dives. "You don't want to do that." So she would never take me. (Sheri)

That's right. People with big jobs would not come in the bars. For one thing, they would be supervisors and they had gay women working for them or could have and didn't know it. And if they were seen there by anybody that worked for them, then they would have something on them. And the next time that boss tried to reprimand that person or fire that person, they could make trouble for them. I had some personal friends that would never come in my bar because of that. And I've had some of their employees come over and ask me, "Do you know so and so and is she gay?" I said, "No they're not." I would lie about it cause I know what can happen. And just because people are gay doesn't make them all nice. (Cynthia)

It's the women that are separating us off, isn't it? We were in the bars together in Pittsburgh and then one woman said, "No, women upstairs and men downstairs" and we stopped going. I used to travel with my two gay friends, guys, we'd travel all over the place, share hotel rooms. We were very close. (Jan)

BARBARA: We don't go to bars anymore. We only did in the beginning because it was new and we met a few people that way.

CHERYL: Did you meet other women in the bars who you felt you had things in common with?

BARBARA: From time to time, yes. But not all that much.

So we all went to Cleveland to a gay bar. It was a disaster. I hated it; it was terrible. It wasn't clean. It was loud; it was smoky. I go to straight bars; I like class. I like nice music and good food. This was worse than the worst hillbilly bar I'd ever seen. That's why I've never been a [gay] bar person. That was my first bar experience. It was dark, it was dingy, and it was in a bad part of town. (Gigi)

I remember one night some straight guys came in and came up and I was dancing with a gay man and so was Kay. And he cut in and was dancing with me and propositioned me. He specifically indicated what he intended to do so I didn't need to worry about getting pregnant. In any case, the proprietor, I think, says something to him and he became very belligerent. So the proprietor called the police and they came in and carted him off. (Claire)

CYNTHIA: I went to the guy's bars and sometimes some of the guy's bar owners would come to my place.

CHERYL: But only during business hours, only while you're open. You all wouldn't go out to dinner together or meet at lunch sometime.

CYNTHIA: No. I had some guys working for me that I hung out with. As far as the owners of the men's bar, I was friendly with them. But I never went to their house or anything like that.

CHERYL: So no network particularly of bar owners?

CYNTHIA: No. When something would happen, like that thing with Miller Beer, they notified me.

GAY COMMUNITY?

In Chapter 7, I explored the issue of word usage, specifically "gay" versus "lesbian." For a number of women, their word of choice is gay for several reasons including the inclusive nature of the word, signifying homosexual women and men together. For several women, however, "lesbian" makes an important distinction for them, separating them from homosexual men. Just what have been the relationships between these narrators and gay men? I assumed that since few of these women are radical feminists, gay men would probably have been present in their lives, and they would not develop an antimale political stance. On the other hand, the lesbian stereotype is one of disliking men or not needing to bother with men. I wondered if the women who had married would be more open to gay men than the women who never married. I could also make a counter argument. In this section of the chapter, I will explore to what degree lesbian space and place was/is important and protected by these women by examining their comments on and history with gay men and their social circles now.

We sort of looked at each other and felt it was time for us to go home. I don't why it should be sort of repugnant to see men kissing each other passionately. (Carolyn)

CHERYL: Do you have as many gay men friends as you do women?

GIGI: More. That was a fellow that called me a while ago, not a woman.

JAN: Then I got hired in the summer theater in Cleveland and ran into more gay people and was hanging around with those gay people, men and women. They were more closeted though, but I became more comfortable in what I was doing and ran around specifically with these two gay boys. One was a dancer and one was a singer in the theater and they are still a couple living in New York.

CHERYL: And now you say you want to simplify your life to where it's only gay people. Will it still be mixed?

JAN: Sure. I have many gay guy friends. Sometimes I get mad at them 'cause they get so gross. One is my dear friend. He is forever asking me if I've got laid yet. I say, "Stop it."

We know some gay guys but we don't really socialize too much with them [which has been the case all through my life]. . . . Within the gay scene, I feel that people can be trusted. I think that I could be a little bit more myself than I usually am with mixed groups and things like that. Although I have a thing, I don't know, like the guys, if the guys are a little bit too effeminate, I sort of like push myself away from them. Maybe I don't want to be associated with them. or things like that. . . . And even when we go there sometimes, it's very awkward to see two guys dancing together. It just seems a little awkward to me. And yet, some of them are so cute and adorable, that it's hard not to really like them as a person. If you sit and you talk to them. (Kate)

Chris says now she knows a few gay boys. Kay M hung out with gay men in several cities including Lake Charles, Louisiana, Denver, and Chicago.

I taught school in Lake Charles and one of my closest gay friends was Michael. We did all kinds of things and I got to know all of the gay fellows. . . . In fact, some of the guys used to call me the Mother Confessor of the Near North Side [Chicago]. There were about seven or eight gay guys in chiropractic school. There weren't many women who were chiropractors. So I would be seen sometimes going out with six or seven guys and we were all going out to the Near North Side. There were two or three gay clubs in that area. (Kay M)

MARY1: I hung around a lot with a lot of the guys.
CHERYL: Have gay men been a part of your life all along?
MARY1: Yes.
CHERYL: Even today?
MARY1: Oh yeah. We have quite a few gay men friends.

Mary1 lived with two gay men after she left a lover, and they paid for her bus ticket to Florida when she decided to start another relationship there. Mary Lou learned about the stock market and computer stock research from a gay man, as did a couple of other women. Four women married gay men, two of them knowingly, with one of those relationships lasting ten years.

MARY2: At one time there were two guys across the street from where I lived and we would get together. And two other guys that I ran around with, that we ran around with. In fact, I remember one time having them over and some gals I knew and the gals didn't say a word. They just sat there and you could tell they were very uncomfortable. So I never invited them back.
CHERYL: Were they straight women?
MARY2: No, they were gay, but they apparently did not approve of gay men. Later on in life and for the last twenty years [I've been] basically with a mixed group all the time. . . . We had a group of friends, mixed guys and gals, that probably were fifty people or more and we were all just very close, all friends, enjoyed each other's company, always got together, always something going on. But the gay issue never came up.

The Gay Olympics held in West Virginia for ten years was attendance by invitation only, all gay. As a contestant entered the door, she or he reached into a box of numbers for male-female partners. Jean says she had very close gay men friends. Pat N relayed the information that when she was gay in Louisiana, she kept almost exclusive company with gay men. Living in New York City in the mid-1960s she knew very few gay men, and went to lesbian bars frequently. Her first eight years living in Germany, she was again in a predominantly gay male environment but with more women than in her Louisiana social group.

NAN: In my middle years I had a lot of contact with gay men. A couple of my best friends were gay and they moved out of the area or they died.

CHERYL: And that accounts for why you have little contact with men now?

NAN: Well, I have contact with heterosexual men more than I do gay men. It's just that my life has changed. I don't need the protection of having to have a man on my arm. A lot of us would accompany each other to functions. I don't feel that need anymore. People have moved on, my life has changed quite a bit, I'm retired now and I'm doing all those things that I want to do and it's mainly with women. When AIDS came out, I was terrified also. I was terrified of hugging a man or kissing a gay man. And my family were afraid to touch me, although I was in the safest group and I explained that to them.

I was very friendly with a number of gay guys over the years, not so much during the long time that I lived in New York. Mostly, I had found in New York, it seems to me that they spent so much time with other men that they didn't have too much use for women, a lot of the ones that I seemed to run across. I could count on one hand the close gay men friends I had.

I said that I had trouble with gay men in New York, finding friends that were long term. But the ones that we have here will probably go on forever. They're very dear and have shown their friendship in more ways than I can say. We were in down in Key West and just had bought this great big motor home, I don't drive it because of my eyesight and they came down from Sarasota and drove it back for us. That's the kind of guys they are. (Nancy)

We have coffees that meet every other Tuesday morning. That's men and women. All of these guys are older guys. They're not thirty years old. I guess they've mellowed in life or whatever. I love them all. (Amelia)

Power of attorney, Mary1 and I both have them. . . . We did have them set up with a couple, men that we've known for years, but one of them died and we don't know whether that would be a problem or not. . . . I have quite a group of gay men friends. Most of them have been introduced to us through other people. We usually have dinner at someone's house. [Sometimes we are in couples.] (Pat M)

We had a lot of gay friends and it was mostly men, mostly the queens. And I always preferred the company of men. I don't know whether or not it was because I thought that way there was no threat or what it was all about. But I just always preferred being around queens. And we had two fellows that we used to go dancing with. So in other words it looked like two couples. But we went to the gay bars of course. (Roberta)

The overwhelming impression is that these women have had much interaction with gay men and like/liked their gay male friends. Gay men have been their tutors, friends, confidants, companions, social chairmen, neighbors. Lesbian feminism of the 1970s, which reasoned that lesbians needed to pull away from men, advocated separatism, and saw gay men as simply men, has very little representation among these women.

Much of this information about gay men, however, reflects activities several decades ago. I collected data on the makeup of their social circles today that will fill out this picture. Eighteen women claim that they currently socialize with lesbians at least 90 percent of the time. Eleven women claim that their social circle now consists of at least 20 percent gay men, and six of those women spend a significant amount of time in the company of straight people. Eight other women said they spend more time in straight company than gay. (I lacked this information for nine women.) Only three of the women who said they have significant numbers of relationships with gay men now were once married.

The quotes above, coupled with the dismay expressed by a number of women over the division implied by the word "gay" between men and women, make it clear that the vast majority of these narrators see themselves as having as much in common with gay men as they do with other lesbians. Some evidence of a gay community rift exists, however.

As these women have aged, their communities of choice have, in many cases, become increasingly focused on other lesbians. After major portions of their lives were spent among straight society it is a luxury of retirement that they can surround themselves with other gay women now. They have also become increasingly politicized about discrimination against women.

I am angry about gay men and what they did to my life. I mean I've met some nice ones at a few mutual parties and I like them okay. Gay men hate women. It's like, they try to act like we're family. No, no, no; they ridicule women. (Marilyn)

Furthermore, the national efforts of gay people to gain recognition and rights have increasingly narrowed efforts to embrace "normal" homosexuals and define out of the movement people who do not otherwise pass as "normal heterosexuals." Gloria says that she doesn't like to see drag. "I don't like to see the degenerates of the gay movement. Bad for the rest of us." Addy and Joyce were just as concerned and unsympathetic about protecting differences.

I think the men make a spectacle of themselves and I think the young women—the young kids—are ruining it. (Addy)

We have gone out of our way to make it better for the gay community and the gay society. And I think [people in parades] go out of their way to tear it down. (Joyce)

This group of narrators largely welcomes the freedom gained for and taken by homosexuals in U.S. society in the past thirty years while simultaneously not embracing the notion of themselves as a part of a national gay community. They have little political interest in earning or keeping legal rights, probably because they have grown accustomed to making do. Many of them lived without community for the first fifty years of their lives, without bars, without marriage and apart from S&M, transgender, cross-gender, sexlessness, polysexed, man-boy love, even AIDS issues. Their view of gay community is an extension of their largely middle-class (and higher) experiences and values. Making the world safe for difference is not a concern of the Whistling Women, while making the world safe for herself has been a looming concern.

CHERYL: So all the fears and family worries and career worries are gone for all these [retired lesbians]?

DOROTHY: They are all gone. And when it comes to family, most people say, Hey, basically they either know what I am or they're smart enough to know what I am, one or the other. And if they can't accept me the way I am, to hell with them. We're just not about to play those dumb games anymore.

> Whistling women
> and crowing hens
> often come
> to a good end

Chapter 9

Conclusion

It is time now to recap the discoveries of greatest significance for social science from this study of forty-four lesbians. The first part of this chapter will do just that. What then remains to be explored is the extent to which the two age cohorts created at the beginning of the study should continue to be treated as separate groups. This topic will be addressed after the review.

NOTES FOR THE CONSERVATIVE RIGHT, GAY STUDIES SCHOLARS, AND OURSELVES

Women do not become lesbians because their mothers worked outside the home, as 61 percent of the moms of the younger lesbians were stay-at-home moms. Nor can lesbians be attributed to feminism since feminism was in a lull from 1930 to 1960 when these women were coming of age and going to college. Bad relationships with fathers is not a significant issue in lesbian identity since only 7 percent of the Whistling Women disliked their fathers. I cannot specify the role of childhood abuse in the lesbian identity since the question was addressed on the questionnaire, which was returned by only twenty women. During the interviews only two women mentioned abuse. However, more women reported abusive husbands. Ninety-three percent of these lesbians reported a religious upbringing. None of these lesbians had lesbian parents. What we can say for sure is that stay-at-home moms and religious, heterosexual loving parents produce many lesbian daughters. Furthermore, of these lesbians who themselves became moms, only one of forty-six children raised by these women is gay today and one not raised by her mother after age six is gay.

If a Whistling Woman wasn't married by age twenty-nine, she never married a man. As a group, the average age of first sexual encounter with a woman was age twenty-five but for once-married women it was age twenty-nine.

This group of narrators has had an average of four women lovers over the course of their lifetimes. Sixty-four percent of these relationships lasted five years or less, 16 percent lasted seven to ten years, and 20 percent lasted eleven to thirty-two years (36 percent lasted longer than the average heterosexual marriage). It seems that lesbians are the opposite of their stereotype, committing to relationships with significant others much longer than is common among the general population. These lesbians stayed in relationships with husbands longer on average than do heterosexual women of their age cohort, and they stay in relationships with women lovers longer than heterosexuals stay together on average.

Divorce failed to change significantly the economic status of narrators who were already in the lower classes or who were already working or who had recently earned an academic degree. It seems that a job did as much for the Whistling Women as did a husband with respect to economic standing in midlife.

In this study it is clear that lower-class or working-class status is not synonymous with butch/fem, nor is lack of education. In fact, 50 percent of the women born into upper-class families in this study identified as butch prior to 1959. More significant, only ten women identified as butch or fem (20 percent), and they were, with one exception, frequent bar-goers. In fact, most of the women in this study were and still are disgusted by butchy women. If gay historians want to explore representative lesbian lives before 1970, they will have to move out beyond the bars to the beaches, bowling alleys, nursing stations, and elementary schools of the era.

Class status was assessed for three periods in these women's lives: status of their birth family, in midlife, and the present. Twenty-one women said their socioeconomic class status was higher when they were working than when they were children, fifteen said it was the same, and five women say they dropped in class standing as working adults. Most of the wealthiest women in this project made their money in real estate, buying, improving or building, and selling houses. Early in life it was more common to support a lover or to merge resources. Now women in partnerships tend to have separate bank accounts while jointly owning assets.

Today, 5 percent of the narrators receive less than $10,000 annually, and 17 percent receive $10,000 to $15,000. The highest annual income among the Whistling Women is $54,000. No significant difference exists in the reliance on Social Security or on rental/trust/royalty income between lesbians and the general population. However, a greater proportion of lesbians have pensions, use stocks for financing retiement, are homeowners, and have disabilities than does the general U.S. population.

But within this lesbian population, a noticeable difference is found between the income makeup of once-married and never-married lesbians. Never-married women are much more likely to have second homes and rental property. Only one once-married woman has a second home. Is it the lack of children among the never-marrieds that makes it possible for them to have this lifestyle, or is it economics?

Nine percent of once-married women currently derive annual income from rentals or mortgages, while 32 percent of never-married do. Fifty-four percent of once-married women have their own pensions; 73 percent of never-married women have pensions. Married women, however, invest in the stock market more commonly than do never-married women, 86 percent versus 73 percent. Given that pensions are the core of a retirement, the once-married women seem to be at a disadvantage in their senior years. Twenty-five percent of the younger once-married women have no pension. I suspect the answer to the second-home question is that the never-married lesbians have a more secure income base than do most of the once-marrieds. The never-married lesbians may also have more familiarity with the real estate market.

Half of the narrators believe that they have maintained their socioeconomic status in the transition to retirement, but 30 percent feel that it has fallen with retirement, most often from middle-class to lower-class status (16 percent) but also from upper class to middle class (7 percent). Remarkably, 20 percent think that their class standing has risen since retiring—a testimony to their ability to negotiate the financial instruments available to them.

Popular activities in retirement are reading and socializing. The Internet is a common feature of each day and home. The Metropolitan Community Church is the favored church of the women in this sample. However, twenty women have rejected religion. It appears that older lesbians are a little less religious than the general population but that they are also more religious than indicated by other studies of lesbians and probably more religious than most churchgoers would assume.

Finally, these lesbian women and hundreds more have created vibrant communities in Florida, Alabama, North Carolina, and Arizona, as well as other places, and national and regional lesbian-focused groups where women their age and younger live and talk together. Over and over again simply one or two women have created a space, implemented an idea, and women have responded out of their need for community. This need for community might be different for gay men, for one researcher could not find any community base among older gay men. Gay men and these women have nevertheless found much solace in one another's company over the years, and many narrators resist the appellation "lesbian and gay" as needlessly separating homosexuals from one another. As these women age, however, they increasingly seek the company of other lesbians. The narrators are typically not sympathetic toward an all-inclusive queer movement. They aren't even politically active in the arena of the more conservative gay rights movement. Only a handful call themselves feminists with many more voting for abortion rights and other issues that benefit working women. Eighty percent of them align with the Democratic party. They are not leaving the party like younger lesbians are.

DO AGE DIFFERENCES MATTER IN STUDIES OF OLDER LESBIANS?

One other social aspect of this study deserves further attention. I have assumed throughout this book that significant differences existed between the narrators based on their birth year and consequently divided them into two age cohorts. It is time now to reconsider this assumption. Although they were born over a twenty-one-year period (1917-1938), they all came of age well before the 1960s, when great social upheavals associated with the civil rights movement, peace movement, free-love movement, women's movement, and finally, the gay liberation movement began and subsequently transformed U.S. society. During their maturation, homosexuals went from fashionable in some social circles or a phase for young girl to a sickness, and point of federal and state government concern. It could be argued that as lesbians, their lives were likely to be more similar than different.

The pivotal points of being a lesbian before 1960 were probably sexuality, living without husbands, suffering discrimination, living without children, and social orchestration, by which I mean living without words, lying, hiding, finding friends, and making community. At the turn of the twenty-first century, we should reconsider the lesbians' lives without men, their incomes, safety, and community. Differences in the lesbian experience both before retirement and since retirement, based on one's decade of birth are explored by topic.

Childhoods: (Abuse, working moms, single-parent households) More of the older women's mothers gave up the care of their children, and more worked while mothering.

Sexuality: Unfortunately, I didn't code the sex questionnaires by age. From the interviews I can extract that the average age for first same-sex sexual experience for older women (and surprisingly for the younger women as well) was twenty-five years old. As for butch and fem, four (27 percent) older women and six (21 percent) younger women identified as butch or fem. All of the fems were found among the younger women. Why there are fems only among the younger women deserves further investigation. Perhaps it is a product of sampling.

Discrimination: Twenty-four percent of the younger cohort reported discrimination based on their sexuality. From among the older cohort four women reported discrimination, or 27 percent. I view these figures as essentially the same, but the type of discrimination differed. Only the mothers among the younger women reported custody battles, which was the only type of discrimination any of the younger married women reported. All of these battles occurred after the start of the women's movement. Perhaps the women's movement gave them the courage to seek dissolution of the marriage, and the knowledge that there were more lesbians than themselves.

Early education: The younger women went away to college more frequently than did the older women (Table 2.6). Twice the percentage of younger women opted to take a two-year or three-year degree, and slightly more younger women completed the bachelor's degree (Table 2.7).

Advanced education: Forty percent of the older women got master's degrees, as did 55 percent of the younger women, clearly demonstrating the greater job requirements in later years. Thirteen percent and 14 percent, respectively, of the women earned PhDs. The older women were able to complete their education in one decade while the younger women were in advanced education classes over a three-decade period.

Marriage: In both cohorts, women married in 50 percent of the cases. The older women married at an average age of twenty-two, and the younger at age twenty. The older women left marriages earlier. The younger women had larger families on average than did the older married women.

Careers: The younger women show a greater variety of degrees than do the older women. Among the older women 20 percent had military experience while only 7 percent of the younger women did. Certainly the lack of a pension is career related and due to longer years in marriage and the jobs entered into by the younger women.

Retirement age: The average age at retirement is essentially the same for both cohorts, age sixty and sixty-one years respectively. Early retirement (before age sixty-five) occurred among 86 percent of the younger women and 60 percent of the older women, a clear difference.

Funding retirement: A greater proportion of the older women receive Social Security and pension payouts, and have investments in the stock market. An equal proportion of the two age cohorts have rental income and are homeowners. A greater percentage of the younger women are receiving disability checks and public assistance.

Sixty-six percent of the older women are living with a partner, and 59 percent of the younger women are so situated. Some significant differences occur in funding retirement with respect to age cohort, but these are even greater when considering marriage status.

Religion: Older and younger women attend the MCC church equally (13 percent versus 14 percent), and are similarly religious or uninterested (47 percent and 45 percent) in religion. A striking difference can be found in the allegiance to "typical" religions (20 percent of the older cohort adhere to typial religions versus 7 percent of the younger cohort). Less dramatic a difference but still noteworthy is the greater proportion of women following alternative spiritual paths among the younger women—34 percent younger versus 20 percent older. (Much more striking are the religious differences between never-marrieds and once-marrieds. Eighteen percent of never-marrieds practice an alternative religion versus 41 percent of the once-marrieds. Fifty-nine percent of the never-marrieds reject religion today while 41 percent of the once-marrieds do.)

Community: Twenty percent of the older women now live in exclusively lesbian communities, while only two of the younger women do (7 percent). Incidentally, only one of the once-married women now lives in a lesbian community. It is undoubtedly significant that once-married lesbians usually have children, and at this point in their lives, in-laws and grandchildren. These women continue to move between the worlds of these family members and their friendship/neighbor communities and activities.

There are no significant differences in political party registration, in technological savvy, or in being "out" between the two age cohorts.

Word usage: Women in the older group are more comfortable with the words lesbian, homosexual, butch, dyke, and queer than are the younger women. For both groups, it was in retirement that they broke their silences.

So, does age cohort make a meaningful dividing line in the case of this study, when examining lesbian lives? Similarities occur in the amount of reported discrimination, the attainment of the PhD, the age at first sex with a woman, the participation in butch/fem, their average age at retirement, the percentage of women who are "out," their Democratic party affiliation, Internet use, rental investments, and home ownership. From the perspective of the younger women differences occur in affiliation as fems, custody battles, going away to college, longer marriages, more children, longer time needed to complete education, lower military enrollment, more atypical religious practices, eschewing life today in an intentional lesbian community, and the words used to label their homosexuality.

I think that age cohort does not matter as much as I thought it would when I designed the analysis. An obvious exception to the downplaying of the age division for future studies would be the division between women who were twenty-five before the 1970s and women who reached that age in the mid- to late 1970s and later, a division between the era of secrecy and silence and the era of publicity and community. Instead, it seems that a more natural social division in studies of lesbian lives is the never-married/once-married division. The marriage differences documented here are often quite significant.

Several e-mails have come my way from Mary1 recently concerning the crazed world perspective of our President Bush and the need for more women to visit the Breast Cancer Site, where a simple click sends a free mammogram for a needy woman (www.thebreastcancer site.com). The Human Rights Campaign has sent me their online newsletter giving me many opportunities to register my opinion about gay marriage. My university department has hired a third lesbian faculty member and a new couple in another department got married in Vermont this summer before moving to Boone. The third annual Queer Film Series on campus is currently underway, and all the most popular TV shows this summer had a gay theme. The U.S. Supreme Court has struck down the Texas sodomy law.

While I have been struck by the vast technological changes my ninety-three-year-old father has witnessed, I am even more aware of the vast social changes the Whistling Women have witnessed in their lifetimes. Alcohol went from forbidden to being sold in grocery stores; blue laws and miscegenation laws have been revoked or ignored; Indians are being paid for land taken over a hundred years ago; homosexuals have gone from being chic to dangerous to chic again; blacks and whites freely mingle in society; blacks and women are paid handsomely to play sports they were forbidden to play three decades ago; women go out in public wearing practically nothing or even just underwear; women keep their maiden names and make babies in at least six ways; sex can kill you; the stock market has been in and out and in and out of favor; job sectors have boomed and busted; and single women can now adopt children, AIDS babies, dogs, and streets.

Islamic individuals with bombs strapped to themselves have replaced the Russian nation's nuclear threat and even the minority crime threat in our fear hierarchy here in the United States. We have earned Arabic hatred partly because lesbians can move about more freely in U.S. society today than they could when the Whistling Women's stories began and more freely than they will be able to in Islamic countries for the foreseeable future. Who could have predicted that we homosexuals would win over the United States and Europe only to unleash the fury of the Islamic world? These stories of lesbians' lives are not finished, and this saga of lesbians in the United States is not over. The greater social acceptance of lesbians in the United States has been fostered by the examples and histories of the lives of Whistling Women. I am hopeful that the social changes of the past six decades will result in a citizenry that embraces and protects all of its members, however different they want to hold themselves out to be, by recognizing the common struggles we all share.

References

Albro, Joyce and Carol Tully (1979) [reprinted]. A Study of Lesbian Lifestyles in the Homosexual Micro-Culture and the Heterosexual Macro-Culture. *Journal of Lesbian Studies* 1(1):55-68.

Almvig, C. (1982). *The Invisible Minority: Aging and Lesbianism.* Syracuse: Ithaca College of Syracuse.

Archbold, R. (1982). Old but Not Alone. *The Body Politic* (December), pp. 25-28.

Bailey, Robert (2000). *Out and Voting II: The Gay, Lesbian, and Bisexual Vote in Congressional Elections, 1990-1998.* Washington, DC: National Gay and Lesbian Task Force.

Beemyn, Brett (1997, Ed.). *Creating a Place for Ourselves: Lesbian, Gay, and Bisexual Community Histories.* New York: Routledge.

Berger, Raymond (1982a). *Gay and Gray: The Older Homosexual Man* Urbana: University of Illinois Press.

Berger, Raymond (1982b). The Unseen Minority—Older Gays and Lesbians. *Social Work* 27:236-242.

Boyd, Nan (1997). "Homos Invade S.F.!" San Francisco's History As a Wide-Open Town. In *Creating a Place for Ourselves: Lesbian, Gay, and Bisexual.Community Histories,* edited by Brett Beemyn, pp. 73-96. New York: Routledge.

Bullough, Vern and B. Bullough (1977). *Sin, Sickness, and Sanity: A History of Sexual Attitudes.* New York: New American Library.

Cahill, Sean, Ken South, and Jane Spade (2000). *Outing Age: Public Policy Issues Affecting Gay, Lesbian, Bisexual and Transgender Elders.* Washington, DC: National Gay Lesbian Task Force.

Calasanti, Toni and Alessandro Bonanno (1992). Theorizing About Gender and Aging: Beginning with the Voices of Women. *The Gerontologist* 32:280-282.

Chafe, William (1972). *The American Woman: Her Changing Social, Economic and Political Roles, 1920-1970.* London: Oxford University Press.

Chauncey, George (1994). *Gay New York: Gender, Urban Culture, and the Making of the Gay Male World, 1890-1940.* New York: Basic Books.

Chauncey, George (1997). The Policed: Gay Men's Strategies of Everyday Resistance in Times Square. In *Creating a Place for Ourselves: Lesbian, Gay, and Bisexual Community Histories,* edited by Brett Beemyn, pp. 9-26. New York: Routledge.

Claassen, Cheryl (1999). Black and White Women at Irene Mound. In *Grit-Tempered: Early Women Archaeologists in the Southeastern United States,* edited by N. White, L. Sullivan, and R. Marrinan, pp. 92-114. Gainesville: University Presses of Florida.

Claassen, Cheryl (2000). Homophobia and Women Archaeologists. *World Archaeology* 32(2):173-179.

Cotten, W.L. (1975). Social and Sexual Relationships of Lesbians. *Journal of Sex Research* 11:139-148.

Dailey, Nancy (1998). *When Baby Boom Women Retire.* Westport, CT: Praeger.

Daughters of Bilitis (1960). *The Ladder* 4:4-25.

Day, Nancy and Patricia Schoenrade (1997). Staying in the Closet Versus Coming Out: Relationships Between Communication About Sexual Orientation and Work Attitudes. *Personnel Psychology* 50(1):147.

D'Emilio, John (1983). *Sexual Politics, Sexual Communities: The Making of a Homosexual Minority in the United States, 1940-1970.* Chicago: University of Chicago Press.

Drexel, Allen (1997). Before Paris Burned: Race, Class, and Male Homosexuality on the Chicago South Side, 1935-1960. In *Creating a Place for Ourselves: Lesbian, Gay, Bisexual Community Histories,* edited by Brett Beemyn, pp. 119-144. New York: Routledge.

Faderman, Lillian (1981). *Surpassing the Love of Men.* New York: Morrow.

Faderman, Lillian (1991). *Odd Girls and Twilight Lovers: A History of Lesbian Life in Twentieth-Century America.* New York: Columbia University Press.

Fedukovich, Deanna (2002). Affirmation in the High Country. Final paper in the course Introduction to Gay and Lesbian Studies, Appalachian State University, Boone, Dr. Cheryl Claassen professor, Spring.

Foucault, Michel (1988). *The History of Sexuality.* Volume One. New York: Vintage Books.

Franzen, Trisha (1996). *Spinsters and Lesbians.* New York: New York University Press.

Freeman, Susan (2000). From the Lesbian Nation to the Cincinnati Lesbian Community: Moving Toward a Politics of Location. *Journal of the History of Sexuality* 9(1-2): 137-174.

Friend, R. (1980). Gayging: Adjustment and the Older Gay Male. *Alternative Lifestyles* 3:231-248.

Frye, Marilyn (1990). Lesbian "Sex." In *Lesbian Philosophies and Cultures,* edited by Jeffner Allen, pp. 305-315. Binghamton: State University of New York Press.

Gagnon, J.H. and W. Simon (1973). *Sexual Conduct.* Chicago: Aldine Publishing Co.

Gratton, B. and M. Haug (1983). Decision and Adaptation: Research on Female Retirement. *Research on Aging* 5(1):59-76.

Gundlach, R. (1967). Research project report. *The Ladder* 11:2-9.

Hall, Radclyffe (1928). *The Well of Loneliness.* New York: Covici Feiede.

Halperin, David (1995). Is There a History of Homosexuality? In *Lesbian and Gay Studies Reader,* edited by Henry Abelove, Michele Barale, and David Halperin, pp. 416-431. London: Routledge.

Henry, George (1948). *Sex Variants: A Study of Homosexual Patterns.* New York: Paul Hoeber.

History Project (1998). *Improper Bostonians: Lesbian and Gay History from the Puritans to Playland.* Boston: Beacon Press.

Johnson, David (1997). The Kids of Fairytown. In *Creating a Place for Ourselves: Lesbian, Gay, Bisexual Community Histories,* edited by Brett Beemyn, pp. 97-118. New York: Routledge.

Katz, Jonathan (1983). *Gay/Lesbian Almanac: A New Documentary.* New York: Harper and Row.

Kehoe, Monika (1989). *Lesbians Over 60 Speak for Themselves.* Binghamton, NY: The Haworth Press, Inc.

Kennedy, Elizabeth and Madeline Davis (1993). *Boots of Leather, Slippers of Gold. The History of a Lesbian Community.* New York: Routledge.

Kennedy, Elizabeth and Madeline Davis (1997). I Could Hardly Wait to Get Back to That Bar. In *Creating a Place for Ourselves: Lesbian, Gay, Bisexual Community Histories,* edited by Brett Beemyn, pp. 27-72. New York: Routledge.

Kerman, Dan (2002). GLBT Seniors to Get Affordable Housing. *Networker* 2(4).

Kinsey, Alfred (1948). *Sexual Behavior in the Human Male.* Philadelphia: W.B. Saunders.

Kinsey, Alfred (1953). *Sexual Behavior in the Human Female.* Philadelphia: W.B. Saunders.

Krieger, Susan (1983). T*he Mirror Dance: Identity in a Women's Community.* Philadelphia: Temple University Press.

Kronenberger, G.K. (1991). Out of the Closet. *Personnel Journal* 70:40-44.

Lee, John (1987). What Can Homosexual Aging Studies Contribute to Theories of Aging? *Journal of Homosexuality* 13(4):43-71.

Levine M.P. and R. Leonard (1984). Discrimination Against Lesbians in the Work Force. *Signs: Journal of Women in Culture and Society* 9:700-710.

Minnigerode, F.A. and M.R. Adelman (1978). Elderly Homosexual Women and Men: Report on a Pilot Study. *The Family Coordinator* 27(4):451-456.

Mitchell, Richard, et al. (1964). Homosexuality and Citizenship in Florida. A Report of the Florida Legislative Investigation Committee. Tallahassee, Florida.

National Defense Research Institute of the Rand Corporation (1993). Sexual Orientation and US Military Personnel Policy. Options and Assessment. Santa Monica, CA: Rand.

Newcomer, Mabel (1959). *A Century of Higher Education for American Women.* New York: Harper.

Newton, Ester (1993). *Cherry Grove, Fire Island: Sixty Years in America's First Gay and Lesbian Town.* Boston: Beacon.

Newton, Ester (1997). The "Fun Gay Ladies." In *Creating a Place for Ourselves: Lesbian, Gay, Bisexual Community Histories,* edited by Brett Beemyn, pp. 145-164. New York: Routledge.

Pollner and Rosenfeld (2000). The Cross-Culturing Work of Gay and Lesbian Elderly. *Advances in Life Course Research* 5:99-117.

Ponse, Barbara (1978). *Identities in the Lesbian World: The Social Construction of Self.* Westport, CT: Greenwood Press.

Quam, J.K. and G.S. Whitford (1992). Adaptation and Age-Related Expectations of Older Gay and Lesbian Adults. The *Gerontologist* 32:367-374.

Rich, Adrienne (1979). *On Lies, Secrets, and Silence: Selected Prose 1966-1978.* New York: W.W. Norton and Co.

Robinson, Minna (1979). Title Unknown. Master's Thesis, California State University, Dominguez Hills.

Schiebinger, Londa (1989). *The Mind Has No Sex? Women in the Origins of Modern Science.* Cambridge, MA: Harvard University Press.

Schmidt, Carol, (1999). RV Parks Offer Flexible, Affordable Lesbian and Gay Retirement Housing. *Outward* (Summer).

Schmittroth, Linda (Ed.) (1991). *Statistical Record of Women Worldwide.* New York: Gale Research.

Sedgwick, Eve (1992). Epistomology of the Closet. In *Lesbian and Gay Studies Reader,* edited by H. Abelove, M. Barale, and D. Halperin, pp. 43-61. New York: Routledge.

Stein, Arlene (1997). *Sex and Sensibility: Stories of a Lesbian Generation.* Berkeley: University of California Press.

Tafel, Rich (2000). Introduction. *Out and Voting II: The Gay, Lesbian, and Bisexual Vote in Congressional Elections, 1990-1998.* Washington, DC: National Gay and Lesbian Task Force.

Thor-Dahlburg (2003). U.S. Funded Center for Gay Seniors to Open. *San Francisco Chronicle,* p. A-5.

Thorpe, Roey (1997). The Changing Face of Lesbian Bars in Detroit, 1938-1965. In *Creating a Place for Ourselves: Lesbian, Gay, Bisexual Community Histories,* edited by Brett Beemyn, pp. 165-182. New York: Routledge.

Williamson, A.D. (1993). Is This the Right Time to Come Out? *Harvard Business Review* 71:18-27.

Wolf, Deborah (1980). *The Lesbian Community.* Berkeley: University of California Press.

Yutema, Sharon (1997). *Americans 55 and Older.* Ithaca, NY: New Strategist Pubs.

Index

Page numbers followed by the letter "t" indicate tables.

Order a copy of this book with this form or online at:
http://www.haworthpress.com/store/product.asp?sku=5158

WHISTLING WOMEN
A Study of the Lives of Older Lesbians

_____ in hardbound at $44.95 (ISBN: 0-7890-2412-8)

_____ in softbound at $19.95 (ISBN: 0-7890-2413-6)

Or order online and use special offer code HEC25 in the shopping cart.

COST OF BOOKS_____	☐ **BILL ME LATER:** (Bill-me option is good on US/Canada/Mexico orders only; not good to jobbers, wholesalers, or subscription agencies.)
POSTAGE & HANDLING_____ *(US: $4.00 for first book & $1.50 for each additional book)* *(Outside US: $5.00 for first book & $2.00 for each additional book)*	☐ Check here if billing address is different from shipping address and attach purchase order and billing address information. Signature_____
SUBTOTAL_____	☐ **PAYMENT ENCLOSED: $**_____
IN CANADA: ADD 7% GST_____	☐ **PLEASE CHARGE TO MY CREDIT CARD.**
STATE TAX_____ *(NJ, NY, OH, MN, CA, IL, IN, & SD residents, add appropriate local sales tax)*	☐ Visa ☐ MasterCard ☐ AmEx ☐ Discover ☐ Diner's Club ☐ Eurocard ☐ JCB Account # _____
FINAL TOTAL_____ *(If paying in Canadian funds, convert using the current exchange rate, UNESCO coupons welcome)*	Exp. Date_____ Signature_____

Prices in US dollars and subject to change without notice.

NAME_____

INSTITUTION_____

ADDRESS_____

CITY_____

STATE/ZIP_____

COUNTRY_____ COUNTY (NY residents only)_____

TEL_____ FAX_____

E-MAIL_____

May we use your e-mail address for confirmations and other types of information? ☐ Yes ☐ No
We appreciate receiving your e-mail address and fax number. Haworth would like to e-mail or fax special discount offers to you, as a preferred customer. **We will never share, rent, or exchange your e-mail address or fax number.** We regard such actions as an invasion of your privacy.

Order From Your Local Bookstore or Directly From
The Haworth Press, Inc.
10 Alice Street, Binghamton, New York 13904-1580 • USA
TELEPHONE: 1-800-HAWORTH (1-800-429-6784) / Outside US/Canada: (607) 722-5857
FAX: 1-800-895-0582 / Outside US/Canada: (607) 771-0012
E-mailto: orders@haworthpress.com

For orders outside US and Canada, you may wish to order through your local
sales representative, distributor, or bookseller.
For information, see http://haworthpress.com/distributors

(Discounts are available for individual orders in US and Canada only, not booksellers/distributors.)
PLEASE PHOTOCOPY THIS FORM FOR YOUR PERSONAL USE.
http://www.HaworthPress.com   BOF04